SOCIAL THERAPY

SOCIAL THERAPY

A guide to social support interventions for mental health practitioners

Derek L. Milne

Northumberland Mental Health NHS Trust and
The University of Newcastle upon Tyne,
Centre for Applied Psychology

JOHN WILEY & SONS

Chichester • New York • Weinheim • Brisbane • Singapore • Toronto

Copyright © 1999 by John Wiley & Sons Ltd,
Baffins Lane, Chichester,
West Sussex PO19 1UD, England

National   01243 779777
International   (+44) 1243 779777
e-mail (for orders and customer service enquiries):
cs-books@wiley.co.uk
Visit our Home Page on http://www.wiley.co.uk
or http://www.wiley.com

Other Wiley Editorial Offices

John Wiley & Sons, Inc., 605 Third Avenue,
New York, NY 10158-0012, USA

Wiley-VCH Verlag GmbH, Pappelallee 3,
D-69469 Weinheim, Germany

Jacaranda Wiley Ltd, 33 Park Road, Milton,
Queensland 4064, Australia

John Wiley & Sons (Asia) Pte Ltd, 2 Clementi Loop #02-01,
Jim Xing Distripark, Singapore 129809

John Wiley & Sons (Canada) Ltd, 22 Worcester Road,
Rexdale, Ontario M9W 1L1, Canada

Library of Congress Cataloging-in-Publication Data
Milne, Derek, 1949–
    Social Therapy : a guide to social support for mental health
practitioners / Derek L. Milne.
        p.   cm.
    Includes bibliographical references and index.
    ISBN 0-471-98726-3 (cased). — ISBN 0-471-98727-1 (pbk.)
    1. Social adjustment.   2. Social networks—Therapeutic use.
3. Clinical sociology.   4. Psychiatric social work.   I. Title.
RC455.4.S67M54   1999
362.2'042—dc21
                                                                                98-41436
                                                                                   CIP

British Library Cataloguing in Publication Data
A catalogue record for this book is available from the British Library

ISBN   0-471-98726-3 (cased)
ISBN   0-471-98727-1 (paper)

Typeset in 10/12pt Palatino by Saxon Graphics Ltd, Derby
Printed and bound in Great Britain by Bookcraft (Bath) Ltd, Midsomer Norton, Somerset
This book is printed on acid-free paper responsibly manufactured from sustainable
forestry, in which at least two trees are planted for each one used for paper production.

This book is dedicated
to my number one social supporters,
namely my wife Judy and my daughter Kirsty

CONTENTS

ABOUT THE AUTHOR

Derek Leslie Milne, PhD, is Director of the Centre for Applied Psychology at the University of Newcastle upon Tyne, where he also serves as Director (Acting) for the Doctorate in Clinical Psychology Programme. He is also a member of the Northumberland Mental Health NHS Trust, specialising in continuing professional development for the Trust's staff.

Dr Milne was elected a Fellow of the British Psychological Society in 1991, partly because of his innovative work in the social support field, such as his work with hairdressers, material of such general interest that it appeared in the science column of *The Times*. In addition to his interest in social support, he teaches and researches in relation to service evaluation, supervision, methods of teaching and training, and evidence-based clinical practice. Relevant prior books include editing 'Evaluating Mental Health Practice' (1987), and writing 'Training Behaviour Therapists' (1986), 'Psychology and Mental Health Nursing' (1993) and 'Teaching and Training for Non-Teachers' (with Steve Noone: 1996).

FOREWORD

By Jim Orford

One of the startling features of the century that is drawing to a close is the rise of psychology and the treatment of mental distress. The numbers of young people in the West now studying psychology, whether as part or whole of a professional training or a degree course, is huge. We all now think psychologically. GPs are asked to face up to research that shows that a third or more of the patients' problems are, in whole or part, mental. The recent 80th anniversary of the First World War armistice reminds us of the discovery of 'shell shock' in the Great War. We now speak of post-traumatic stress disorder.

Our thinking has changed. But what is the nature of our thinking about mental distress? The century has been dominated by Freud and the post-Freudians, by behaviourism and behaviour therapy, by the client-centred humanistic school of thought, by Gestalt and numerous other therapy types, and latterly by cognitive-behavioural treatment—the now ubiquitous CBT.

All have their adherents and all their successes. What they all have in common, though, is their focus on the individual sufferer as the locus of the problem and the focus of the treatment. What is wrong is the way the *individual person* thinks, was brought up, responds to cues, or feels about herself. Treatment therefore consists of taking the person to a place of refuge, or at least privacy, and administering treatment, nowadays usually in the form of psychoactive medication or an extended conversation with a counsellor or psychotherapist. The thinking and the therapies are person-centred.

Voices have always been raised against this individualist bias and the clamour those voices are making is getter louder. One set of voices reminds us of cultural diversity. As British society, like many others, becomes more multicultural, the individualism of dominant psychological ways of thinking, emanating largely from the USA, one of the most individualistic countries in the world, becomes ever more apparent. Many societies are more collectivist in their thinking about human nature and human distress: they don't need to invent social support, it is part of their identity, part of the definition of being human. Another set of voices belongs to those who have bemoaned the lack of preparation of mental health personnel for the move from hospital to community. Instead of reorienting to thinking of distressed people in a community context, some complain that services have simply been relocated, bringing with them all their individualistic, person-out-of-context assumptions and methods. Another set of voices, now deafening, informs us of the strong and if anything strengthening link to be found between social class and ill-health, both physical and mental. Not only is there a social gradient to health, with those of lower social class—whether judged by poverty, material deprivation, employment position, job status or education—being the less healthy, but there is now evidence that overall, a society's health is poorer when there is greater inequality. Until recently in the UK we had a government that tried to minimise, even deny, these findings. We now at least have a government that recognises them, is prepared to talk about them, and has coined the term 'social exclusion'.

Yet another set of voices is those of innovative thinkers in the mental health field and in psychology who have challenged the conventional individualistic wisdom. One thinks of Burkitt (1991), a social psychologist, who wrote:

> The view of human beings as self-contained unitary individuals who carry their uniqueness deep inside themselves, like pearls hidden in their shells, is one that is ingrained in the Western tradition of thought ... [this] image of humans ... is totally inappropriate for the study of personality. In order to truly understand the human self, [this] vision of humans ... must be dispensed with. (pp. 1, 189)

A strong voice, recently raised in support of this same position is that of Prilleltensky. In his book, *The Morals and Politics of Psychology* (1994), he has a chapter entitled 'Abnormal psychology' in which he traces the development of the field over the last 40 years. He sees a profession having taken place from an *asocial* approach, through an enhanced awareness of its *microsocial* elements, to an increased alertness to macrosocial variables. In the asocial approach the problems are formulated in terms of individual defects:

> The medical model, in either its organic or psychodynamic version, captures the essence of the asocial stage ... Environmental factors are not entirely disregarded, but they are given only secondary priority and remain largely in the background ... the individual is too frequently dissociated from the wider systems of society that shape his or her behaviour extensively, thus creating an ahistorical and asocial image of individuals. (p. 99, 100, 102)

Prilleltensky is equally critical of alternative perspectives that have become dominant in the mental health field, including the behavioural and the systemic viewpoints. Both promised to address wider, social factors in mental health, but in practice both have remained highly restricted to a consideration of individuals and the microsocial environments immediately surrounding them.

For many years I have been teaching community psychology to clinical psychology trainees. One exercise they carry out is to construct a formulation of a present problem—usually presented by an individual person in distress—in social or community terms. I have always found the result encouraging, since they generally have no difficulty in identifying social factors that are likely to be important. Recurring factors included poverty, poor housing, lack of affordable and convenient transport, lack of recreational facilities, and threats to health and safety such as mugging and drug use in the neighbourhood. These are the kinds of factor to which psychological formulations have traditionally been blind.

Several of the presenting problems that trainees were attempting to formulate involved parents, often single mothers, whose children had been presenting with a variety of 'symptoms'. Their poor financial resources, housing and local facilities impacted on them as individuals and upon their family systems in a number of ways. One was in terms of lack of space in the home, and in particular the inability to provide separate space for functions such as feeding, sleeping and play. Another recurring point was the difficulty of maintaining close and harmonious links between home and school which has been argued, again, are vital for child development (Bronfenbrenner, 1979). Maintaining good links between the child's worlds at home and at school is never easy, particularly when, as was sometimes the case, parents were self-conscious about their lack of literacy skills or low socioeconomic status compared to teachers. If the school was more than a walk away and there was an absence of affordable and convenient transport, these difficulties were compounded. A central issue was lack of available and adequate social support. Families, including immigrant families who needed all the support they could get, had often lost significant sources of support by moving away from others or because of the death of key relatives. Poverty, and the poor housing and lack of transport that often goes with it, often seem to deprive families of the ability to organise social support for themselves that is easier with better material resources. A further factor was prejudice and the feeling of stigma that attached to some members of minority ethnic groups and to people who had been diagnosed as having a 'mental illness'.

But in practice trainees usually revert to the dominant individualistic perspective under the pressures of working in mental health settings that operate as if they were unconscious of the social constraints on people's lives. Indeed it has been suggested that there is a kind of 'social unconscious' which affects us all, whereby we are unaware most of the time how our actions and ways of thinking are shaped by social circumstances. we assume we are free agents—rugged individualists. But for mental health professionals to continue to make this mistake runs the risk, to use the title of Ryan's (1971) classic and highly readable text, of *Blaming the Victim*.

Derek Milne's voice is amongst those of the innovators in thinking about mental health and how we can respond to it. In this book he encourages mental health practitioners to think differently, to think social, to think laterally, and to leave behind our hitherto total reliance upon purely person-centred ways of understanding and responding to psychological distress. His voice, however, is one of experience. He knows the problems. His stance is not one of criticism, nor revolution, nor of unrealistic expectations. Through citing numerous examples both of work done by himself, his colleagues and students, and by others who have reported their work in all sorts of professional and academic journals that most of us have difficulty in getting access to or simply do not have the time to read, he builds his argument for extending practice into what he calls 'social therapy'. The latter, thankfully, is not a new brand of therapy that one can find packaged in a manual but rather a name that he has cleverly invented to refer to a panoply of approaches and projects which have in common the strengthening of people's social support.

His choice of social support as the central idea around which to organise this book is well made, For one thing there is now a great deal of good writing on the subject, both conceptual and empirical. On this literature he draws extensively. Social support also has the merit of helping us bridge the gulf between a purely individualistic way of thinking of mental health, and a more contextualised way. Social support can be thought of, at one and the same time, as a property of individuals, and a characteristic of social systems. Network diagrams are often drawn with focal individuals in the centre. The amount of an individual's social support can be counted up as if it were a personal characteristic. Social support may even be construed as simply a product of an individual's social skill in acquiring or using it. On the other hand, the potential to use the idea of social support to characterise the nature of neighbourhoods, blocks, places of work, schools, is boundless.

Another distinct advantage of social support for Derek Milne's purpose—which is to ease us all gently in a direction we should be going but are resisting—is that it is a kindly notion. Unlike power and empowerment, which are often taken as the core ideas in community psychology, and which he might have chosen as his core themes, social support has connotations of care, togetherness, positive health—the kinds of values to which mental health workers can most easily relate.

Not that this book is not extremely challenging. It is. I remember the anger aroused amongst psychotherapist colleagues when I first tried to draw their attention to work on the therapy-like support offered by such community agents as bartenders and hairdressers. No-one who is at all precious about their mental health professionalism will be entirely comfortable with the contents of this book. Not only does the author remind us of Cowen's (1982) early work on hairdressers, and bring it up to date for us, but with numerous examples he breaks down the diversions between experts and lay people, professionals and non-professionals. He exhorts us all to think in terms of building support for those in distress, and seeking out sources of social support wherever they are to be found. At one point he takes us on a tour down his local high street, ticking off all the places, from the GP's surgery to the florist and the vets where social support might be found. He concludes that sources of social support to draw on when we are mentally distressed are all around us, and we should reorient our practices to harness them.

References

Bronfenbrenner, U. (1979). *The Ecology of Human Development: Experiments by Nature and Design*. Cambridge, MA: Harvard University Press.

Burkitt, I. (1991). *Social Selves: Theories of the Social Formation of Personality*. London: Sage Publications.

Cowen, E. (1982). Help is where you find it, *American Psychologist*, **37**, 385–395.

Prilleltensky, I. (1994). *The Morals and Politics of Psychology*. Albany, NY.

Ryan (1971). *Blaming the Victim*. New York: Random House.

PREFACE

There are a number of reasons for writing a book that attempts to encourage and support mental health professionals to review and redirect their work by engaging in more 'social therapy'—i.e. intervening to promote social support processes in the community. Firstly, from a broad perspective there is the faltering and flawed progress of community care. Although many countries have managed to reduce dramatically the proportion of patients in psychiatric hospitals (e.g. one third of hospitals in the UK have been closed), there has been a disappointing lack of success in creating adequate alternatives either in Europe or in the USA (Leff, 1997). In the UK, problems have included insufficient resources, lack of finance, perverse social security policies, organisational fragmentation and confusion, and inadequate staffing arrangements (Audit Commission, 1986). This report recommended 'radical changes', including acknowledging innovative 'champions' of care; delegating responsibility to the operational level; integrating services and professional groups; defining responsibilities in terms of much smaller areas—the local neighbourhood patches; and developing social support systems in these patches. For example, encouragement was given to coordinating and mobilising voluntary resources so as to form an important element of community care. It was noted that some of the most cost-effective and flexible services were provided by voluntary organisations (e.g. 'Homestart' and 'Crossroads' carer support schemes for older or disabled adults). The Commission concluded that 'it is little short of amazing that *any* successful community-based schemes have been introduced' (p. 73), given the range of formidable obstacles to effective care practices.

Secondly, from a professional perspective it is evident that we need to recognise and respond to these issues, as the demand for help with mental health needs shows no sign of abating. This need cannot be met by mental health practitioners working in their conventional ways (Christensen & Jacobson, 1994). In addition, the emergence of a 'managed care' approach to mental health services, with its emphasis on minimising the provision of professional help, is likely to limit the interventions of formal helpers with individual sufferers (Sarason, S.B., 1981; Humphreys, 1996). Meanwhile, we have seen the emergence of a new generation of non-professional therapists who are capable of making cost-effective interventions. These changes require a fresh appraisal of traditional professional practice in the mental health field, one that is presented constructively in this book as 'social therapy'.

Thirdly, unlike several of its predecessors, this book does not, however, rely on exhortation to facilitate innovation in the practices of mental health professionals. To do so would be psychologically naïve: professionals also face 'formidable obstacles' to innovation. Rather, the onus is placed repeatedly upon a careful formulation of professional behaviour, in order to understand why certain practices persist in the face of counter-evidence, but also to acknowledge important developments. Such a psychologically reflexive angle, allied to an accessible summary of this evidence, provides a much firmer basis for professionals to re-appraise their practice. More in keeping with its immediate predecessors, the present book also provides many current models and methods to stimulate the much needed imagination and innovation.

It appears that arguments for a more imaginative approach to care in the community are growing ever stronger. They have long been linked by researchers to a recognition of the social and political context of distress and coping, but mental health practitioners have tended towards a mentalistic or intrapersonal account of psychological distress. This is corroborated by their patients, who also tend to attribute their distress to their own faulty thinking and irrational actions: 'despite the evidence for social causation, persons seldom experience their own agency and actions to be externally caused' (Fryer, 1998, p. 81). This illustrates one of the formidable obstacles to innovation. It appears to me that the clearest implication is for mental health professionals to become more involved in social therapy, but there are also implications for the way that professionals provide conventional therapy.

This book will detail this option from a psychological perspective, starting at a basic introductory level, in order to promote our 'one-to-many' work as supporters or 'therapists' of the 'many-to-many' social supporters. It is an option that avoids the naïve notion that mental health professionals can somehow change the social environment on a large scale single-handedly. Rather, it recognises, formalises and builds upon the work that many professionals already undertake, christening it 'social therapy' so as to accord it due status and record its continuity with 'one-to-one' work.

ACKNOWLEDGEMENTS

Reflecting the three main forms of social support, for 'informational support' I would like to thank my brother-in-law Dr Duncan Gray for help on the Hippocratic Oath, Nonnie Crawford for the stimulating parallels between the models of dental health and of social support, and several colleagues for their thoughts on the term 'social therapy' (including Pat Corrigan, Ivy Blackburn, Sue Hingley, Ian James and Roger Paxton) as well as on other material (especially Chris Lozinski and David Moseley).

Under the heading of 'practical support' must come gratitude to my employers, the Northumberland Mental Health NHS Trust (and particularly my manager Roger Paxton) for approving the necessary secretarial and library support, provided generously by Barbara Kirkup, Angela Clasper (Secretaries) and Pauline Ward (Librarian). The Trust's information officer (Anne Liddon) also helped to improve the clarity of several chapters. Much appreciated additional secretarial support was provided by Clare Costello and Barbara Mellors at Newcastle University.

Finally, the essential 'emotional support' came from my family (Judy and Kirsty Milne); from my good neighbours Joe and Anita Dickinson; and from several colleagues, including Peter Britton, Dale Huey, Richard Marshall, Mark Papworth, Colin Westerman and Jim White.

PART 1

The theoretical, practical and professional context

It appears that only a very small proportion of those with mental health problems ever see mental health professionals. Yet, somehow, such people manage to cope—how can this be understood? and what implications does it carry for mental health practitioners? Is help, formal and informal, simply 'where you find it' and distinguishable only by such factors as where and from whom one receives it? The next two chapters suggest that professionals do indeed provide a distinctive form of coping assistance. They also acknowledge the complementary nature of social support, and highlight how professionals can extend their traditional roles so as to foster the availability and quality of social support.

Chapter 1

INTRODUCTION

'SOCIAL THERAPY' DEFINED

Terms like 'social therapy' have, of course, been used before, either to describe practical efforts to engage patients in interpersonal interactions as part of occupational therapy, or as an aspect of a major therapeutic approach (e.g. social skills training in behaviour therapy). Similar terms have also been coined in relation to social support, such as 'social system psychotherapy', 'social network therapy' or 'social network intervention' (Herink, 1980). However, to my knowledge the term 'social therapy' has not been used in the present sense previously. This use refers primarily to how professionals intervene interpersonally to facilitate the functioning of social supporters (e.g. caring for the carers) and so as to improve the environments in which support occurs (e.g. 'expressed emotion' in families) in order to enhance a community's capacity to care. This incorporates the three defining features of a therapy, namely a basis in the helping relationship, the use of psychosocial methods to improve thoughts, feelings and behaviours, and administration of the therapy by a specially trained professional (Strupp, 1978). These methods should have a sound theoretical underpinning, be derived from a substantive body of knowledge and be open to appropriate empirical research. I believe that the social therapy described in this book meets these criteria.

However, it is recognised that the term does not fit neatly into the conventional therapy mould. For instance, rather than being clearly differentiated from other therapies, it is more of an integration of several approaches. Similarly, it is appropriate even when there is no overtly troublesome condition, in contrast to part of Strupp's (1978) definition. Also, unlike conventional therapies, social therapy is not necessarily restricted to particular formats (e.g. work with individuals), contexts (e.g. clinical settings) or 'doses' (e.g. 10 sessions) (Roth & Fonagy, 1996).

Counterbalancing its weakness in relation to these criteria, the term social therapy carries the benefit of legitimising a wider role, one that most mental health professionals engage in at least occasionally; of recognising explicitly the social context and content of all therapies; of linking individual psychopathologies to social phenomena (e.g. consider social phobia, agoraphobia, sociotropic depression, attachment and personality disorders); and of highlighting the role of social causation in psychopathology (i.e. just as cognitive therapy aims to alter faulty thinking, so social therapy is directed at faulty social actions). For these reasons the term social therapy seems warranted, as well as possibly serving to attract attention to a less favoured area of professional practice, much needed attention at a time when there is a growing obsession with conventional therapeutic activity.

THE CASE FOR A FRESH INITIATIVE

The preface summarised the principal arguments for a more systematic and imaginative approach to care in the community. Consider one aspect in more detail, namely the irresistible rise of the therapists employed to provide psychological help to individuals with mental health difficulties. There was a time during the 1950s and 1960s when only psychiatrists delivered psychological help, with clinical psychologists limited to a supportive role as diagnosticians (largely in the form of IQ and personality testing). Following the successful involvement of psychologists in therapy since the 1970s, the last decade has witnessed a dramatic snowballing of the range and number of non-psychologist therapists (NPTs). There are several critical reasons for this psychological health care explosion, particularly the power of market forces allied to growing evidence that therapists who are not psychologists can achieve equally good clinical results.

Table 1.1 summarises these and other reasons for the dramatic diversification of psychological health care. These amount to a powerful argument for psychologists to limit this role as therapists and in addition to engage in such challenging activities as clarifying and developing ways to support the social supporters. It is only by means of such 'indirect' work that psychologists (and others) can begin to deliver the benefits of a psychological approach to the communities that surround their traditional emphasis on 'direct' work (i.e. 'face-to-face' or 'one-to-one' therapy).

Social support refers to the provision of informal help in order to try and meet someone's psychological needs. It is provided by almost all community members to one another and it consists structurally of informational, practical and emotional assistance (e.g. sympathetically listening to a neighbour) and companionship. From a functional angle, increasing evidence attests to the vital role that such social support plays, either in 'buffering' individuals from the full force of stressful life events, or in more generally helping them to feel cared for or better able to cope.

Table 1.1   Five major reasons why psychologists cannot and should not resist non-psychologist therapists (NPTs). (Based on Hayes *et al.* (1995); Humphreys (1996)

1. 'Worldliness'	Unlike psychiatry's historical block on psychology, present day attempts to argue for a professional 'guild' will occur in an environment where policy makers and the public are now cynical about the role and motives of professionals (e.g. 'managed care').
2. Economics	Declining resources and the 'internal market' mean that competitively priced services that achieve good results will grow in prominence.
3. Evidence	Studies of professional training indicate that NPTs are equally effective (for some problems/clients)
4. Self-defeating	History teaches us to develop and diversify what we offer, while disseminating the fruits of our work to others.
5. Immorality	How can psychologists justify creating monopolies that lead to more expensive and less readily available services? This is particularly immoral if the aim is to enhance the prestige and monetary needs of psychologists as a group.

A summary of the evidence for these points and more on the detailed aspects of social support is provided later in this chapter and again in Chapter 3.

WHAT TO EXPECT FROM THIS BOOK

The book also recognises that mental health practitioners need to understand those factors that influence or determine their own professional behaviour if they are to realise their potential in the social support sphere. It follows that a sympathetic analysis and formulation is needed, rather than yet another exhortation or rebuke for failing to engage adequately in community psychology (cf. Bender, 1976). Despite years of cajoling from experts, why do mental health professionals not adapt their practices more imaginatively? As one would expect, it is surely because there are a number of important costs and consequences to such a reorientation. To illustrate, an early analysis by Froland *et al.* (1981) noted inadequate preparation and training for alternative forms of practice, as well as negative attitudes towards sharing skills and conducting projects with non-professionals. More recent analyses indicate that little has changed (e.g. Rachman, 1995). We need to recognise that there are, therefore, good reasons for the apparent inflexibility of professionals, while seeking ways to supplement the traditional one-to-one approach with more effective and appropriate models of neighbourhood practice. This book attempts this difficult balance by means of building on current approximations to a community approach (e.g. carer support; health education); by applying psychological principles reflexively to professional practice; and by providing information, evidence and concrete examples to prompt role development.

Adopting an historical perspective, this initial chapter examines the nature of social support in relation to several dimensions and outlines some of the practical applications of social support in the mental health field. The roots of a community-based orientation to one's work are then analysed, leading to conclusions about our professional role in supporting social supporters. Chapter 2 then details who has been involved in doing what within the social support approach, beginning again with the historical background and recounting the staggering array of non-professional helpers who have at times teamed up with mental health professionals to develop informal helping relationships in the community. A summary of the results of this collaborative endeavour will be provided, leading to an outline of the logical range of possibilities for professionals in this particular branch of community work. Examples of how this might proceed will be offered and constraints on some of these possibilities will be duly recognised. However, the tone is positive and up-beat, recognising what has already been achieved by mental health practitioners and pointing out how this can be strengthened.

Chapters 3 and 4 go into more detail, in an effort to develop our understanding of the nature and influence of social support. A detailed analysis is provided of how models of social support link in to formulations that are dominant in the mental health literature, particularly transactional coping theory. A major part of our understanding of social support must be based on careful measurement of the relevant variables, and in Chapter 4 a summary of the available instruments is provided. This will help practitioners to construe social support, and will equip them with some readily available tools for measuring social support in their own context.

Section 3 (Chapters 5 to 7) is concerned with the practical social support work that mental health practitioners can undertake, and is defined at three levels. Firstly, 'clinical' interventions are those that overlap with routine professional activities and include the way that social support and a community orientation can make individual therapy more effective and acceptable. At the next level, that of the 'proximal' interventions, I examine the more systemic attempts that professionals have made to tackle relevant social support issues. The level of analysis is that of the school, the workplace and family or friends. Finally, 'distal' interventions concern how professionals can tackle (or at least recognise) such determinants of mental health as material and social deprivation, health education and environmental design. In all three chapters case studies will be provided to offer mental health professionals accessible and realistic ways to develop their practice. As before, these are underpinned with theory, to promote reflection and action.

In the final section (Chapters 8 and 9), I turn to the evaluation of social support interventions, examining how the three levels of work outlined above can be assessed. Such evaluations can provide corrective feedback to the practitioner, or represent evidence of the effectiveness of this work to service purchasers or others. Emphasis will be placed on the conventional definitions for a quality service in mental health and on the more user-friendly methods of quality evaluation (such as client satisfaction surveys or simple observational analyses). In particular, attention is given to the importance of establishing a highly collaborative relationship with those individuals in the community who have a major stake in the work that the mental health professional is undertaking. In the final chapter some of the main threads of this analysis will be drawn together, to highlight how mental health practice must develop if it is to prove more successful in addressing the vast demands placed on formal services and on informal helpers. Considerable stress will also be placed on the implications for the initial and continuing professional development of professionals.

DEFINING SOCIAL SUPPORT

Social support lies at the heart of community care and so should be analysed from a number of different perspectives. As this book is written by a clinical psychologist, the main angle taken will be that of community psychology. Table 1.2 indicates eight principles of community psychology, as summarised by Orford (1992). All of these principles apply to the case of social support and will be reflected at different stages in the book.

The most fundamental aspect of this set of principles is that the well being of individuals is not simply due to some kind of personal weakness or strength, but rather it is assumed to be a function of the interaction between that individual's characteristics and the environment. As Orford (1992) put it in his preface, 'community psychology is about understanding people within their social worlds and using this understanding to improve people's wellbeing … it is a branch of the academic study of psychology and at the same time a branch of the helping professions … ' (p.vii). Such a formulation recognises that mental health status interacts with a number of fundamental pillars and practices within our society, many of which transcend the individual. To be specific, one explanation of mental ill health includes the idea that it is due to 'social causation'. This explanation points to material and structural deficiencies in society which create inequalities in resource (e.g. income) and lead to relative disadvan-

Table 1.2 The principles of community psychology

1. Assumptions about causes of problems
   An interaction, over time, between person and social settings and systems, including the structure of social support and social power.
2. Levels of analysis
   From micro-level to macro, especially at the level of the organisation and the community or neighbourhood.
3. Research methods
   Include quasi-experimental designs, qualitative research, action research and case-study methods.
4. Location of practice
   As near as possible to the relevant, everyday social contexts.
5. Approach to planning services
   Proactive 'seeking out'; assessing needs and special risks in a community.
6. Practice emphasis
   On prevention rather than treatment.
7. Attitude to sharing psychology with others
   Positive towards formal and informal ways of sharing, including consultation.
8. Position on working with non-professionals
   Strongly encouraging of self-help and non-professionals and seeks to facilitate and collaborate.

From Orford (1992)

tage and a vulnerability to the unequal impact of hazardous jobs. An alternative view is that mental ill health is a result of 'social selection', that is, people who have mental health problems are liable to drift into these more hazardous and less well-resourced occupations, since their personal coping repertoires mean that they cannot keep up with their more competitive contemporaries. Jobs are a very good example of the rich tapestry which enfolds community care, since they provide social horizons beyond the immediate family and friendship links; because they enforce participation in collective purpose and serve in significant ways to define one's social status; and also because employment demands reality-orientated activities and enforces experiences which meet fairly enduring human needs (e.g. for time structure, purposeful activity, and social contacts). Such functions have profound implications for mental health, including knowing one's relative position in society (Jahoda, 1988). There is a high association between unemployment and poor mental health such that, for example, psychiatric 'caseness' has been found to be 2.7 times higher amongst the unemployed and parasuicide 9 times more frequent (Orford, 1992). But are these associations due to social causation or social selection? Jahoda (1988) has concluded that 'to state psychiatric conclusions individualises an issue that is essentially a social one … the cure lies not in individual therapy but in the creation of jobs' (p. 21). This is a clear example of a community or environmental orientation to mental health, stated in unusually strong terms. Sadly, this orientation has been marginalised in the mental health field, despite overwhelming evidence that an approach that recognises the impact of social inequality on health is both valid and urgently needed (Williams, 1996; Wilkinson, 1996).

A related issue concerns the link between mental health and one's material circumstances. Studies repeatedly indicate a strong link, similar to that in relation to unemployment. For example, Phillimore *et al.* (1994) studied census data from 1981 to 1991 and rank ordered 678 wards on an index of material deprivation. This was composed of unemployment, car ownership, housing tenure and overcrowding. Standardised mortality ratios were then calculated for the counties of Cleveland, Cumbria, Durham, Northumberland and Tyne and Wear. The results indicated quite clearly that mortality differentials widened between the most affluent and deprived fifths of wards during the decade. Phillimore *et al.* (1994) concluded that 'these results emphasise the case for linking mortality patterns with material conditions, rather than with individual behaviour' (p. 1125). It is this sort of evidence, and that only some 7% of people with a psychological problem in the community receive specialist help (Goldberg & Huxley, 1980), that requires mental health practitioners to review their emphasis on therapeutic work and which suggests that they should pursue activities with a greater community orientation. A very good vehicle for this work is social support, a kind of crossroads between the material and social worlds we inhabit. As Wilkinson (1996) put it:

> To feel depressed, cheated, bitter, desperate, vulnerable, frightened, angry, worried about debts or job and housing insecurity; to feel devalued, useless, helpless, uncared for, hopeless, isolated, anxious and a failure: these feelings can dominate people's whole experience of life … It is the chronic stress arising from feelings like these which does the damage. It is the social feelings which matter, not exposure to a supposedly toxic material environment. The material environment is merely the indelible mark and constant reminder of the oppressive fact of one's failure, of the atrophy of any sense of having a place in the community, and of one's social exclusion and devaluation as a human being. (p. 215)

WHAT IS SOCIAL SUPPORT?

In a classic paper, Cowen (1982) defined social support as informal interpersonal help with emotional problems. This definition recognises the importance of human relationships in order to cope successfully with stressful life events. In addition, social support has long been recognised as a routine way of meeting psychological needs and of enhancing the quality of life, i.e. something that is not necessarily linked to crises or adversity (Cutrona, 1996). These needs have been labelled attachment (a close relationship that allows nurturance, unconditional assistance and safety), social integration (sense of belonging), social validation (recognition of identity and competence), and guidance (advice and information) (Weiss, 1972; Caplan, 1974). Therefore, social support can be defined as any informal human interaction that meets these psychological needs or which helps individuals to cope with adversity (Heller *et al.*, 1986). More will be said about this broad definition in Chapter 3, since it incorporates two schools of thought on social support.

There is a greater consensus about the importance of social support amongst researchers. For example, in contrast to prevailing professional views about the salience of formal help, Cowen suggested that it was a myth that people with psychological problems always get expert help and a myth that only experts can help them. Rather, he suggested that the facts of the matter were that only about 1% of those with psychological problems ever see experts and that some 35% of the population have psychological problems, yet appear to get better. Cowen suggested that social support was one major way that psychological problems were resolved, and he drew attention to various groups who might be critical to the provision of social support (over and above family and friends, who may be regarded as the prime providers). These were hairdressers who offer support and sympathy to distressed customers, bartenders who provide advice to their clients, and lawyers who help clients to clarify their feelings (e.g. in divorce cases).

The process of providing social support appears to include three fundamental mechanisms of help, namely emotional support, informational guidance and practical assistance, although various other mechanisms have been suggested by researchers. For example, it is also defined in terms of non-directive support (including providing information and self-disclosure) directive guidance (including goal setting, advice and practical help), tangible assistance (e.g. lending or giving resources, taking care of things) and positive social interaction or companionship (eg. membership of a team or club; social events). According to Cowen (1982), in the case of hairdressers this involved offering support and sympathy, trying to be lighthearted, listening, presenting alternatives, telling customers to count their blessings, and sharing personal experiences. Additional qualities of hairdressing which illustrate some of these social support mechanisms have been provided in workshops with stylists (e.g. Milne & Mullin, 1987). At the commencement of one of these workshops the stylists were asked to list the qualities of a 'good' hairdresser and indicated the following:

- showing interest in the client
- being helpful by listening and making the client feel special
- being patient
- having an outgoing personality

- being confident yet polite
- being sympathetic and trustworthy
- being communicative
- sharing feelings.

These strategies may come as a surprise to some mental health professionals, because of the apparent overlap between the methods social supporters such as hairdressers use and those used by professionals (as a result, it is often argued, of significant training). Surprised or not, professionals might also suggest that even if these methods were comparable, the real difference between them and social supporters lies in the severity of the 'presenting problem'. However, even on this count the results of Cohen's research in America in 1982 and UK work undertaken by the present author suggest that this difference may be exaggerated. The list of problems faced on 33% of contacts by Cohen's clients included:

- difficulties with child management
- physical health
- marital distress
- depression
- anxiety
- work problems.

Additionally, in the workshops that the present author has conducted, specific examples cited by hairdressers from recent experience included the customer describing attendance at a funeral, a friend dying, getting married, boyfriend problems, a screaming baby, a hyperactive child and a spouse having an affair. Of course, such terms do not necessarily indicate mental health difficulty or the severity of the 'presenting problem'. However, there are indications from an analysis of 'psychiatric caseness' that indicate considerable overlap. For example, Milne et al. (1989a), in their study of helping six ex-clients to function as social supporters, found that psychiatric caseness was comparable to a clinical sample, even though few of the 14 individuals receiving this help were using formal mental health services.

The overlap between formal and informal help

Social support can also be understood in terms of its process and outcomes, as per formal psychotherapy. In general terms, as indicated in the above examples from hairdressing, social supporters are inclined to use a number of tactics which approximate to counselling. In one local study, designed to analyse the overlap between the speech patterns of stylists and therapists, the Helper Behaviour Rating Scale (HBRS) was used to measure the respective speech patterns (Hardy & Shapiro, 1985). This indicated that stylists made use of speech patterns that were characteristic of formal therapy across the full spectrum of categories measured by the HBRS. Like therapists, stylists asked questions, suggested things that might be done to deal with problems and even commented with equal frequency on what was going on in the 'here and now'. However, there was no significant overall correlation between the stylists' and therapists' patterns of speech, indicating that they had different helping styles. In essence, this local study and other pieces of research suggest that there are some important overlaps between therapists and social supporters, such as hairdressers. This is most evident in relation to the informational and emotional aspects of helping. But by contrast psychotherapists tend to provide a distinctive approach, featuring the unconditional valuing of clients, the provision of more reassurance, more exploratory and interpretive work, with less advice giving. Table 1.3 summarises some of these differences between social supporters and psychotherapists (Milne, 1992b).

There are major theoretical debates about how exactly social support, however provided, comes to operate on the wellbeing of the individual. This is discussed in chapter 3, but in essence suggests that social support may act as a 'buffer' (between the stressors experienced by the individual and their mental health), as well as providing a 'main effect' of bolstering an individual's esteem and coping repertoire.

Table 1.3 can be amplified by the findings of other researchers, which indicate additional parallels and differences between social supporters and therapists. Winefield (1987), for instance, suggested that clients in both contexts expected to benefit as a result of interpersonal interaction (e.g. through receiving personal attention). As a result of such interaction, benefit was thought to arise from adaptive learning in a context where the client feels valued. On a more negative note, Winefield noted that the lack of benefit might similarly be attributed by both helping groups to the personal characteristics of the clients, as in the lack of a match (or 'therapeutic alliance'). However, Winefield felt that important differences existed, including:

- The theoretical basis for the work (therapy having breadth and depth; social support being seen as a 'conceptual morass');
- Reciprocity or give and take in social support; unilateral help in the case of therapy;
- The relative expertise and training of the helpers;
- The costs of the help (including also accessibility and stigma differences);
- The number of helpers available (as Cowen indicated in 1982, these are far more numerous in the case of social supporters);

Table 1.3 Common and distinctive elements of social support and psychotherapy

Variable	Common	Social support	Psychotherapy
Type of problem	considerable (e.g. child management and health)	Minor practical and emotional problems	More severe emotional problems
Form of help	Considerable overlap of informational and emotional help	Practical: more questions, advice and information	Client unconditionally valued and more reassurance, exploration and interpretation
Function of help	Self-esteem enhancement; to provide information	Relieve practical difficulties	Enhance adaptive coping
Consequences of help for helper	Mostly feel good	Reciprocity: more negative reactions?	Employment; job satisfaction
Sources of help	Range of people	Mostly family and friend/s but extremely diverse in all social settings? 'Socioculturally similar' important?	Mostly professional and in formal settings; socioculturally dissimilar
Mechanisms of help	Enhance coping: direct and indirect (buffer and main effects)	Equally buffer and main effect? Via practical and emotional strategies	Mostly buffer (i.e. stressor related) via specific adaptive coping strategies

- The number of help settings that are available (again, innumerably greater in the case of social support);
- The forms of help that are provided. As discussed earlier, therapists have a distinctive profile which excludes such important characteristics of social support as tangible or material assistance. Differences may also exist in the respective outcomes achieved by formal and informal helpers; and
- The result of receiving help.

Underlining the final difference above, in a local study (Milne *et al.*, 1992a) the help provided by hairdressers, friends, relatives and a clinical psychologist were compared for a sample of 40 outpatient clients of the clinical psychologists in the study. A significant difference was obtained in the adequacy of the help provided by these four groups, with psychologists rated by clients as most helpful.

We will return to the vexed issue of the outcomes of professional versus non-professional help in the next chapter.

Results of social support

Thus, while it seems clear that formal help as provided by a therapist has a distinctive profile, there is also evidence of overlap with social support in some key areas. And since we know that therapy works, we also tend to expect benefits for the person receiving social support. Conversely, one might predict that, since social support tends to include some tactics about which professionals would have reservations (e.g. trying to be lighthearted), there may also be some negative impacts on clients. In a similar way, since the social supporters are not normally provided with training or support themselves, one might anticipate some adverse consequences for them at times in providing support to others. Evidence for all three types of consequence exists.

The benefits of receiving social support include feeling supported and obtaining sympathy. This can result in increased awareness, recognition of similarities and increased expressiveness or communication. There may also be the 'ventilation' or off-loading of anxieties and concerns.

The value of such support, characterised by a close confiding relationship in which there is trust and the free expression of feelings, was charted famously by Brown & Harris (1978) and will be detailed at several points in this book.

Turning to the second consequence, from personal experience most readers will be aware that supposedly supportive social interactions may also be unpleasant or unhelpful in some vitally important respects. A clear and well-established example of this is the phenomenon of 'expressed emotion' (EE), being a negative or intrusive attitude expressed by relatives about a client (see Atkinson & Coia, 1995, for a summary). EE reflects the emotional 'temperature' within a family, including critical comments, hostility and emotional over-involvement. Studies indicate that high EE creates significant stress upon the individual and is associated with higher rates of distress, most typically in terms of the relapse rate of clients diagnosed as having schizophrenia. Exacerbation of symptoms has also been a way of measuring the negative impact of this dimension of social 'support'.

EE helps to explain the counter-intuitive negative impacts of social interaction in relation to schizophrenia, and similarly adverse effects have been noted in terms of depression. Veiel (1993), for example, conducted a prospective study with 168 depressed psychiatric inpatients, who were assessed one and seven months after discharge from hospital. He found that female clients who were recovered at the point of discharge seemed to deteriorate within what appeared to be a 'good' support environment. It seemed that subtle pressures and demands may have been responsible for the deterioration.

Thirdly, there can be negative impacts of social support on the supporters themselves. In his seminal work Cowen (1982) noted eight negative reactions amongst his sample of hairdressers to their supportive role, including feeling trapped and depressed. For such reasons, Coyne and DeLongis (1986) suggested that we needed to give far more attention to the so-called 'reverse buffer effect', namely the negative aspects of social involvement such as emotional overload, verbal abuse and betrayed confidences. Against such an effect should be counterbalanced the less often recognised positive effects of providing support. For instance, the literature tends to dwell on the high price of caring for a dependent person, assuming that there is no reciprocity or recompense. If this were true, many more carers would surely abandon caring. On this logic, Grant & Nolan (1993) surveyed 726 members of the UK's National Association of Carers, finding that 60% of the respondents identified at least one source of satisfaction from their caring role. Most frequently cited was altruism—i.e. pleasure in the act of giving to their dependent, and in helping to maintain the dependent's dignity and self-esteem. Additional benefits included being appreciated, improved affinity, repayment, honouring vows, and meeting needs for nurturance.

Who helps?

A final way of making sense of social support is structural. This includes thinking about who provides support and in this sense it might usefully be recognised that theoretically we are probably all social supporters at some stage during the average day. At such times, there is reason to suppose that effective support is most likely to come from socially similar others who themselves have faced and addressed (relatively successfully) the different stressors of concern. In making this observation, Thoits (1986) suggested that this would be because of greater empathic understanding and more importantly (from a theoretical and practical perspective) because the coping strategies that these supporters use are a relevant model for the distressed individual.

This is but one of the many social variables that could be introduced into a structural analysis. Others have been indicated by Newcomb and Chou (1989), whose work suggested that in addition one had to take account of the quantity of support that is provided, the family or social setting within which it occurs, how the support is organised and finally the adequacy or quality of the support. These will be discussed in more detail shortly, as well as cropping up repeatedly in this book. In relation to the support variables, Newcomb and Chou also recognised a number of variables associated with the individual receiving social support. This included their status with respect to their medication, finances, health, relationships, mental health and employment characteristics. When linked to the preceding outline of support, these variables produce a bewildering array of potential interactions, which illustrates the complexity of social support.

Levels of help

If this were not enough complexity, it is also necessary to recognise that formal and informal help can occur at different levels of intensity or sophistication. Table 1.4 illustrates this point, taking the counselling continuum as a case in point.

Table 1.4   The helping continuum in relation to counselling, ranging from the informal role played by social supporters to the formal one fulfilled by therapists.

Type of help	Examples of providers	Process of helping
1. 'Social support'	Hairdressers, bartenders, shopkeepers.	Giving emotional, informational and practical assistance
2. 'Informal counselling'	Health Service receptionists; lawyers.	Probing, minimal verbal response, information giving
3. 'Semi-formal counselling'	Special teachers, occupational therapists, nurses and other mental health professionals as an integral part of other activities.	Structuring statements, reflection and restatement
4. 'Formal counselling'	Trained counsellors.	Interpretation, summary, confrontation, self-disclosure, goal-setting
5. Intensive psychotherapy	Psychotherapists (e.g. clinical psychologists and nurse therapists).	Including cognitive behaviour therapy, psychoanalytic psychotherapy, systemic therapy, etc.

Similar structural analyses have been provided in relation to therapy, as in it occurring as 'type A' (the kind of psychological help such as expressing interest and reassurance that is proffered by all professionals), 'type B' (the kind of psychological help provided by more specialised providers of psychological help, such as community psychiatric nurses) and 'type C' (that form of help provided by those with extensive professional training, such as nurse therapists or clinical psychologists: Department of Health, 1996). Again, it should be recognised that although such structures describe the typical situation, each of us will at times operate at different levels and indeed possibly occupy the role alternately of helper and helped. In this vein, Goldberg & Huxley (1980) highlighted the importance for general practitioners to show what the World Health Organisation referred to as a 'tolerant attitude', and which might be more clearly defined in terms of showing understanding and consideration, dispensing sympathetic explanations, and providing reassurance, advice and support in the context of an intimate doctor–patient relationship. This has been referred to as 'simple psychotherapy' and fits with level 2 on Table 1.4. Such simple psychotherapy, if extended and applied intelligently at the community level, provides the basis for important changes in the way that mental health services are delivered. Other terms that reflect this process historically have included 'social system psychotherapy', 'network therapy', 'ecological therapy', 'general systems therapy' and 'support systems' (Milne, 1992b). In short, social support is an inextricable feature of almost all human interaction, although professionals tend by definition to try and limit its role in the way they work.

Quantity versus quality of social support

Returning to the variables listed by Newcomb and Chou, it is worth recognising that, in the history of analysing and attempting to improve social support, there have been two fundamentally different approaches. The first has emphasised the quantity of social support as the critical determinant of individual mental health and has used the 'social network' as its fundamental unit of analysis. In this view, the size, composition and reciprocal nature of one's social network is critical if one is to understand wellbeing. The classic way of analysing this model has been to record the number and frequency of critical life events in an individual's life and to relate these to supportive interactions. For example, Brown et al. (1986) measured negative self-esteem and social support in relation to some adversity. It was noted that when husbands failed to support their partners during adversity there was a greater likelihood of an episode of depression for the partner. Numerous other studies have also indicated an important relationship between life events and support networks (Brugha, 1988).

However, more recent research suggests that while the network is a necessary condition for effective social support, the sufficient condition is that the support is *adequate* to the needs of the individual. In this functional sense, the critical features of support are its adequacy in relation to the individual's needs. Therefore, it can be seen that a wide range of possible ways of meeting an individual's needs exist. Some people function best in relative isolation (i.e. have a small support network) while others require more numerous contacts to meet their needs. In this sense the network is a social 'map' of the possibilities for support, whereas social support as such refers to the functions that are served when individuals within this network interact (e.g. transactions involving emotional concern or instrumental aid). To illustrate, in their study of a sample of 210 older adults, Revicki & Mitchell (1986) confirmed the view that social support consisted of both the quality (instrumental) aspect of support and the quantity (network) element. Studies of this kind will be reviewed in more detail and from a more contemporary perspective in Chapter 3; and instruments reflecting the different approaches are detailed in Chapter 4.

PRACTICAL APPLICATIONS OF SOCIAL SUPPORT IN MENTAL HEALTH

Even if one is sympathetic to the argument that the role of professionals be extended to include a greater emphasis on social support, it is not apparent what exactly should be done. For example, what might a psychologist contribute in the case of material deprivation, such as homelessness? Shinn (1992) provided four replies to this taxing question, commencing with the importance of studying those individual factors that make people vulnerable to stress, as in the coping strategies of children in homeless families. A second task is to study the interface between individuals and social policy, including how well protected individuals are in rented accommodation. Thirdly, mental health practitioners can employ longitudinal research designs to clarify the pattern of homelessness. To illustrate, in a previous study it was found that, once homeless, very few individuals were able to obtain sustainable housing again without outside assistance. Lastly, Shinn (1992) suggested that professionals can study and try to modify those factors that influence how individuals obtain and sustain a home, such as their coping strategies and ability to elicit support from social services or community organisations. In a more routine way, professionals can collaborate with housing associations and voluntary organisations to develop strategic and operational management (see Goss, 1996, in a special journal issue devoted to housing).

In a wider-ranging and hard-hitting account, Smail (1991) suggested that practitioners needed to develop a 'radical environmentalist psychology of help'. This included recognising and addressing the impact of public values on ourselves as well as our clients. It might also include political activity designed to shift values which are harmful to mental health (e.g. valuing individualism and relative personal wealth derived from successful competition). Secondly, Smail (1991) felt that professionals should address ideological influences concerning the use of power. In this sense the mass media as well as individual practitioners may perpetuate false realities, such as the one that says individuals who cannot cope with their work are automatically treated as deficient and in need of stress management. By contrast, an environmental analysis might suggest that structural causes (such as media images of the individual) have a more important part to play than the blaming of the individual for failing to cope with unbearable situations. In a similar vein, Smail argued that we should explicate class disadvantages, such as poverty and a sense of inferiority, which run through and partly explain a person's ability to cope. Finally, we are urged by Smail to tackle some of the more proximal influences, such as an individual's school, work or housing that touch our client's lives directly. Practitioners should recognise how individuals can be empowered to influence proximal environments, or at least encouraged to recognise their powerlessness in many situations. Smail suggested that the distress of which clients complain may often be a completely understandable and appropriate reaction to powerlessness, and so should be recognised as such by therapists, rather than attempting to treat them for failing to adapt to their impossible predicament.

What other things might mental health practitioners do in the community? Prior to the more detailed analysis of homelessness that he provided in 1992 (see above) Shinn (1987) listed a range of activities, which are summarised in the next chapter (especially Table 2.1). This includes supporting the pastoral care role of ministers of the church, helping Governments to design better environments, assisting teachers in their educational work on mental health, facilitating the work of voluntary organisations and getting involved in such activities as enhancing the quality of working life (Table 1.5).

These roles will be discussed in more detail in later chapters. However, it is not the style of this book to simply amplify the cases for more imaginative or appropriate ways of working. Rather, the aim is to try and build from current practice, while recognising that powerful environmental forces also bear down on the professional. It follows that a more understanding and psychological analysis is needed, if innovation is to occur.

Table 1.5 Supportive roles for mental health professionals in relation to social support in the 'proximal' environment (Shinn, 1987)

Setting	Roles
1. Religious	Support 'pastoral care' programmes (e.g. the 'extended family' for abused children); learn from those with experience of providing pastoral care
2. Government	Influence building and general environmental design
3. Educational	Staff and parent education in mental health matters ('primary prevention'); facilitating the learning environment
4. Voluntary sector	Assist organisations to develop. Foster self-help groups. Research what works and for whom
5. Workplace	Increase worker participation and reduce 'burnout/stress' by enhancing the quality of the work environment; challenge organisational norms that 'blame the victim' (e.g stress management)

THE PROFESSIONAL CONTEXT

Despite powerful arguments for role and service innovation and the range of exciting opportunities that exist for mental health practitioners, social support interventions have been sporadic and limited in impact. This requires an explanation. As a rule, mental health professionals are trained for a traditional one-to-one role as a therapist, which can lead to frustration and role crisis when they are encouraged to participate in community interventions, such as in supporting social supporters (Mosher & Burti, 1994). The lack of appropriate skills, incompatible values, excessive professional expectations, mixed feelings amongst professionals in sharing their skills, and the shift to proactive needs assessment at a community level are prominent obstacles to a professional shift away from one-to-one work (Mosher & Burti, 1994; Orford, 1992).

Such considerations led Froland *et al.* (1981) to devote a whole chapter of their book on helping networks to the costs and consequences of collaboration between professionals and social supporters. Amongst the headings they considered were:

- *Staff effort*. The amount of time spent working through help mediators will tend to increase while the style of work will become more informal and unstructured.
- *Co-ordination*. As a community programme becomes less formal (e.g. fewer meetings) then difficulties in co-ordinating staff and helpers can emerge.
- *Recruitment and training*. Once service systems move away from the traditional formal patterns of training and recruitment, fresh difficulties

may emerge (e.g. to what extent is training appropriate for social supporters?).

- *Supervision of supporters.* In a similar sense, to what extent should formal staff be involved in reviewing, monitoring and supervising helpers? Who should assume overall responsibility for the task that supporters perform?
- *Payment.* This concerns the extent to which supporters are provided with funding of payment or reimbursement for out of pocket expenses.
- *Back-up services.* In what other ways should formal therapy services support informal helpers in their work?

In a survey, Froland *et al.* (1981) found that of all these various costs and considerations the 30 agencies surveyed placed most of their resources into the provision of staff effort and back-up services. By contrast, they found that only three of the 30 agencies always provided staff who would supervise or monitor helpers, and only four agencies where professional staff helped to coordinate the informal support activities. Seven of the agencies never used formal procedures for recruitment and 11 never used any explicit training for the helpers.

More recent analyses of these costs of collaboration include tension of confusion over respective roles (Wilson, 1994); departing from traditional, peer-endorsed circuits and developing a more visible and accessible presence in the community (including daily rounds of bars, cafés and small restaurants!—Guay, 1994); and attitudinal objections to the former UK Government's community care initiative, because it was viewed as 'a top down, imposed, technocratic solution to reduce public spending' (Rachman, 1995).

Although challenging, these styles of professional interaction with social supporters need to be weighed against the need to expand our workstyles and the results that can be obtained. In their interesting analyses, Froland *et al.* (1981) went on to consider some of the specific consequences for agencies of their work with informal helpers. A range of outcome criteria for assessing the partnerships were considered, including improving accessibility to services, providing more responsive services that yield higher client satisfaction and self-sufficiency, reducing hospitalisation, and providing control to local informal groups. Although not all of these criteria apply equally to all of the 30 surveyed agencies, probable beneficial outcomes were reported on the majority of criteria by at least half of the responding agencies. Overall, the programmes showed some desirable impact in relation to all of these criteria, except possibly client self-sufficiency. This led Froland *et al.* (1981) to conclude that there were positive results from collaboration with informal helpers.

Similarly, more recent research confirms some important pay-offs for grappling with the challenges of collaboration in the community.

Rachman (1995) reported that social work managers recognised the challenge and opportunities for acquiring new knowledge and skills (although their staff fear the erosion of their traditional skills and a consequent disempowerment of their clients). Guay's (1994) two demonstration projects on citizen involvement in relation to a wide range of health and social problems (including homelessness and drug abuse) necessitated just this kind of role change and versatility, but yielded satisfaction in terms of successfully implementing a novel and ideologically attractive form of community care (i.e. the 'helper therapy principle', in which some clients are converted into social supporters: Reissman, 1990). In her review of self-help groups and professionals, Wilson (1994) noted that the latter group can get invaluable help with aspects of their work for which they have little time or expertise: a complementary relationship can be established, which can not only lead to success based on collaboration over social support interventions (as per Guay, 1994), but which can also foster consumer choice and feedback, so facilitating the evolution of more acceptable and effective services. Also, Mowbray (1990) suggested that 'assertive community treatment' (ACT) represented a good example of community psychology at work, making rewarding use of professionals' existing repertoire (e.g. systems work) while being consonant with professional ideals (e.g. promoting competence and integrating services).

Such encouraging evidence for the value of social therapy would lead one to expect that mental health professionals would be well disposed to this style of work. Unfortunately, it appears that while there has been a move to providing more responsive and community-based health care for those with mental health problems, it doesn't equate with a community orientation (Orford, 1992). Evidence for this is found in the papers published in such prestigious journals as the *American Journal of Community Psychology* and the *Journal of Community Psychology*. Over a 10 year period (from 1973 to 1982: a total of over 700 papers), only 8% incorporated a level of analysis beyond the individual. More recently, adherents of environmentally biased approaches (such as behavioural psychotherapy) have asserted that they have developed approaches well beyond those envisaged 20 years ago, and that an impressive array of work had been undertaken. In order to assess these claims, Milne & Ridley (1994) analysed a random sample of papers appearing in Behavioural Psychotherapy throughout the 1980s. A number of questions were addressed in that review, including whether this literature was environmental in its focus. In order to classify research in this way, Smail's (1991) breakdown of clinical, proximal and distal levels of activity was adopted. It was found that for all articles appearing in the journal during the 1980s ($N = 259$) 77% were clinical in focus, followed by 22% with a proximal focus and only 1% having a distal focus. To make matters worse, of the proximal articles 24% were theoretical, as were all three of the distal articles in the sample. The authors concluded that behavioural research, at least as reflected in that particular journal, had been only modestly environmental during the 1980s and there was no trend for it to become more environmental over time.

Since this finding could have been due to an understandable bias by researchers towards the more researchable topics, a survey of practitioners who adopt a behavioural approach in the UK was conducted (Milne, 1994). A survey questionnaire was sent to a random sample of 30% of the members of the relevant association (BABP: $N=396$) during 1992 and a useable response was received from 191 of these individuals, a 48% response rate. The same question and tripartite breakdown as used for the above survey of research was repeated, and replies from the surveyed group of behavioural psychotherapists indicated that direct clinical work represented 58% of their work followed by 29% at the proximal level and only 13% emphasising distal work (i.e. health education, social support interventions, etc.). In a related question the respondents placed slightly more emphasis in formulating clients' problems at the clinical level, i.e. in terms of internal or personal reasons (54% of respondents), and that these were held to explain the presenting problem more than were external considerations such as the work environment or family reasons (46% of respondents). In keeping with these findings, the instruments used by practitioners indicated that while interviews with the client were conducted on 93% of occasions, assessments of the client's environment (e.g. the Ward Atmosphere Scale) were used on only 18% of occasions.

CONCLUSIONS

From the foregoing account a number of conclusions can be drawn about the provision of social therapy. To begin with, it has been the clear finding of surveys that the majority of those who have mental health needs are far more likely to be in receipt of informal help than the ministrations of a professional helper (Cowen, 1982; C. Barker, et al., 1990). Secondly, such informal help does appear to ameliorate the need, although it in turn may create difficulties for the supporter (the reverse buffer effect). By implication, professionals have at least two roles opening up for them, firstly to attempt to understand whether they are providing the right sort of help to the most needy clients; and secondly to consider whether some of the clients shouldn't be those who provide (but are negatively affected by) the giving of social support to needy others in the community. In addition, in this chapter it was recognised that a wide and fascinating range of activities are also possible for professionals in relation to proactively supporting social supporters, ranging from work in the school to the work place.

Although there are definite costs and consequences attendant upon working at this community level, we must continue to develop support systems so that professionals foster care in the community. This book is intended to promote such a shift towards a more community-orientated approach, based on a sympathetic formulation of the traditional caution of mental health professionals towards such work. Somehow, we need to do more to tackle the 'unhealthy societies' (Wilkinson, 1996) that contribute significantly to the welfare of our unhealthy patients. This book suggests how these traditionally separate realms of the material and the personal can best be regarded as inseparable, and details how mental health practitioners with this heightened understanding can engage in more systematic and imaginative forms of social therapy.

Chapter 2

CHALLENGES AND OPPORTUNITIES FOR PROFESSIONALS

THE REALM OF POSSIBILITIES

As a crucial dimension of community care, social support interventions have been a central part of a revolution in the way that professionals theorise about the best ways to deliver mental health services. Numerous imaginative visions of such methods have been presented during the past three decades, together with invigorating suggestions about how formal and informal care givers can unite in creative collaboration, so as to produce more appropriate forms of help. This vision has been truly multidisciplinary, with contributions from social work, psychology, nursing, psychiatry, education and other disciplines.

Before turning to a more sobering account of the realities of social support practice in the community, the chapter begins with a sketch of key elements of this vision of a better society, since, if nothing else, this recognises what is possible. Such ideals also serve a valuable purpose in providing a truly three-dimensional context for the work that we undertake in the challenging context of community care. In particular, we need to adopt a broad, or ecological perspective concerning our social environment, one that recognises the complex historical and environmental influences operating on us all. Such a perspective allows one to understand how socially supportive behaviours arise, how they function, and what role professionals can play in this sphere.

The term 'ecological' was used by Garbarino (1983) to indicate a key interest in the way that individuals interact with their immediate environment (the ecological niche) so as to affect and respond to each other, in a process of mutual adaptation. Exactly how we should construe this reciprocal process is the subject of the next chapter, which disentangles the different models and mechanisms of socially supportive behaviour. For the moment, however, we simply assume the many forces, operating in a multifaceted and multilevelled way, affect the individual. A clear example is the notion of 'environment press', which refers to various forces or stressors operative in an environment and shaping the behaviour of individuals in their settings. Various terms have been used in relation to this pressure, including the notion that 'behaviour settings' coerce people in particular environments to be increasingly congruent with the situational demands that are present in that given setting. Moos (1976) referred to this as the principle of *progressive conformity*. It should be recognised that this particular analysis applies to professionals as well as to clients and may therefore be an appropriate element in the psychology of professional behaviour, a major theme in this book. Such conceptions of our behaviour take us out of the traditional therapy clinic to the wider world that influences human functioning. The possibilities are similarly vast, because it introduces such a different level of analysis into the way that professionals conceive of their work. To cite Lewins' classic formulation of human behaviour, if we are to understand that behaviour is a function of the person in interaction with the environment, then it follows that one can complement the individual therapy for the person with interventions that address either the environment in which the person behaves, or more probably the *interaction* between the individual and his or her environment. One critical implication of this ecological and developmental perspective is that of empowerment. This refers to the role professionals have in enabling individuals or groups to engage in activities that sustain or restructure their environment. This relationship is negotiated and reciprocated over time, but it is recognised that a number of consequences of this relationship will be unpredictable. In this sense, the popular metaphor of the Russian doll, with its set of nested structures each inside the next, is an inadequate way of construing the individual in his or her ecological niche. While the nested relationship does have credence, it lacks the interactive quality that a truly ecological framework would suggest.

What, then, have been the aspirations and visions in the literature that are relevant to social therapy? A principal and possibly defining characteristic of this vision has been *prevention*. Perhaps best characterised by the work of Caplan (1964), a range of primary, secondary and tertiary preventive activities have been enumerated. Primary refers to reducing the incidence of mental health problems in all aspects of a community, while secondary prevention refers to limiting the duration of a significant number of those problems that do arise. Finally, tertiary prevention is limiting any impairment or handicap that may result from a mental health problem. In essence, prevention is proactive, by contrast with the traditionally reactive secondary or more likely tertiary intervention of therapy for the individual with mental health problems. It is orientated to what needs to be done now to minimise complications in the future and is a clear example of how an environmental orientation can complement a clinical one by recognising the continuity between the past and the present.

A classic example of preventive mental health work of this kind is the training of children in interpersonal cognitive problem solving (ICPS). This consists of almost 50 different 'game' activities designed to teach ICPS. The first of these is the ability to develop different ways of solving a problem, then to anticipate the consequences of actions for oneself and others, and then finally to be able to think of ways of achieving goals or modifying a course of action at different stages depending on accumulating evidence (Shure & Spivack, 1979). Groups of children who received the ICPS intervention obtained favourable results, as in acquiring more of the problem-solving skills than did control children, and in achieving better adjustment ratings (e.g. impulsive children becoming more tolerant of frustration).

Visions of training and skill-sharing

A second major dimension of the vision that has characterised the community care initiative has concerned training. Professionals would need to adopt new roles to be successful in preventing mental health problems and would need some role development to function as social therapists. To take as an example the discipline of clinical psychology, a traditional role has been that of the limited partner of a higher status professional group (i.e. psychiatrists), working in relation to a limited range of activities (almost entirely concerned with assessment or diagnosis in response to requests from psychiatrists), and only gradually altering as psychologists developed and applied new psychological knowledge (Humphreys, 1996). As a result, clinical psychology practice extended to embrace a range of other activities, including consultancy work, training other professions in psychological methods, organisational development work, and, most conspicuously, the advent of a range of sophisticated therapies to be administered by expert professionals. It also included the development of lower technology psychological interventions, such as self-help materials (Christensen & Jacobson, 1994). As Humphreys (1996) emphasised, this progression opened up a universe of alternative professional activities.

Although such activities as skill sharing cause concern to many psychologists, Humphreys argued that the most adaptive way to cope with a challenging new professional environment (e.g. characterised by growing pressure to contain costs and to establish adequate help providers at lower costs) is to recognise that it also creates opportunities. Training for all professionals needs to reflect the changing environment, and to address some of the fundamental questions that are thrown up by the emerging alternatives. For example, if psychologists were not able to do psychotherapy, what else might they do? Or, supposing that there is an important role remaining for therapy, what are the fundamental complementary services that they should provide? In essence, Humphreys and others (e.g. Levy,

1984) suggest that their training and practice would be more productively orientated around broader concepts, such as human services psychology, as opposed to that of the traditional emphases on individual level treatment for tertiary mental health problems. This new vision of training would pull together good practice and sound theory from all the relevant disciplines, and operate at different levels within the community. The prime focus would be on using our collective knowledge to promote human wellbeing at the social, community, family and individual levels (Humphreys, 1996). Similarly, Peterson (1995) suggests that all professions need to direct their energies towards meeting the fundamental needs of society by creating new services, rather than by investing energies in preserving current practices or professional advantages.

Perhaps as a result of having its own relatively clear vision, psychology has grown in a way that has been described as both vital and astonishing (Fox *et al.* 1985). Building on the impressive accomplishments of this particular profession, Fox recognised the need to continue to develop the vision and the training. As a result, they offered 20 proposals towards a revolution in the training of psychologists, moving from the current practice of defining specialities by client group (e.g. learning disability or adult mental health) to functionally defined specialities, such as community psychology. Another fundamental proposal was to prepare people as 'practitioner scholars', so as to enable individuals to integrate the developing knowledge base with their practice throughout their careers. That is, students should be required to demonstrate both effective professional functioning and the ability to consume and apply results of new research in order to resolve the emerging problems of professional practice. Peterson (1995) argued that those who train professionals should themselves be 'reflective educators' in the training field: they should treat the education of professionals as a science rather than an art, using evidence as the basis for their practice. In a subsequent article, Fox (1994) buttressed the views of Peterson and others by suggesting that the continued growth and development of professional training ultimately may stand or fall on the integrity of the training systems that prepare them.

Whether or not training has managed to keep pace with the vision, the related question of the content of any such training arises next. What should mental health practitioners be trained to do in the community? In broader terms, Gale (1997) suggested that his programme would include the following:

- seeking to enhance human experience and self esteem, and to understand human nature;
- using such understanding as a precondition for intervention;
- developing interventions designed to enhance human relationships, the world of work and the creation of prosperity;

- ensuring each individual achieves his or her potential and that communal harmony is developed by better understanding of the causes of conflict; and
- applying scientific models and methods in order to achieve the foregoing.

Visions of practice

As a result of such visions of training and of community intervention, the potential range of activities in mental health practice has been mapped out. Table 2.1 indicates in more concrete terms how mental health practitioners could usefully be deployed to foster social support, in keeping with this vision.

Table 2.1   A summary of some of the social support interventions undertaken to date

Intervention strategy	Goals	Methods
Enhance personal networks	Expand clients' range of social support and resources	Consult with existing supporters; assist existing efforts; establish new networks (e.g. support groups); employ, train and supervise support workers
Develop voluntary resources	Recruit and enable companions and non-professional helpers/therapists	Clarify and support existing services; assist other resources to develop; select, train and supervise helpers/therapists'; research, what works, how it works, and for whom
Support mutual aid networks	Establish peer support groups and relevant activities	Liaise with current self-help groups; develop new, complementary groups in conjunction with voluntary sector (e.g. church)
Promote organisational functioning	Enhance the quality of working life	Encourage worker initiatives (e.g. gain sharing) and participation in decision-making (e.g. teachers and parents). Facilitate the 'learning environment'; change organisational norms that 'blame the victim' (e.g. 'stress management' workshops)
Foster community empowerment	Create local task forces to address neighbourhood needs	Provide forums and facilitate appropriate initiatives; support opinion leaders; co-ordinate activities (e.g. influencing building and general environmental design)

Based on Froland *et al.* (1981), Heller (1990) and Shinn (1987)

An early example of the realities of practice: the community mental health centre

Progress from institutional psychiatric care to the development of community mental health centres (CMHCs) has been a major initiative in North America. Following a Bill passed in October 1963 authorising federal funding for CMHCs, it was legislated that the following features would characterise CMHC services. They were to be:

- comprehensive (providing inpatient, outpatient, emergency and partial hospitalisation care, as well as consultation and education services);
- accessible (available 24 hours a day to all residents of a limited geographical area regardless of ability to pay);
- coordinated with other relevant agencies;
- able to provide continuity of care; and
- orientated towards prevention, through consultation and education, with both agencies and the public.

In 1977, the CMHC programme was supplemented by a community support programme, heralding a fundamental shift from facilities and the services that existed in them (i.e. the CMHCs) to support networks for individual clients. In essence, the community support programme promoted a decentralised and de-bureaucratised approach, introducing a systems view of community mental health (Mosher & Burti, 1994). Key elements were having a responsible team; providing halfway houses and supervised or supported apartments; providing outpatient therapy, vocational training, social and recreational opportunities; and attending to family and social network dimensions.

The community support programme in the USA demonstrated recognition of the need for professionals to operate at the interface between traditional individual care and the social context in which clients live. However, progress has not been smooth: only some 750 of the 2000 CMHCs that were proposed are actually in operation (Mosher and Burti, 1994).

Current examples of the realities of practice: assertive community treatment (ACT) and early intervention programmes

As part of the community care programme, the large psychiatric institutions were closed or substantially reduced in size and greater emphasis placed on coordinating psychiatric and social care in the community. In North America and Europe the favoured solution has become the 'case management' approach (also known at times as 'care management' and the 'care programme approach'), which became a statutory obligation on health and social services in the UK and an indispensable element of community care in the USA. In this approach, each mentally ill person is assigned a 'care manager' who assesses needs, develops a care plan, arranges for suitable care to be provided, monitors the quality of care provided and maintains contact with the client (Holloway, 1991).

One version of case management, ACT, has emerged as an alternative to acute admission to a psychiatric hospital (Stein and Test, 1980). Its distinctive features are multidisciplinary team working (there is little emphasis on team members carrying case loads), low staff:client ratios, providing all interventions themselves and, of particular relevance to the present book, providing these interventions in the community and in the clients' own homes. In the case of clients with schizophrenia, a relevant variation is PACT, the programme of assertive community activity that emphasises vocational activity as both intervention and outcome (Test et al., 1985). Using this approach, there is frequent contact between professional and client and an emphasis on monitoring. This makes it possible to recognise the early signs of relapse and therefore to arrange an 'early intervention'. This targets young vulnerable clients in order to try to prevent or limit social, psychological and mental deterioration, particularly over the first five years (the 'critical period') since an initial psychotic episode. The main interventions are pharmacological and psychosocial (e.g. cognitive therapy: Birchwood and Tarrier, 1994). ACT, PACT and the early intervention approaches therefore represent a welcome move to provide appropriate interventions and care in the community context in which clients live. This will no doubt improve their effectiveness, although the evidence to date on ACT is damning, perhaps because it is not implemented consistently (Marshall et al., 1996). For example, these reviewers concluded that although case management clients were slightly more likely to maintain contact with psychiatric services, it led to a doubling in the rate of hospital admissions and no evidence that it improved clinical or social outcomes.

It is perhaps worth distinguishing between *case* and *care* management at this juncture. Case management (including variations on it, such as ACT and PACT, as detailed above) focuses on the mentally ill and arose as part of the de-institutionalisation programme in the USA during the 1980s. It is typically a Health-Service-led initiative, whereas care management concerns the coordination of services to all those with health or social care needs in the community. In the UK, care management succeeded case management as a result of the Community Care Act of 1991. This includes those with mental health problems as well as physical disability and illness. It deals primarily with practical needs, such as mobility around one's home (e.g. providing special aids, respite care for carers or a home help). Social workers are the main providers of care management, which is local-authority led. But National Health Service (NHS) (e.g. occupational therapists), voluntary or private sector personnel may also be involved, depending on local arrangements. Case management, care management and the care programme approach (CPA) are formal arrangements for providing community care, and revolve around an identified individual key worker or care manager who helps to assess individual needs, clarify the available resources that might assist patients, arrange for such assistance to be provided, and monitor its adequacy. The CPA emphasises the targetting of resources, the continuity of care and the coordination of care for the severely mentally ill within the community, and came about in 1990 following the Spokes enquiry into the death of a social worker at the hands of a psychiatric patient. All three forms of community care also recognise the importance of social support (for example, the information booklet on care management available to individuals in Northumberland refers to the local authority's commitment to ensure the client has 'meaningful contact with other people', to support the client's carer(s) where necessary and to help address 'strained relationships' in the household). Latterly a legal obligation has been placed on Local Authorities to ensure that carers' needs are assessed in their own right. Such needs are defined carefully in an individualised care plan. In sum, all are processes for arranging a needs-led package of services for an individual, encompassing health and social care needs. However, it should be noted that there are a variety of ways in which care management has been interpreted and implemented, at least within the UK; also, while there is compelling evidence to support the clinical case management approach (e.g. PACT), care management is costly and appears to have few benefits for patients (Burns, 1997b).

Because of the overlap between case and care management, there have been joint NHS–Social Services efforts to organise an integrated arrangement to address mental health needs, which subsumes the more specialised care programme approach (CPA). Where this has been introduced (e.g. Northumberland), the staff of the different agencies work together in networks or integrated teams, sharing the work and a service base within a given neighbourhood.

REALITIES THAT IMPAIR THE VISION

Professional infighting

Instead of seeing the larger picture and grappling with collaborative approaches that might realise the vision of a truly integrated community mental health service, professionals appear to have spent most of their energy defending their respective patches. The clearest historical example is perhaps that of psychiatry, which monopolised psychotherapy, largely to the benefit of psychiatry, and was detrimental to society because it actually created a shortage of needed services (Gilgen, 1982). This was the case even though there was no clear evidence that psychiatrists were any more effective at psychotherapy than were the other providers. However, psychiatrists argued that it was not ethical to allow the newer professions to deliver psychotherapy unsupervised by psychiatrists, as they lacked 'proper' training. According to Humphreys (1996) several important lessons can be drawn from the phase that began in the 1940s with psychiatry's dominance. Principal amongst these was the idea of a professional guild, underpinned by an assumption that the interests of psychiatry and welfare of society at large were one and the same (as in protecting society from the therapeutic attentions of those lacking qualifications deemed appropriate by psychiatrists). Nowadays psychiatry can be perceived to have overestimated the extent to which its monopoly served the public interest, and as Humphreys put it, the interests of psychiatry now appear self-serving (Table 1.1 refers to this issue).

Psychiatry has not been alone in trying to establish professional guilds so as to exclude other groups from coveted practices. In the USA doctoral-level clinical psychologists may look askance at their masters-level colleagues, who in turn can question the credibility of non-professional therapists. But declining resources and increasing public cynicism about the motives of professionals suggest that these professionally built boundaries will be hard to sustain. Perhaps in the short term these changes are unlikely to prevent continued building of professional fortresses. They may even exaggerate perceived differences, due to the pressure to claim distinctive contributions and thereby to stake out patches of the mental health field for one's own profession.

A related pressure on professionals which may also lead to the building of professional fortresses has been the legislative reforms and the implementation of different policies for care in the community. Such reforms have raised questions as to whether they represent a real opportunity for innovative services, or are simply a different form of service rationing and a device to deprofessionalise care. Rachman (1995) referred to this as a *technocratic* solution to reduce public spending. Her analysis, based on a review of several hospital-based social work services for adults with health and social care needs in four local authorities in England, indicated that each authority had responded differently. This included variations in whether care managers or social workers were employed. Because of such reasons, change was proceeding slowly, as none of the authorities were enthusiastic. While managers were found to be more optimistic and saw the changes as challenging, workers were more pessimistic, fearing that professional practice would be eroded and users would be disempowered.

Perhaps a final example of the professional in-fighting can be seen in the strongly hierarchical system established by psychiatry and maintained by a succession of increasingly well-qualified professional groups. The professional drift towards ever-increasing periods of training and ever-heightening levels of qualification can readily be construed as serving professional self-interests, but this probably runs counter to the needs of society. This tension must be part of the explanation for the difficulty professionals have in letting go of traditional beliefs and practices (Russett & Frey, 1991) and one of the main impediments to a truly comprehensive and innovative community care system.

The perceived threat of non-professionals

Meanwhile, disabled by in-fighting and self interest, the professionals are vulnerable to the growing competition from non-professionals. In the past, when professional authority was unchallenged, the idea that non-professionals might have a valid role to play would have been scorned. The advent of more critical and cost-conscious times (as detailed in Table 1.1) has also meant that evidence of effectiveness has begun to replace professional opinion as the basis for deciding the relative value of the contribution made by non-professionals. The evidence for their relative contribution is actually quite stunning for the self-important professional groups, as I hope the following brief review indicates.

Durlak (1979) and Hattie et al. (1984) were amongst the first to review the relative effectiveness of professionals and non-professionals. They concluded that the clinical outcomes achieved by the latter group were equal to or even better than those obtained by professionals. Although many of the studies included in these reviews had serious methodological deficiencies (e.g. concerning who was defined as 'non-professional'), there was nonetheless a sense of disbelief in the professional community, not least amongst those with a stake in the training of professionals.

Subsequent reviews, spurred by this disbelief, applied ever more stringent analyses, but the evidence continued to favour the non-professional, usually defined by exclusion—i.e. anyone was labelled a 'non-professional' who had not received a formal training for professional practice as a therapist through a recognised career in nursing, psychiatry, psychology, social work, etc. (Harchik et al., 1989; Faust and Zlotnick, 1995).

However, while these reviews may have supported the claim that:

> Clients who seek help from non-professionals are more likely to achieve resolution of their problem than those who consult professionals. (Hattie et al., 1984, p. 534)

they left open the possibility that this is because non-professionals see more 'treatable' clients. To clarify matters, what is required is a randomised controlled trial in which comparable clients are randomly allocated to professional and non-professional therapists. In addition, other important differences will need to be addressed, such as the clinical settings in which therapy is provided and the nature of the interventions that are provided (presumably 'evidence based' versus 'commonsensical'). Up until now, the comparative evaluations of the two groups of helpers have oversimplified such issues, and have also assumed that experience equated with expertise and that training meant competence (Beutler and Kendall, 1995). Perhaps when such research has been conducted the threat the professionals perceive will be replaced by a greater recognition of the opportunity that non-professionals offer as co-workers in community care.

To illustrate, in the UK there is an opportunity to develop in a systematic way the role of untrained mental health support workers, who could work in community mental health teams (A. Murray *et al.*, 1997). These support workers would receive close supervision, ongoing guidance and specific training as appropriate (e.g. on the effects of medication or on housing issues). This would enable the support worker to provide a complementary input to that of the professional, assisting patients with their practical needs (e.g. daily living skills and daytime activities) and providing a vital social support resource. The Sainsbury Centre review (A. Murray *et al.*, 1997) indicated that the patients regarded the support workers favourably, finding them more accessible and in tune with their needs. Their results also suggested that they were much more frequently involved in social and emotional support than other members of community mental health nurses (e.g. establishing and sustaining social networks; being available out of hours; and helping patients to communicate with family members). It seems evident that mental health practitioners could usefully invest some of their energy by developing and supporting these support workers, who could fill an important social support void in the service spectrum.

Mental health professionals as double agents

At a more systemic level, the kinds of tensions that exist between the professional disciplines and between professionals and non-professionals can be seen to be reflected also in the relationship that exists between any such professional group and society at large. This relationship makes professionals the carers of their clients, while at the same time these professionals are the agents of the social system, serving the needs of the society that employs and accredits them (Goldiamond, 1978). This need not be problematic, in the sense that a lawyer is not only defending a client but is also simultaneously an officer of the court. Goldiamond asserted that most of our interventions belonged in this category, labelled 'congruent'. He argued that it was in instances where there was incongruence that problems can arise.

A clear example of incongruence lies in the provision of stress management techniques to individuals who are asked to operate in an unacceptably stressful environment, or in offering staff training to nurses who already perform heroics in maintaining a caring environment, while coping stoically with reductions to their staff:client ratios (see Table 2.1). Many other illustrations could be provided and most readers will be acquainted with some such dilemma, one in which they are in effect placed as agents of some element of society so as to regulate or 'blame the victim' of an unacceptable environment. Further examples have been provided by Gelsthorpe (1997) in a particularly practical and helpful account. He noted that most professionals cope with incongruence by leaving a job and accusing the stayers of collusion, or by staying but accusing the leavers of abandoning colleagues and clients. In place of such polarised and often polemical relationships, Gelsthorpe proposes that we consider three questions in relation to the incongruence:

1. Is the practice socially acceptable or socially sanctioned?
2. Does the practice occur on an individual level, a local level or a national level?
3. Does the practice fall within your own professional sphere of competence?

In answering these questions we can clarify the appropriate reactions to a 'double agent' situation.

We all need to be alert to the possibility of incongruence in our work as double agents, and this can be seen to be a particularly threatening dimension of social therapy. Active involvement in novel forms of community care carries with it fresh tensions concerning role boundaries, not to mention those relating to the appropriateness of certain professional roles in society. To illustrate, consider how some neighbourhood interventions can entail interchangeable roles for psychologists, educators and researchers; and can necessitate frequent rounds of visits to the given community citizens in order to support such typical clients as landlords, waiters or laundromat attendants in their role as 'natural helpers' (Guay, 1994). Most professionals would feel threatened by such a strikingly different way of doing one's work, in part because the risk of incongruence is less clearly circumscribed than in our more conventional roles. Thus, it can be seen that our relatively uncharted function as double agents in relation to social therapy is another possible impairment to the visions of innovative and effective community work.

COPING STRATEGIES FOR PROFESSIONALS

Given that there is a gulf between many of the possibilities and realities of community care, we need to consider a number of intermediate steps. To illustrate, P. Henderson and Thomas (1987) have identified a nine-stage process to what they prefer to call 'neighbourhood work'. This includes the 'entry' phase, getting to know the neighbourhood, clarifying roles and building appropriate organisational systems. In traditional professional systems these challenges would normally be relatively minimal and could be guided by well-established procedures, but in neighbourhoods the professionals will need to adapt or develop their skills. A case in point has been described by Reynolds *et al.* (1996), who developed a day centre for people with mental health problems in London. A key task was to communicate effectively with the people in the neighbouring properties, several of whom were concerned that clients using the centre would be dangerous, or at least disrupt local community (e.g. shopping custom). Following public consultation meetings, the staff, neighbours, police liaison officers, church representatives and parents and governors from the local girls' school collaborated to form a 'neighbourhood steering group'. Lessons drawn from the experience included the importance of informing and involving neighbours at every stage, seeking practical success quickly and setting standards for responding to complaints. As Henderson and Thomas (1987) emphasised, we do need to find this range of relevant coping strategies if we are to address the growing importance of community work. For example, they note the trend towards early retirement and to a higher proportion of older people in the population, trends which, when allied to policy shifts in the direction of care in the community, lead to more people spending more of their time at home and in their neighbourhood.

So how are we to cope? One set of options can be generated by adapting and building on what we already know and do, as in identifying relatively manageable chunks of community work that are not too far removed from current practice, such as work with the families of people with a mental health need (e.g. see Scott and Leff, 1994). Similarly, we might tinker with our training programmes, boost the emphasis on relevant theory, or model a portion of our practice on clear and feasible examples (such as Guay, 1994). A second set of options can emerge from a more radical re-think, one in which we apply the principles and methods of mental health practice to ourselves. Such a reflexive application is surprisingly rare and so can appear to reflect an elitist stance, as if the theories that we have of human behaviour somehow excluded ourselves. As Bernstein (1995) has stressed, this can make us look somewhat ridiculous, in addition to representing a failure to harness and apply what we know about human beings as effectively as we might.

To illustrate, most professionals would probably subscribe to a self-control or self-regulation model of practice, in which clients are encouraged to observe themselves systematically, to set appropriate improvement goals and to alter their behaviour so as to influence favourably their social interactions. This work would take full cognisance of the environmental context (Egan, 1990; Sturmey, 1996). If such a fundamental approach were taken to professional self-development it would be likely to lead to more successful outcomes for us too. In the chapters that follow, many constructive and successful examples will be provided in order to show in detail how professionals can be reflexive and thereby find a compromise between the possibilities and the realities. This helps them to cope more effectively with their changing roles.

PART 2

Understanding social support

Social support can appear unrelated to the routine work of all mental health professionals, as in defining any social concerns as the separate business of the social worker. In the next two chapters it is proposed that this is a myopic and fallacious perspective, since social support is an integral component of the way people attempt to cope with mental health problems. It follows that social support merits the full attention of all mental health practitioners, and, as this includes careful assessment, a summary of suitable instruments is presented.

Chapter 3

MAKING SENSE OF SOCIAL SUPPORT

INTRODUCTION: IS STRESS HARMFUL?

People have long recognised the important role that is played by stress in their lives, one that is typically regarded as harmful or negative. Stress tended to be used to refer to internal events that were experienced as unpleasant (e.g. a headache or a worry), while the term stressors was used to refer to events that were external to the individual (e.g. work demands). Both stress and stressors were regarded as negative, i.e. as being personally or culturally undesirable changes, necessitating adjustment (Brown & Harris, 1978). Because the distinction is of little functional value, the terms stress and stressor will be used interchangeably in this text.

The early research of the 1960s assumed that there was a direct and straightforward link between such stress and the problems that it appeared to cause, in the form of a subjective experience of strain or distress (e.g. symptoms of anxiety or depression), and in terms of the more objective signs of dysfunction (e.g. illness states or inability to maintain a job or a relationship). Up until the 1970s or so, most psychological and psychiatric theories treated the social environment as a source of stress to which the individual was required to accommodate or escape (Heller, 1979). Numerous studies reported a strong relationship between major life events and psychological distress: individuals who had experienced many life events consistently reported higher numbers of psychological symptoms (Thoits, 1982). Negative (i.e. culturally or personally undesirable) life events had the largest impact, though desirable events also contributed to distress. This early view of stress overlooked the part played by individuals in either modifying the stressors or in reacting differently to a given stressor: the simple 'black box' notion of stress in and distress out was exemplified in the attempts to measure the number of stressors and rank order their severity, in the form of a list of major life events (e.g. Holmes & Rahe, 1967). However, the amount of variance in distress that was explained by the amount of stress measured in this way was typically less than 10%, and individuals showed highly idiosyncratic reactions to stress

(Holohan *et al.*, 1996). For example, some people remained healthy or even flourished, despite the presence of major stressors; while others appeared to be overwhelmed by a minor life event. Survival during some of the most major events anyone could imagine experiencing make a particularly powerful contribution to the idea that stress is not the cause of distress. During the Second World War, for example, prisoners in concentration camps were exposed to brutal and degrading living environments, ones that included forced labour, malnutrition, disease and the threat of imminent death. Yet many prisoners managed to cope with the severe stress in a way that prevented them from experiencing the kind of distress that the early theories would predict. For example, the prisoners dug escape tunnels and resisted interrogation, preserving some critical aspects of their self-image (Moos & Schaefer, 1993). The Holocaust was perhaps the extreme stressor, described as the ultimate test of human adaptability. Perhaps because it was so traumatic a large range of coping strategies were deployed, many of them as extreme as the stress (e.g. loss of an anchor in reality and the lack of a conventional social structure). On the 'negative' side they included identification with the aggressor, regression and daydreams of revenge and more positively on focusing on day-to-day survival, the development of support groups, and taking risks for others (Kahana *et al.*, 1988).

One explanation for the lack of success in predicting distress from knowledge of the stressors impinging on an individual was that of measurement error: with the development of better instruments, surely the expected relationship would emerge, strong and clear? However, some 25 years ago our understanding of how stress related to distress changed fairly dramatically. Instead of attributing the problem to poor measurement, researchers began to realise that the instruments had been sound enough, and it was the understanding of the stress process that was the weak link. Crucially, it became recognised that fundamental variables mediated between stress and distress, which explained the poor correlations of prior research. Known by different names, these mediators seemed to consist of a mixture of coping responses and resources, which worked in some yet to be determined way to moderate the impact of stress on distress. Figure 3.1 depicts these two early formulations of stress. Of great significance to our understanding of how people coped with stress, the new version recognised that these moderating influences could result in the resolution of or adaptation to the stress.

MODELS OF STRESS

Stating one's reasoning on stress in the explicit form illustrated in Figure 3.1 represents an important aspect of research and clinical practice, namely

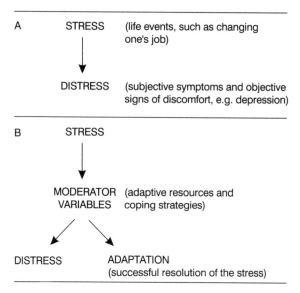

Figure 3.1   The initial view of the link between stress and distress (A), which was succeeded in the 1970s by a formulation incorporating moderating variables (B)

the construction of a theoretical model. Just like a physical model of a bridge or a plane, theoretical models allowed one to tease out and test the critical aspects of a phenomenon, leading into a cycle of discarding those parts that did not appear to work or make sense and developing those aspects that provided a better fit with reality. Models are, therefore, a crucial way of representing what we know in a form that encourages progress (Warr, 1980). Models are also used in clinical work, for the same reasons. For example, Beck's model of cognitive therapy posits important relationships between stressors and distress that are moderated critically by the individual's way of thinking about events (Beck, 1991). In clinical practice the terms 'clinical formulation' or 'problem analysis' would tend to replace 'theoretical model'. However, they are functionally equivalent activities.

Because models and formulations play such an important role in how we construe, tackle and evaluate the way that we meet scientific and therapeutic challenges, they will be centre stage in this chapter. Not only will this help us to crystallise the different perceptions of stress, moderators and personal adaptation, but it should also serve as the platform for intelligent mental health practice (i.e. there's nothing as practical as a good theory).

Given the large number of models that have been proposed as explanations of the stress process, this chapter adopts a chronological approach in order to provide a relatively coherent and intelligible account of the significant developments to the model. Starting as we have with the earliest scientific formulations (Figure 3.1), I next highlight the main increments to these formulations, bringing us up to the present day. Areas of difficulty with these successive models are noted at each developmental stage, as are some of the practical implications for mental health practitioners. To illustrate, according to model (a) in Figure 3.1 all practitioners could be expected to do to assist individuals would be to try to either remove or minimise the stress or the distress. Examples include social work interventions that are intended to improve a person's environment (e.g. better accommodation) or psychiatric interventions designed to alleviate symptoms (e.g. antidepressant tranquillisers). By striking contrast model (b) in Figure 3.1 opens up a whole range of therapeutic options, ones that attempt to improve the ways in which an individual moderates stress (e.g. Beck's cognitive therapy). The implications that follow from this model are vast, including how much emphasis we should place on our living environments and social relationships, how mental health services should be organised, and how the associated responsibilities and costs should be apportioned. In short, the way that we model the stress process is related directly to the politics and practices of community care.

SOCIAL SUPPORT AS A STRESS-MODERATING VARIABLE

Time and again the social and psychological literature attests to the importance of social support, but authors have had more difficulty in making sense of how it works. Early reviews of this literature noted how the company of a 'significant other' was associated with fewer adverse impacts of stress, when compared with the health outcomes of those who were relatively unsupported (Cassel, 1974; S. Cobb, 1976). These two authors believed that the research evidence was sufficiently clear and sound to encourage initiatives designed to mobilise social support (e.g. teaching patients how to give and receive support). Less emphasis was given to reducing the stress.

Thus, social support was regarded as the protective buffer or mediator between stressful life events and personal distress or illness. Its role as a mediator was founded on informational feedback, in the form of signs and signals from close family and friends about how to correct deviations from 'normal' functioning (e.g. how to view or react emotionally to stress). At a more profound level, such support was also regarded by Cobb (1976) as conveying the information that the supported individual is cared for, loved, esteemed, valued; and belongs to a network entailing mutual obligation in these respects.

As noted by Gottlieb (1983), these early formulations accentuated the individual's perception of positive affect and feedback as the essence of social support, while offering little by way of an explanation of how we come to perceive support in this highly subjective way. It is a version of social support that is also very limited, in terms of not fully recognising who else might play a supportive role, or of acknowledging other ways in which support can be provided (e.g. tangible or practical help). Therefore, Caplan (1974) offered a more comprehensive version of social support in which the supporters also help individuals to mobilise their psychological resources to address emotional distress (e.g. by offering cognitive guidance), share tasks and furnish extra resources (e.g. providing extra money or materials). Moreover, Caplan (1974) recognised that a range of social support could occur in a wide range of settings, from institutions to the High Street; and could be provided by an equally diverse variety of helpers, from the formalised network or mutual help group to the informal support provided by strangers at the bus stop. Like his contemporaries, Caplan (1974) saw valuable roles for mental health professionals in stimulating and forming partnerships with these supportive groupings in society, helping them to identify new resources and to build alliances with other similar groups.

INTEGRATING SOCIAL SUPPORT AND PERSONAL COPING STRATEGIES

Caplan's (1974) account of social support was, therefore, considerably broader than those provided by Cassel (1974) or Cobb (1976), and suggested that social support was all around us, almost always positive (helpful), and readily recognisable. Gottlieb (1983) addressed these assumptions in a more comprehensive and transactional model of social support, one that recognised that:

1. Individuals learn to react to certain stimuli as stressors—this provides the basis for the situational specificity and physiological variations in some reactions (or non-reactions), as in people who are sensitised or habituated to some events (e.g. relaxed about public speaking).
2. In addition, there are stable personality factors that interact with the perception of stressors, such as an individual's self-esteem and locus of control.
3. Stressors are appraised by individuals, in a primary way to evaluate the threat posed by a stressor, and in a secondary way to judge their potential coping resources.

4. These stressors are not solely the major life events that were emphasised in earlier research (e.g. changing jobs or moving home) but also consist of everyday 'hassles' and 'uplifts'. Indeed, daily hassles and uplifts are a better predictor of psychological distress than are major life events.
5. Stressors should not be construed as unilaterally assaulting passive, insentient individuals. Rather, they may be anticipated or even controlled, such that their impact is significantly modified. For example, Gottlieb (1983) cites how air traffic controllers who are given breaks at will cope better with stressors. Furthermore, Gottlieb (1983) recognised that participation in a social network was not always helpful or empathic to its members, being capable also of generating conflict and imposing demands. Therefore, he cautioned against a romantic view of social support, arguing that we need to balance the 'sustaining' and the 'discordant' influences that stem from social interactions.

In summary, social support was regarded as intersecting stressors and psychological distress at four possible junctures: through the stress buffering effect noted by Caplan (1974) and others in the 1970s, which Gottlieb (1983) identified in two stages (i.e. between stressor and distress, and between distress and health outcome); intersections were also possible in terms of a direct preventive function, shielding people from exposure to adverse stressors; and in a general way by enhancing morale and health. These four intersections are marked on the Gottlieb model of social support (1983), shown in Figure 3.2. Also explicit in this model is a fifth interaction, one in which social support transactions were fostered by individuals' coping resources.

Bearing out Gottlieb's (1983) model of social support, some famous sociological research on depression, conducted by Brown and Harris (1978), also led to the conclusion that the changes caused by stressful life events were not in themselves significant. What really affected these stressors were the perceptions that people had of these events: 'everything turns on the meaningfulness of events' (p. 275). Also, short-term stressors, even ones bringing severe emotional torment (e.g. the near-death of a child), did not contribute to depression. Rather, it was longer-term threats (i.e. of at least one week's duration, but usually much longer) associated with loss and disappointment that impacted on depression. Brown and Harris (1978) also found evidence to suggest that these major stressors were not additive, as assumed by early life-event researchers. It appeared that their sample, drawn from Camberwell in London, were not at increased risk of depression when one versus several minor or major stressors were compared, except again where multiple stressors were perceived as connected in some way, i.e. part of the same problem (e.g. pregnancy associated with bad housing, a poor marriage, or a quite trivial event that 'brings home'

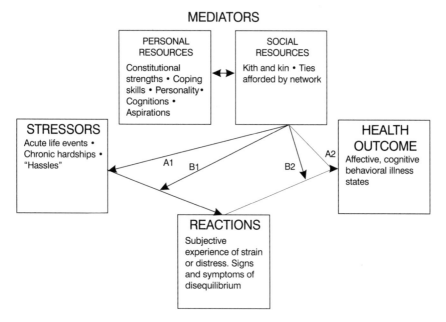

A1: Direct effect of social support, e.g., prevents exposure to certain stressors; induces more benign appraisal of threat

A2: Direct effect of social support, e.g., boosts morale and sense of well-being

B1: Buffering effect of social support, e.g., preserves feelings of self-esteem and sense of mastery when exposed to adversity

B2: Buffering effect of social support, e.g., protects against depression when stressful reactions occur

Figure 3.2 Gottlieb's (1983) model of social support, identifying four ways that social support could intersect the relationship between stressors and distress. Copyright ©1983 by Sage Publications Inc. Reprinted by permission of Sage Publications Inc.

the symbolic significance of a major loss or disappointment). In essence, the power of stressors appeared to reside in their role in causing individuals to reassess their identity and the meaning or purpose of life. For this reason, Brown and Harris (1978) referred to minor and major stressors as 'provoking agents', i.e. not necessarily sufficient to cause depression, though probably influential in terms of when depression occurs.

The inadequacy of provoking agents or stressors to explain depression led Brown and Harris (1978) to posit a second variable, that of 'vulnerability factors', especially the lack of employment and of the social support of a close confiding relationship. Again, these factors alone (plus the early loss of a parent and three or more children at home) could not cause depression but each greatly increased the risk of depression in the presence of a provoking agent.

Provoking agents and vulnerability factors were therefore regarded by Brown and Harris (1978) as risk factors. To these they added 'symptom formation' factors, in order to explain the type and severity of symptoms once an individual is depressed, such as previous experience of an episode of depression or past loss of one's mother before age eleven. Taken together, these three factors provided a social–psychological theory of depression, one that is consistent with and elaborates aspects of the model in Figure 3.2.

SOCIAL SUPPORT AS A 'MAIN EFFECT', THERE TO FOSTER COPING

Many psychologists researching social support have also alighted on the idea of vulnerability, although the preferred terminology was that of social support as a buffer or protection against stress, as noted in the model that Gottlieb (1983) constructed (see Figure 3.2). Two major ways in which social support could operate were summarised in a major review of the literature (Cohen & Wills, 1985). Firstly, social support could have a beneficial effect on wellbeing only when people are under stress, the so-called 'buffering' model. According to this view social support protects individuals from potentially harmful stressors (this buffering process is labelled B1 and B2 in Figure 3.2). Alternatively, it was argued that social support could have a beneficial effect irrespective of whether people are under pressure. This was labelled the 'main effect' model, because evidence in support of this perspective came from a statistical main effect of support with no stress × support interaction. In practice, a main effect would operate in individuals enjoying membership of large social networks and receiving regular positive experiences in a set of stable, socially rewarded roles in a community. This would be mediated, it was posited, by individuals' experiencing positive affect through the community's recognition of their self-worth (process A2 in Figure 3.2). As Lazarus and Folkman (1984) put it,

> ... it is usually assumed that being embedded in a social network is essential for people to feel good about themselves and their lives. The classic work of Bowlby on attachment emphasises that even infrahuman species such as monkeys form close attachments to other members of the species and are distressed by separation and loss ... without ongoing social relationships, much of the meaningfulness of human existence is lacking or impaired. Viable social relationships make possible identification and involvement—the opposite of alienation and anomie. (pp. 245–6)

The link between this main effect of social support and physical wellbeing was thought to occur either through the impact of social support on immune system functioning or through its influence on health-related behaviour patterns (e.g. alcohol use or seeking professional help). The main effect model was thought to be most powerful in a situation between receiving little or no social support and receiving moderate levels of support. Beyond such moderate levels of social support was a threshold, beyond which few further benefits were observed.

SOCIAL SUPPORT AS A STRESS BUFFER, SERVING TO PROTECT

The alternative model was one in which social support intervenes in such a way as to protect an individual from a stressor. This could arise by reducing the effect of a given stimulus or even preventing a person from appraising it as stressful, by redefining the potential for harm or by bolstering the person's perceived ability to cope with the stressor (this is labelled as process B1 in Figure 3.2). A second possible buffering intersection lay in the individual's coping responses, in relation to an event perceived as stressful. This could take the form of reducing the emotional reaction (e.g. taking a tranquilliser or practising a relaxation technique) or by reappraising the stressor (e.g. reducing its importance). This process is labelled B2 in Figure 3.2.

The Cohen and Wills (1985) model was therefore consistent with the one elaborated by Gottlieb (1983), but a fresh box was included to incorporate appraisal processes between the stressor and social support. These processes were firstly the individual's recognition of an event as a stressor, followed by an appraisal of its stressfulness, in terms of such factors as the demand or threat that the stressor posed. This cognitive component was presented in the Gottlieb (1983) model, but was not as strongly emphasised. Gottlieb's account of social support also differed in terms of having the judgement of stressfulness linked explicitly to the individual's capacity to cope (rather than to apparently inherent properties of the stressor, such as 'demand', as did the Cohen and Wills (1985) model). Conversely, Gottlieb's (1983) formulation placed a broader emphasis on an individual's personal resources, incorporating constitutional strengths, personality factors and one's aspirations, in addition to the coping strategies recognised in the Cohen and Wills (1985) model.

PERCEIVED SUPPORT: PART OF A MULTICOMPONENT PROCESS

In a review of research during the late 1970s and early 1980s, Heller et al. (1986) lamented that, despite a decade of social support research, there was still only a limited understanding of how social ties were health protective. They attributed this to the dominance of demonstration projects and correlational studies that lacked an adequate model. While these had provided the evidence to show that social support was a moderator of stress, they had not fully explained social support. In particular, to provide the necessary explanation Heller *et al.* (1986) asserted that the social support model had to be broken down into its component parts, instead of being treated as if it were a single phenomenon, in the same sense that one would not now study 'personality' as if it were unitary. The key question was to explain how these components or social support factors produced their beneficial effects: what exactly were these factors, how did they relate to one another, and what were the mechanisms that resulted in personal benefit?

Based on their review Heller *et al.* (1986) suggested that one of these factors was *perceived* support. This referred to

> a generalised appraisal that individuals develop ... in which they believe that they are cared for or valued, that significant others are available to them in times of need, and that they are satisfied with the relationships they have. This perception was not anchored in any specific relationship, nor does it necessarily refer to the perceived effectiveness of help given in any particular stress-related transaction. (p. 467)

Also, unlike the Gottlieb (1983) model, the emphasis was shifted still further away from social networks, and other summaries of the *actual* support provided to an individual, to the *interpretation* of any social support. The mechanism for the positive effect of perceived support was thought by Heller *et al.* (1986) to be the enhancing of self-esteem through how one believes others value one ('reflected appraisal'). Figure 3.3 depicts their elaboration of the Gottlieb (1983) model (Figure 3.2). Note that this model is based also on the research that they reviewed, so it is only for convenience that is labelled 'the Heller *et al.* model'. However, in keeping with Gottlieb (1983), the model underscored the role that social support can play in facilitating coping. The critical differences lay in:

- removing 'cognitions' from Gottlieb's (1983) panel of 'social resources' and treating it as a separate component, responsible for the interrelation between social support and coping; and
- placing coping strategies explicitly alongside social support as a potentially independent influence on one's wellbeing.

PERSONAL COPING STRATEGIES

By recognising the interactions between social support and coping, Heller *et al.* (1986) made it logical to draw on the concepts used in the literature

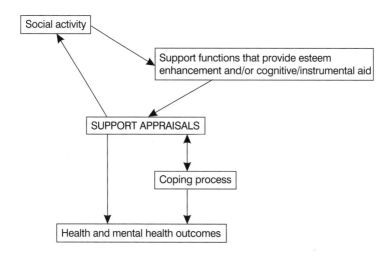

Figure 3.3 The Heller *et al.* (1986) model, emphasising the centrality of the appraisals people make of their social support. Copyright ©1986 by the American Psychological Association. Reprinted with permission.

on personal coping strategies as part of a more comprehensive model of social support. Coping refers to 'constantly changing cognitive and behavioural efforts to manage specific external and/or internal demands (i.e. stress) that are appraised as taxing or exceeding the resources of the person' (Lazarus and Folkman, 1984, p. 141). Two major forms of coping with stressors tended to dominate the early scientific literature. 'Problem-focused' coping involves taking direct action in relation to one's internal or external environment to remove or alter stress appraised as threatening; while 'emotion-focused' coping consists of thoughts or actions intended to alter or limit the distress that results from stress. (More recently, as we shall discuss in the next chapter, several sub-categories of these two broad categories have been defined, and indeed 'emotion-focused' coping has tended to be re-labelled as 'avoidance-based' coping.) Prior to this scientific literature there were psychoanalytic formulations of cognitive processes, in the form of ego operations, that were also deemed critical to wellbeing. These resolved conflicts between an individual's impulses (e.g. aggressive instincts) and external reality, as in defensive security operations (distorting reality). In functional terms, these were also coping mechanisms (Moos and Schaffer, 1993).

Defined in this way, the fundamental parallels between social support and coping became apparent, as in both being directed at changing or managing a stressful situation. In practice, they would usually operate in combination (Thoits, 1986). Thus, an individual could moderate the effects of a stressor by acting to elicit social support (e.g. by using the problem-focused coping strategy of requesting information on the stressor), leading to a cognitive reappraisal of both the stressor and the emotional support that was available from a significant other. Because of the transactional nature of these components and processes (symbolised by the bidirectional arrow in Figure 3.3), numerous other combinations of social support and personal coping were recognised as possible. However, certain patterns or relationships were noted, as in the primacy of the esteem-enhancing component of social support as the mechanism regarded increasingly as fostering health maintenance; and in the primacy of practical assistance plus esteem-enhancement (e.g. through showing empathic understanding) as a facilitator of personal coping strategies. Thoits (1986) suggested a further refinement to this interactive model. Because both social support and coping serve the functions of ameliorating or changing stress, she proposed that the coping strategies people use to deal with stress in their own lives are also the strategies they use to assist others in need. Thus, she relabelled social support as 'coping assistance', being the active involvement of significant others in people's efforts to deal with stress. Indeed, given this integrative version of the psychological process of helping, it was not just kith and kin who could provide coping assistance: Thoits noted that this could also be provided by professional therapists, referring to it as 'the purchase of social support'. Therefore, friends, family, professionals and others (e.g. bartenders and hairdressers) were regarded as potential sources of social support, because all could serve the key functions of (for example) suggesting alternative ways of perceiving or handling stressors, and could at times participate directly in helping an individual's own coping efforts (e.g. by assisting in the re-interpretation of stress). This integrated formulation allowed Thoits (1986) to argue that both social support and coping were actually based on the same underlying model—the personal and social processes whereby we meet our psychological needs.

The parallels between therapy and social support were elaborated by Winefield (1987), who joined them under the shared function of help provision. These parallels included expected benefits to the recipients and similar mechanisms of benefit (especially new learning in a supportive relationship). However, important differences were noted, including rather separate theoretical bases and different provider–recipient relationships (e.g. the relationship was not expected to be reciprocal in therapy). She teased out the implications for practitioners, particularly the need to enhance clients' support elicitation skills and the importance of offering assistance to the supporters of the client.

In keeping with the psychotherapy literature's emphasis upon the 'core conditions' (e.g. empathy and concreteness) necessary for successful therapy, Thoits (1986) teased out the importance of empathic understanding in social support. She argued that this was most likely to arise when the support is provided by socially similar people—i.e. those who 'have faced or are facing the same stressors, and who have done so or are doing so more calmly than the distressed individual' (p. 420). This sociocultural and situational similarity between the helper and the helped was thought to enhance the likelihood of the effective perception and reception of empathy (i.e. 'someone who really understands'). However, Thoits (1986) noted that a difficult balance had to be struck, since people who react significantly more or less strongly to a stressor than does the person receiving the social support may be avoided—a relatively narrow band of acceptable emotionality was thought to exist, since we don't want to end up as a result of social support feeling more upset (by a supporter who exaggerates the stress) or more inadequate (by a supporter who calmly faces the stress).

Sociocultural or situational similarity was not always deemed critical, however, as other attributes of a helper may compensate or even carry greater value for an individual. A case in point for Thoits (1986) was the expertise of the therapist, whose specialised skills and knowledge may override the criteria applied to informal helpers. An interesting account of the accumulated wisdom of mental health practitioners has been provided by J. Smith *et al.* (1994). Defined as 'expert knowledge in the fundamental pragmatics of life', wisdom was regarded as consisting of five elements: a rich factual knowledge about life and how people develop; an equally impressive knowledge about how to proceed—strategies for how to act on stressors; knowledge about the context for life events (e.g. how relationships work); knowledge about how different people hold rather different values, goals and priorities; and a capacity to recognise and manage uncertainty (e.g. being aware that there is no perfect solution and recognising the need to plan for unexpected eventualities). When Smith *et al.* (1994) tested this formulation with a sample of younger (mean 32 years) and older (mean 70 years) clinical psychologists against other professionals (*not* from the mental health field, e.g. administrators and architects), they found that the psychologists did indeed show more 'wisdom' than the comparison group (judged by experts' ratings of their 'think aloud' response to two written wisdom-related dilemmas—e.g. coping with unemployment). However, contrary to their expectations, there were no age-related differences in wisdom for the two samples of psychologists.

As these examples and Figure 3.3 illustrate; Heller *et al.* (1986) and Thoits (1986) construed the process of social support as 'complex and cumulative': each component in the model tends to influence each other component as part of a network of feedback loops. In this way, the appraisals one makes of support may determine subsequent social interactions (stressors, in this model), which draw on a succession of different coping strategies (e.g. initiating, maintaining, then closing a conversation), leading to feeling good about oneself. As a consequence of this formulation, it was clear that it was not social activity as such (i.e. a stressor) that explained the health outcome (e.g. distress), as originally construed in the 1960s (see Figure 3.1). Also, the 'moderator' panel in the 1970s model could now be broken into its components, as detailed in Figure 3.3. Of paramount significance to Heller *et al.* (1986) in this reformulation was the way that individuals perceived and interpreted social support. In this sense, social relationships were understood as being processed through a kind of cognitive–emotional filter. This gave a value to both the social interactions (e.g. whether to think of a specific instance of help as valuing or devaluing one's personal worth) and to the related personal coping strategies that were deployed (e.g. whether judged to be enhanced or diminished by the social support process). Emerging from this cumulative transaction was a further appraisal of whether and when further help was needed.

As before, the development of the social support model carried fresh implications for mental health practice. If the benefits of support were not simply a result of appropriate social ties, then setting up peer support groups (described as the 'current fad' by Heller *et al.* in 1986) was unlikely to prove optimally effective. According to the new model, the *meaning* of the social activity to the individual had to play a more salient role, and it followed that the facilitation of relevant personal coping strategies during social activity was at least as valuable as any general sense of belonging, in terms of the resultant sense of wellbeing. A concrete example would therefore be to help individuals in therapy groups to re-interpret and modify their social interactions, i.e. developing more adaptive cognitive and behavioural coping strategies.

In summary, the reformulation of Heller *et al.* (1986) recognised that *both* the buffer and the main effect models of social support were to be expected to operate and indeed that one should anticipate that they function interactively in relation to a stressor. Furthermore, their summary of research findings up to that point led them to recognise that not all social support had a positive effect, possibly in part because those who provide the social support feel anxious or threatened by the plight of the support recipient. As well as providing an overdue antidote to the romantic view of social support as invariably positive, this served to incorporate the social supporter as a vital tier in the model, what they referred to as a 'glaring omission' in the social support literature up to that point (p. 464). Linked to this broadening of the social support model, Heller *et al.* (1986) noted that the traditional dichotomy between 'clinical' and 'healthy' research participants now made little sense, since the social support model made equal sense of both groups (and so, e.g. the findings from research with one might readily benefit the other). Similarly, they also foresaw the need to broaden and supplement the concept of social support, so that it approximated the full range of psychologically important aspects of social life (e.g. meaningful employment).

A further conceptual development at around this time actually moved in the direction of narrowing the social support model. In her review paper, Thoits (1982) drew attention to the way that the distress attributed to stressors might best be viewed as distressing because they interfered with social support (e.g. a change of job or residence, so depriving someone of emotional support). And if negative or stressful life events were to be understood as stressful fundamentally because they altered the social support upon which a person's psychological wellbeing depended, then the notion of stressors as life events or life changes could be dispensed with as an explanatory factor! In sum, distress might best be regarded as a function of alterations to the initial level of social support. Thoits (1982) therefore overturned the formulations of the 1960s, which had placed the primary etiology at the feet of stress, replacing it with a model in which social support operated as the primary determinant of distress.

THE 'REVERSE BUFFER' EFFECT: SUFFERING AS A SOCIAL SUPPORTER

This broadening and deepening of the social support model also led to growing recognition of the negative aspects of social support for those who provide the coping assistance, the so-called 'reverse-buffer' effect (Coyne & Delongis, 1986). This was characterised in terms of emotional overload, verbal abuse and betrayed confidences. A subtle example has been provided by Lane & Hobfoll (1992), who analysed how people with a physical illness coped with their chronic breathing difficulties in the context of social support. It appeared that as these individuals experienced more symptoms (e.g. congestion and fatigue) and losses to their functional capacity, so they became more outwardly angry (e.g. irritable and obstreperous). The next stage in this process was for immediately increased anger in the social supporter, resulting in unhelpful interactions and a need on the part of the supporter for professional debriefing, especially around the issue of irritability. Similar findings have been reported in relation to depressed patients, who also tend to alienate their social supporters (Coyne, 1976).

SOCIAL SUPPORT THAT DOES NOT HELP

Just as supporters may helpfully suggest that individuals in distress re-interpret stressors positively, so in theory they can unhelpfully propose a more catastrophic interpretation. Instead of normalising and hence calming the reaction to a stressor, would-be social supporters may suggest abnormality and recommend that professional help is sought as a matter of urgency, so accentuating the stressor. Similarly, apparently supportive family members may systematically avoid open discussion about a particular incident, or may minimise, criticise or even trivialise efforts at coping. In another example, the supposed supporters may offer assistance in their own personal way of coping, but this may be taken to excess. In making these observations, Thoits (1986) noted that offering a drink or a smoke is one of the first responses helpers make to try and relieve upset, which, if overused, can actually cause additional problems (e.g. abuse of alcohol leading to perceptual disturbance, interpreted as evidence of madness). Thus, the negative consequences of social support may be intentional or unintentional, a factor that may make a significant difference to how someone interprets an episode of failed support.

Perhaps the best-known example of problematic social support in terms of mental health services is that of 'expressed emotion', which is discussed in Chapters 1 and 6. This refers to critical comments, hostility and emotional over-involvement in families of those with schizophrenia, a form of stress and associated with increased distress for the sufferer (e.g. evidence suggests that symptoms are exacerbated and lead to higher rates of relapse). It is thought that the mechanism for harmful support include stressors that imply strong emotions, embarrassing experiences, or events that may evoke social disapproval. Additionally, a process of social comparison may exacerbate stress because people in a social network demonstrate maladaptive coping strategies, by adverse comparison with others, and even by 'contagion' (the spread of an intense level of distress to others—as in 'burnout' at work) (Buunk & Hoorens, 1992). Other ways that social support can turn out to be unhelpful include a lack of reciprocity (creating a feeling of indebtedness on the part of the recipient), undermining feelings of competence and control, threats to self-esteem (e.g. challenging a support recipient's value of self-sufficiency), and simple incompetence (e.g. saying the wrong thing at the wrong time). Unhelpful aspects of social interaction are touched on again in the final chapter.

THE CURRENT MODEL OF SOCIAL SUPPORT

While the earlier models of social support had highlighted the negative consequences of exposure to stress, and at best had recognised a neutral outcome in the form of 'adaptation' or problem 'resolution', one notable emphasis that characterised social support formulations in the 1990s was the inevitability of some *positive* outcomes. Again, it was not that this was absent from earlier accounts of the stress process: the classical literature is peppered with stories designed to underscore the personal virtues derived from facing adversity; and pre-scientific theories in psychology also recognised the possibility of personal growth arising from stressful encounters. For instance, Maslow (1970) used the term 'growth motiva-tion' to refer to an individual's urge to enrich experience and expand hori-zons, in order to fulfil personal potential (the need to 'self-actualise'). Similarly, psychoanalysts noted that alongside a drive to reduce tension there is also a need for novelty, excitement and mastery of one's environ-ment. This was very similar to the roots of behavioural thinking in Darwin's evolutionary theory, in which the struggle for existence was fuelled by positive and creative efforts at adaptation. Furthermore, the early scientific literature contains empirical evidence to support these views. Haan (1977), for instance, found that individuals who had experi-enced major changes in their earlier life were more tolerant of ambiguity and showed more empathy in their later years. Moos & Schaffer (1993) also speculated that exposure to stress provides the opportunity to improve one's problem-solving skills and to rely more appropriately on others for support, leading to such outcomes as wisdom, tolerance and respect for others. In short, scientific progress in terms of understanding the transactional stress process is not very different from progress in other fields, more typically akin to a series of waves than a dramatic break-through. Some of the ideas that took root in the 1990s were noted many years previously—they were simply not as salient at that stage.

How was this more positive emphasis incorporated into social support models? Note, in Figure 3.4, the explicit recognition of a positive outcome of the transactional stress process in the term 'wellbeing' (panel 5), even though the other panels are fundamentally as per the 1980s model (Figure 3.3).

This 1990s model also incorporated some important developments, reflecting a further decade of research activity. Stressors were placed in a social–ecological context, regarded as the environment for the most important life events (including physical health and finances). Reflecting the logic of Thoits (1982), life stressors were accompanied in panel 1 by social resources (i.e. social support, including the active participation of family and friends, including work colleagues). In parallel, panel 2 includes an individual's demographic and personality characteristics. This includes gender, psychological vulnerability and stable patterns of tack-ling stressors, as a result of experience. Together, these two panels can be regarded as moderating variables, factors that exercise a general influence on stress transactions. Neuchterlain (1987) referred to these broad sets of factors as 'environmental potentiators and stressors' (e.g. high EE), 'environmental protectors' (e.g. social support), 'personal protectors' (e.g.

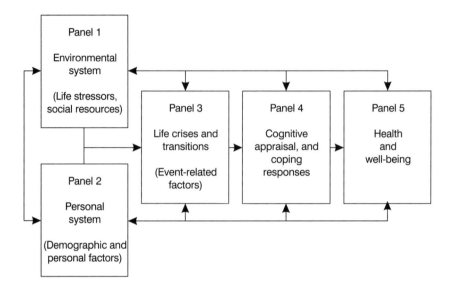

Figure 3.4   The positive social support model of the 1990s (Moos & Schaefer, 1993). Reprinted with the permission of The Free Press, a Division of Simon & Schuster from *The Handbook of Stress* (2nd edn). Edited by Leo Goldberger and Shlomo Breznitz. Copyright ©1982, 1993 by The Free Press.

medication) and 'personal vulnerability factors' (e.g. reduced cognitive processing capacity). As a consequence, the way that focal stressors are appraised and tackled (panel 4) varies over individuals and over time. If successful, this mediating transaction leads to wellbeing, but if there is some form of maladaptive coping it leads to distress. On this reasoning, coping responses (panel 4) are the mechanism of change, determining health outcomes (panel 5).

Another elaboration of the Figure 3.3 model is the greater number of bidirectional arrows, intended to indicate that transactions occur between all variables, including the impacts and the reciprocal feedback on outcomes. The model is also intended to emphasise that individuals are active agents, in deciding how to appraise events and in making selections from amongst the available coping responses (Brewin, 1995). This judgement is based on a prediction of the likely consequences for the individual, which the model would imply as entailing some complex cost–benefit judgements. Therefore, this 1990s model of social support is fundamentally different from those of the 1970s and 1980s in terms of directionality, complexity and causality. As a result, individuals are placed at the centre of events, cognitively empowered to take control of their psychological destiny, which is as likely to be positive as negative.

Part of the complexity of the model lies in its recognition of the role of individual differences. To illustrate, Moos and Schaffer (1993) summarised studies examining the contribution of gender, age and personality factors, ones which they thought indicated reliable variations in the transactional stress process. One of the gender studies, for example, found that women are more likely than men to use avoidance coping strategies, such as a hostile reaction, distraction, passivity or wishful thinking, at least in terms of more severe stressors. Similarly, older adults have been reported to rely more on distancing (e.g. resignation), confrontation (e.g. venting frustration) and less on social support. Older adults have also been found to display less flexible coping strategies than their younger counterparts, although men in a sample of 60 were more flexible than women (i.e. made more systematic use of a wide variety of coping strategies in different situations): more flexibility was associated with greater wellbeing and achievement, and was negatively correlated with distress and alienation (Lester *et al.*, 1994). As regards personality factors, Moos and Schaffer (1993) cited research pointing to important individual differences due to competitiveness, extroversion or impulsiveness. In one particular study, those who scored highly on optimism, control and self-esteem were more likely to rely on active coping and planning.

A second way in which the social support model in Figure 3.4 is more complex than its predecessors lies in its broadening so as to incorporate work life. Values and coping strategies that operate at work can influence other social interactions, such as the way that high autonomy, support and trust at work may transfer to similar values at home, and to a general emphasis on self-direction and active coping.

PRACTICAL IMPLICATIONS

What implications does the social support model in Figure 3.4 have for mental health practitioners? Fortunately, another feature of the last decade of research has been an increase in naturalistic, longitudinal studies, which provide a much better guide to practitioners than do the traditional correlational studies with students. In one of these, the coping strategies used by people with depression were monitored following treatment. At the one-year follow-up assessment, participants who placed more reliance on problem-solving and less on emotional discharge had better outcomes. This pattern was confirmed at re-assessment during a four-year follow-up, with the benefits being less depression (e.g. fewer physical symptoms) and more self-confidence (Swindle, *et al.*, 1989). Similar research with problem drinkers further indicated that the use of multiple methods of coping was vital to improvements, with a definite bias towards those that involve active cognitive and behavioural coping. Also, the best outcomes tended to occur when these multiple methods of coping were deployed in a versatile and appropriate way: even the generally adaptive strategies could prove maladaptive if used rigidly or inappropriately. For example, active cognitive forms of coping (e.g. considering alternative ways to deal with a stressor) if used in the absence of active behavioural coping (e.g. implementing a selected option for dealing with a stressor) could be expected to lead to distress. However, practitioners should always evaluate the success of coping strategies in terms of their functional relationship to wellbeing or distress. There are times when the apparently maladaptive coping strategies are optimal, as in the use of emotion-focused coping under circumstances where nothing useful can be done to change these circumstances (e.g caring for someone with a dementia) (McKee *et al.*, 1997).

Out of these clinical studies and the underpinning social support model, mental health practitioners should recognise several practical implications. These include the importance of:

- assessing the full profile of a clients' coping repertoire, so as to define strengths (active cognitive and behavioural strategies) and weaknesses (avoidance strategies), and doing so in the context of the adequacy of a client's social network;
- using this profile in relation to the clients' perception of key stressors, in order to also judge appraisal processes (e.g. for defensive distortions to reality);
- relating these to the background variables (the environmental and personal systems) so as to gauge the appropriateness of the coping strategies that are being used; in particular clinicians should attend to the possibility of negative aspects of social support, as these can have a greater impact on clients' coping than positive support (e.g. being socially isolated due to faulty coping; or feeling dependent and so low in confidence: see Schreurs and de Ridder, 1997);
- developing active problem-solving skills (cognitive and behavioural coping strategies) and discouraging emotion focused approaches; and
- encouraging clients to extend their adaptive coping repertoire, and to use it in a flexible, appropriate fashion. Drawing attention to the actual or likely consequences of particular attempts to cope is a critical way to judge whether a strategy is appropriate or not.

(Please note that a range of instruments that can be used to carry out these and other assessments are summarised in the next chapter).

THE NEXT DECADE

Good conceptual models are characterised by their elegance (refinement), explanatory power and the predictions they stimulate, amongst other things (Warr, 1980). Judged by such criteria, the last four decades have witnessed progressively better models of social support. A recurring feature of this development has been that the successful elements of earlier models are incorporated into later ones, such as the link between stress and social support. Indeed, a feature of the unfolding models of social support is that they are not mutually exclusive, as most authors appear to argue: it is not a case of 'main effect' or 'buffer', but of complex interactions that vary significantly depending upon the nature of the situation (Pierce et al., 1996). By analogy, consider the example of fluoride, which was originally introduced into the public water supply to protect teeth against decay (i.e. a buffering function). Subsequently it was found that fluoride also served a 'reparative' function, facilitating the tooth's own capacity to deal with plaque (i.e. the main effect). Moreover, the protective and reparative functions of fluoride appeared to interact in a complex but mutually beneficial way. Therefore, this analogy suggests that the buffer and the main effect models may not only occur concurrently, but may interact in a mutually beneficial way.* By implication social support may be thought of as the fluoride of mental health!

No doubt this pattern of building on earlier models will continue, but what features can we anticipate? Perhaps the next stage will involve a move to more explicitly hierarchical models, set out in this way to emphasise that some variables are more important than others, at least for a given analysis. As the variables are increasingly viewed as bidirectional and circular in their causal relationship to each other (i.e. not the sort of simple cause-effect relations of the 1960s model), then in practice this might best be depicted by modifying the size of the model's panels, rather than by arranging the panels in a particular sequence. In addition to rank-ordering the variables in the model, such a development should also lead to the removal of some variables from at least some analyses. At present, the successive models tend to simply 'bolt on' new variables for which some supportive evidence has been found, thereby becoming too flabby and inclusive. To illustrate, Liang and Bogat's (1994) analysis of the role of culture in relation to social support resolved that the impact of stress on adjustment was moderated by both the main and buffering effects of social support, in conjunction with the participants' personality (defined only in terms of locus of control). Culture was placed above these two variables as a factor having a general bearing on how social support and locus of control will operate, which were placed in the middle of their hierarchy. All variables were found to operate in a combined, systemic way. Logically, this model of social support is preferable to the one in Figure 3.4 because of its greater refinement (i.e. fewer, more precisely arranged variables) and at least equal explanatory and predictive power.

---

* I am grateful to Nonnie Crawford for this analogy

For these reasons, and because science usually moves towards such elegant solutions, I expect that the next decade will witness the acceptance of models such as the Liang and Bogat (1994) one.

As a footnote to the growing recognition that coping and social support are intertwined, it has been advocated that future research continues to elucidate at least four apparent links (Schreurs & de Ridder, 1997). Firstly, and the best known, is that seeking social support may be regarded as a coping strategy; secondly, social support may serve as a resource for coping (e.g. influencing the choice of a particular coping strategy and developing the skill with which it is used: their review of research suggested that this link was probably the strongest). A third link is one in which social support is regarded as dependent on coping, as in an individual's ways of eliciting support. This recognises more clearly how maladaptive coping (e.g. ventilating negative affect) can be associated with the reverse-buffer effect and with the thinning of a person's social network. Lastly, Schreurs & de Ridder (1997) proposed a novel link in which coping and social support were considered jointly at a systems level, as in how a family or a couple cope.

A second prediction I'd like to make is that the temporal relationship between the panels will become an important research focus. Drawing on the literature from the study of therapy process, one would expect that the social support field will follow a progression from defining the key variables to recognising critical features of the timing with which they come into play. That is, in relation to a given stressor, the *immediacy* or *latency* of social support may be as important as its nature. Put in concrete terms, the adequacy of emotional or informational support, for example, will in part be a function of how spontaneously (or otherwise) it is offered. A related and more important aspect concerns the *appropriateness* of this timing. More appropriate (i.e. acceptable and helpful) social support will be characterised by an intelligent complementing or meshing of the behaviour, thoughts and feelings of the supported person and the social supporter. In the therapy literature this has been termed 'responsivity'—the systematic inter-linking of the variables in effective therapy with the client's moment-to-moment functioning (Stiles & Shapiro, 1989). Other interesting possibilities that follow from applying the findings from therapy process research to the field of social support include greater attention to the quality or competence of the social support intervention, as in defining and observing the degree of skill or the amount of adherence to a particular method (see Waltz *et al.*, 1993). Such close and systematic scrutiny of what is done in the name of social support may well reveal important reasons for inconsistent findings, as has proved to be the case in therapy research.

Whether or not these two predictions regarding the emerging theory of social support are accurate, predicting how mental health practitioners will respond to the growing body of evidence on the importance of social support is a more problematic issue. Even mainstream clinical research can have disappointingly little influence on practice, unless researchers and practitioners collaborate as true problem-solving partners (Sobell, 1996). By implication, a limited but potentially valuable role for this book is to present clinically meaningful research findings (e.g. from longitudinal field studies) in a way that encourages local applications. The chapters in Part 3 are the clearest examples of this emphasis. Before detailing them, I next set out how mental health practitioners can measure the key variables in the social support model, an essential prerequisite for successful social support activity with clients living in the community.

Chapter 4

MEASURING SOCIAL SUPPORT

INTRODUCTION: FROM MODELS TO MEASURES

The previous chapter provided a brief history of attempts to explain social support. How should practitioners use these models in their work? In essence, models are tentative theories or hypotheses, providing the logical framework for practitioners to target and measure the key social support variables. This helps them to assess, formulate, intervene and evaluate whatever they do in relation to social support. Therefore, models are a good guide to what to measure and should be integral to formulation (whether of an individual clients' problem or of a community system), providing information to a degree that informal methods of assessment rarely do. For example, such information can be more wide ranging or systematic than that from clinical interviews alone, as well as providing a quantification of the problem.

This chapter provides an outline of instruments designed to assess social support from three relatively distinct perspectives. These are the broadly sociological approach of measuring an individual's social network; the more psychological perspectives which focus on the observable, more objective interactions and functions of social support; and lastly the subjective experience of the adequacy of social support. Each of these perspectives represent a complementary way to make sense of and to measure social support, and all are congruent with but spell out the general model of social support presented at the conclusion of Chapter 3. In addition to outlining some of the representative instruments that are proposed by the adherents to these approaches, I will add some colouring in terms of the context and findings that these researchers reported. The reliability and validity and the sampled instruments will also be described.

Following on from these three substantive sections there will be smaller sections on the characteristics of a 'good' measure of social support; and a conclusion that notes the general status of measurement in social support.

MEASURING SOCIAL NETWORKS

History is littered with attempts to measure social support by means of a diverse range of instruments, differing with respect to the perspectives adopted (subjective versus the supporter's view), the operationalisation of social support (e.g. social network or perceived adequacy) the emphasis on specific versus global assessments, and the methods that are employed (e.g. questionnaire or direct observation).

The traditional way to formulate how social support affected an individual has been to construct a social network analysis or 'sociogram', in order to define someone's social 'embeddedness' or 'personal community' (Procidano, 1992). This was based on such features as size, composition, integration, linkages, geographical dispersion, density and homogeneity of an individual's social world. The sociogram provided a structural profile or configuration of that person's access to family, friends, colleagues, neighbours and others who were thought to be significant, and led to conclusions about the necessary amount and nature of social support, the so-called 'adaptive quotient' (Gottlieb, 1983, p. 58).

The social network approach held great appeal because it provided a way to study people's adaptation to life in communities and served as a basis for developing broad-based prevention programmes. If the determinants of psychological distress were affected by the 'social surround', then strengthening the social support systems would be expected to reduce vulnerability, increase personal coping and heighten the sense of community (Mitchell & Trickett, 1980). These two authors traced the origin of the concept of a social network to British social anthropologists, who used mathematical graph theory to describe the social field of individuals when the prevalent structural concepts of role status and territorial location proved inadequate to capture the rich social interactions in the villages that were studied. Sometimes social networks are analysed in terms of formally recognised social units, such as a church or a self-help group; and at other times it is recognised that people make use of both formal and informal social resources in a way that forms unique support configurations. For example, instruments such as the Significant Others Scale (see below) invite the client to identify a series of key role relationships.

In terms of recognised units, consider the role of the church as a social setting. This is a community facility which is accessed by a large proportion of the population (e.g. 40% of American's frequent church on any given Sunday: Jacquet, 1984). From the perspective of social support, attending church may be anticipated to provide a sense of meaning, hope, a shared world view and involvement with like-minded others from the neighbourhood (Maton, 1989). In a study of three large but rather different Christian congregations in the American midwest, Maton (1989) had participants maintain a seven-day 'congregational involvement' log of all members of their congregation with whom they had contact each day, together with the provision and receipt of social support. This network analysis indicated that involvement in the church did indeed contribute to the members' sense of wellbeing, derived from high levels of tangible social support that appeared to serve as a buffer against stressors. Part of the benefit, it was conjectured, derived from feelings of security and a sense of belonging to a caring community. This caring community was systematically encouraged to provide formal and informal support by its highly respected and influential leaders. Also, individuals who were willing to receive or provide this support may have felt selectively drawn to this church community, so reinforcing the support function. Maton (1989) speculated that members also benefitted from 'spiritual support', i.e. a sense of being helped by a loving and caring God.

Some light is shed on the value of church attendance by analyses of related peer-support groups. Galanter (1988) described 'Recovery Inc', a self-help group dating from the 1930s and designed to help its members to cope with mental health problems (especially 'nervous breakdowns'). The group consists of weekly two-hour local meetings for about 12 people, some 90% of whom were ex-mental health service clients (e.g. 39% had taken major tranquillisers). Each meeting includes listening to audio-tape recordings of the inspirational leader (Dr Abraham Low, a Chicago psychiatrist), followed by presentations and discussion by group members. In this sequence, stressful incidents are described, then the group spots problematic thinking patterns that led to distress. These patterns are corrected by reference to Dr Low's maxims (e.g. 'symptoms are distressing, but not dangerous'). Key features of the success of the Recovery Inc groups include highly supportive members, group leaders available over the phone between meetings, strong commitment to the movements ideology, the infusion of hope, and the opportunity for identification with similar others. Galanter (1988) had 356 Recovery Inc members complete a Social Cohesiveness Scale, an eight-item measure of how the respondent felt about other Recovery members, as compared to non-members. Items included 'they care for me' and 'I enjoy being part of their activities', rated on a five-point intensity scale. Results indicated strong social cohesion, not just to those people whom the respondent knew well, but also towards the overall membership. Unlike religious sect members, however, Recovery members retained their affiliative feelings towards the non-members that they had identified, indicating that Recovery members remained integrated within their communities. Also, additional assessments suggested that social cohesiveness made a significant contribution to their mental health. Galanter (1988) concluded from these data that Recovery Inc could conceivably serve as an adjunct or even as an alternative to the care of mental health practitioners, but cautioned that the kind of intense affiliation it engendered can also present problems (e.g. by developing a pseudo science justifying counter therapeutic regimes, or creating an intense dependency: Galanter, 1990).

Turning to the idea that people access a range of such supporters as fellow church or group members, consider next a study that analysed twelve different sources of support used by students, ranging from the formal (e.g. boss, doctor/dentist) to the informal (e.g. parents, boyfriend/girlfriend) (Cauce & Srebnik, 1990). Each support provider was judged by the students in terms of their similarity or difference, using a short (15 item) Likert-style adjective rating scale. These adjectives included 'loving', 'warm', 'intimate', 'formal', 'sharing' and 'dependable'. The results indicated that two dimensions characterised the social support providers and their relationships to the students, namely those of intimacy and relevance (i.e. involvement in daily life). Thus, bosses were found to be high on relevance but low on intimacy, while doctors were low on both dimensions. Amongst the informal providers, friends were highest on relevance and intimacy, while the nuclear family was less relevant (the students were living away from home) and moderately intimate (see Figure 5.1). Cauce and Srebnik (1990) concluded that these students did have a series of separate support systems, which they perceived to have varying degrees of intimacy and relevance.

Turning next to clients with mental health problems, there have been several studies concerned with the importance of their social networks. Early research has indicated that schizophrenia sufferers who had multiple hospital admissions had smaller and less connected networks, attributed to the antagonistic attitudes and reactions of friends, together with the clients' impaired social competence (e.g. failure to reciprocate). However, careful measurement of the social networks of those with an enduring mental health problem has suggested that professionals may need to reconsider what constitutes a serviceable network. For example, Harries, et al. (1984) adopted a multidimensional scaling approach, based on both the observed and perceived client networks, which indicated that the clients' networks did not correspond to those that were perceived by staff, what they referred to as a 'hidden society'. They noted that clients' challenging behaviours often accompanied disruptions to this inconspicuous network. Another interesting and particularly carefully developed instrument from the early 1980s was the Interview Schedule for Social Interaction (ISSI; S. Henderson et al., 1980). Although designed primarily to assess the availability and perceived adequacy of social support, its 52 items also measured the availability of attachments and social integration. In relation to the challenging client behaviour noted by Harries et al. (1984), Henderson and his colleagues suggested that the ISSI could be used to evaluate attempts to improve an individual's network. More recent research has developed these kinds of analyses. For example, Metzer *et al.* (1994) used the Social Network Schedule (SNS), a semi-structured interview that allows sociograms to be drawn over time of who confides in whom, who is friends with whom, and who would miss whom if they left (Dunn, *et al.*, 1990). Leff and his colleagues in the Team for the Assessment of Psychiatric Services (TAPS) near London have also administered the SNS to clients moving out of Friern and Claybury psychiatric hospital groups. In one of a series of TAPS studies, O'Driscoll *et al.* (1993) collected SNS baseline data from 488 clients. These data indicated a median network size of six people in both hospitals. For Friern clients this included two friends, one confidant and three active relationships (figures are medians, again). Similar findings were reported for the sample from Claybury Hospital. One year later some of these clients had been resettled into community accommodation, and a comparison with a matched group who had remained in hospital indicated that the 'leavers' had more diverse social networks that contained a higher proportion of contacts identified as friends. These friends came from the relatives of friends or carers, neighbours, or contacts made at social clubs (J. Anderson *et al*, 1993). The authors believed that this was the first prospective, controlled research design to examine changes in the social networks of long-stay psychiatric clients. They noted that the development of a relatively complex and locally integrated social network is associated with lower risk of relapse amongst schizophrenia sufferers in the community.

Metzer *et al.* (1994) also found that a move out of hospital and into new accommodation in the community was associated with more cohesion (i.e. closer ties) and more reciprocity. Figure 4.1 illustrates some of their data. In keeping with the earlier point about people establishing a flexible configuration of supports, Metzer *et al.* (1994) reported some signs that the re-establishment of social contacts in the local community loosened the social network in the residences.

Continuing the theme, there is also evidence that as the social network increases so the likelihood of hospitalisation decreases. Using the Social Network Schedule (as above), Becker *et al.* (1997) were able to determine the social network of over 100 patients with a severe mental illness, relating this to their use of services (e.g. out-patient appointments and social-worker support) and their hospital isolation. Their findings 'provided substantial evidence in favour of the social network association hypothesis' (p. 18), i.e. that a patient's network size was related to the likelihood of inpatient treatment. Similar findings have been reported using the Life Events Interview, which includes questions about a patient's social network size, network composition and the duration and frequency of network relations (Holmes-Eber & Riger, 1990).

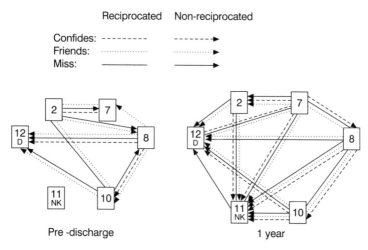

Figure 4.1 A network analysis, illustrating how a move from a psychiatric hospital to a community home and the arrival of a new patient (11 NK) altered the social network of five patients. ('Confides' refers to feeling able to share feelings on worries; 'friends' refers to whether another person is viewed as a friend; and 'miss' refers to whether a person would be missed if no longer present.) Reproduced from Metzer *et al.* (1994) by permission of Carfax Publishing Ltd, PO Box 25, Abingdon, Oxfordshire OX14 3UE.

A variation on simply graphing the links in a person's social network is to estimate some of the important qualities in these links, such as their power relationships. Hagan and Smail (1997) provided a clinical illustration of mapping the powers and resources available to clients ('assets'), as well as the severity of pressures to which they may be subjected ('liabilities'). The assets are coloured black and the liabilities red, in relation to material resources, personal resources, home and family life, and social life. Shading is also used where limiting factors operate.

In summary, the measurement of an individual's social network is relatively straightforward, can be conducted with a range of user-friendly instruments, and yields data that are associated with mental health. However, the network approach is insufficient: there is increasing evidence that structural characteristics of social support are only weakly related to both the adequacy of support and with distress (B.R. Sarason, *et al.*, 1990). For example, it is evident from clinical observation as well as from research studies that not all contacts in a social network are helpful, making it necessary to also analyse the interactions within networks, and especially the resulting outcomes. This is, therefore, the focus of the next section.

MEASURING SOCIAL INTERACTION

Following network analysis, the second major tradition has been to measure supportive interactions, usually taking the form of an assessment of the consequences of social support. In this sense, social interaction measures focus on the *functions* that social support can serve, whereas social network measures concentrate on the *form* of social support bonds.

According to Procidano (1992), the most popular instrument in this category has been the Inventory of Socially Supportive Behaviours (ISSB: Barrera, *et al.*, 1981). This is a 40-item scale, based on a broad conceptualisation of social support that includes practical assistance (i.e. 'tangible' help e.g. sharing tasks and providing money, materials or skills). Barrera *et al.* (1981) generated the 40 items for the ISSB from a literature review, drafting them so that they referred to specific supportive behaviours, were widely applicable and omitted reference to psychological states (i.e. adjustment or distress). The ISSB has a five-point response format, encouraging respondents to rate the frequency with which they had received each of the 40 social support items on a scale from 'not at all' (score 1) to 'about every day' (score 5). The response is based on events occurring during the preceding month. Illustrative items include 'did some activity together to help you get your mind off things'; 'talked with you about some interest of yours'; and 'let you know that you did something well'. Barrera *et al.* (1981) then assessed the reliability and validity of the ISSB, which is summarised below (in the section on 'what makes a good measure?').

While Barrera *et al.* (1981) clearly viewed the ISSB as a measure of social interactions and so carefully defined the 40 ISSB items to reflect the central functions served by social support, they did not tease out its main factors. Therefore, in a subsequent paper Barrera and Ainley (1983) carried out a factor analysis of the ISSB, finding evidence for the factors 'tangible assistance', 'directive guidance' and 'emotional support'. In addition, they conjectured that there was a fourth factor, 'positive social interaction'. A more sophisticated approach to factor analysis, FACTOR EP, was therefore applied to the ISSB by Walkey *et al.* (1987). This requires that the emerging factor structures are replicated across independent groups of people. Only if the number and type of factors is clearly and consistently replicated across groups are they said to be stable or 'real'. Walkey *et al.* (1987) had 370 students from Arizona, 179 students from Chicago, and a sample of 106 students from Wellington, New Zealand, complete the ISSB twice, one week apart. Applying the FACTOR EP analysis led these authors to conclude with Barrera and Ainley (1983) that the ISSB contained the first three factors identified above. This meant that the ISSB was best regarded as a measure of these three specific types of social support, rather than as a general measure of social support. They noted that future research might add some new items to the ISSB in order to measure 'socialising' (the 'positive social interaction' factor), since theory would suggest that it too is a specific dimension of social support.

As discussed in Chapter 3, there is significant overlap between social support and coping, which makes the use of coping instruments relevant. For example, in addition to being the recipient of social support from others, as measured by the ISSB, effective coping behaviour includes efforts to seek or elicit social support. This aspect of social support is assessed by such instruments as the Ways of Coping Checklist and the Coping Responses Inventory.

The Ways of Coping Checklist (WOCS), can be administered as a questionnaire or as an interview (Lazarus & Folkman, 1984). The WOCS was designed to provide a detailed summary of specific social support thoughts, feelings and behaviours, in relation to a stressor specified by the client. The 66 WOCS items were generated from research and experience, and addressed the two loosely defined functions of emotion-focused or problem-focused coping. Examples of the former with a social support emphasis include the items 'I tried to keep my feelings to myself' and 'I let my feelings out somehow'; while the items 'talked to someone to find out more about the situation' and 'I apologised or did something to make up' are illustrative of the 'problem-focused' style of coping. All items are rated on a four-point frequency scale, from 'not used' to 'used a great deal'.

More recently, Moos (1990) has provided an updated variant of the WOCS, called the Coping Responses Inventory (CRI). The CRI contains 48 items covering eight subscales, one of which is 'seeking guidance and support'. The CRI can be administered as a self-report questionnaire or as an interview. Respondents indicate the frequency with which they have enacted the identified behaviours during the past year on a four-point frequency scale, from 'not at all' to 'fairly often'. Unlike many other instruments, the CRI responses are related to a specific problem, as identified by the respondent. Illustrative items from the six-item social support subscale are 'talk with your partner or other relative about the problem', 'try to find out more about the situation' and 'pray for guidance or strength'. As these items indicate, Moos (1990) explicitly recognises in the CRI's design that coping behaviours may be adaptive ('approach coping responses') or maladaptive ('avoidance coping responses'), and the evidence tends to suggest that the latter are at best only initially adaptive (as in 'pray for guidance or strength'). The full CRI is available for clinical or research use in a portfolio of accessible mental health instruments (Milne, 1992a). This portfolio also includes the complementary Significant Others Scale (Power et al., 1988), which, as discussed in the earlier section of this chapter, allows one to define up to six 'significant others' in relation to the 'actual' versus the 'ideal' emotional and practical support.

A third example of a coping instrument with a social support component is COPE (Carver *et al.*, 1989), which helpfully is also available in an accessible portfolio of health psychology instruments (Weinman, Wright and Johnston, 1995). Unlike the two coping instruments mentioned so far, COPE can be used to assess both how individuals handle specific situations as well as how they are disposed to general (i.e. 'state' versus 'trait') coping. However, like the WOCS and, CRI, the COPE assesses how frequently people seek or use guidance (or information) and emotional support.

A useful summary of several popular social support instruments has been provided by Bowling (1991). These are the Inventory of Socially Supportive Behaviours, the Arizona Social Support Inventory Schedule, Perceived Support from Family and Friends, the Social Support Questionnaire, the Interview Schedule for Social Interaction, the Social Network Scale, the Family Relationship Index, the Social Support Appraisals Scale and the Social Support Behaviour Scale, the Interpersonal Support Evaluation List, and the Loneliness Scale. For each of these instruments, Bowling (1991) provides sample items, information on the scoring procedure, and information on reliability and validity.

Observational measures of social support

So far, the measures that have been summarised are dependent upon self-report, either by means of a questionnaire or a structured interview. There are clinical situations when clients are unable or unwilling to comply with a self-report format, or where a more objective assessment approach is preferable. As Dunn *et al.* (1990) noted, there is also an understandable caution in accepting as reliable the reports of people with a psychiatric diagnosis, people who have spent many years in hospital (although it should be noted that, following a comparison of observational and self-report data from such clients, they concluded that 'the patients' judgement was at least as reliable as healthy people's recall of actual social events'—p. 847). However, the purpose of an observational assessment may be the same as for self-report instruments, and the first example provides a relatively straightforward observational approach to network analysis. This is the Dunn *et al.* (1990) study, which partly devised an observational system in order to validate the Social Network Schedule (SNS—described earlier) and partly used the system to carry out a naturalistic assessment of the quality and quantity of the social interactions of a group of long-stay psychiatric patients. They devised four social behaviour categories for their observation system, consisting of 'helpers' (who tidy up and help other patients etc.), 'friends' (a cohesive group of companions) and 'nuisances' (who do not initiate socal interactions). Observations focused on a sample of 12 people in the hospital club, indicating that a self-regulating social hierarchy, developed entirely by the patients, was in operation. This hierarchy was defined by each patient's quality and quantity of social contacts (e.g. 'helpers' had the most frequent contacts, 'asocials' the fewest). The complexity of each patient's social network was calculated by totalling the number of different patients that were contacted during the 10 one-hour observation sessions, and from calculating the proportion of time that each patient spent in social activity. The network size ranged from 2 to 19, with a mode of 8 (i.e. similar to the SNS results), while the time spent in social interaction ranged from 0% to 75%.

The second example of an observation approach focuses on the central issue of social support elicitation (Winefield, 1984). Support elicitation behaviours can usefully be related to the functions that they achieve, in the classic interactional approach to understanding social support. The first example incorporates this emphasis by adapting the three factors defined above for the ISSB.

The Support Observation System (SOS; Milne & Netherwood, 1997) was developed on the basis of the helping behaviours that therapists use with their clients, as encapsulated in the Helper Behaviour Rating scale (HBRS: Hardy & Shapiro, 1985). To the relevant HBRS items (e.g. 'information' and 'self-disclosure') were added the more conventional social support ones of emotional support, tangible assistance and positive social interaction. Being an observational tool, it was also deemed necessary to include the categories 'negative talk', 'nothing happening' and 'other'. These 13 SOS categories were recorded by a non-participant observer, using a sampling technique (partial interval recording) to code live interactions in two hairdressing salons. In this way, the observer recorded the frequency of each category of speech. Furthermore, the clients' utterances were classified according to their broad subject matter (e.g. general or personal information) and the stylists' speech was coded using the same SOS categories. This is illustrated in Table 4.1, which summarises the overall profile of the stylist's speech.

This interactional analysis of social support provided a rich account of the unfolding client–stylist verbal interactions over 20 minute periods, allowing the relationship between the two parties to be analysed. The results of applying the SOS to clients and stylists in a salon in a large, traditional psychiatric hospital and a salon in the neighbouring town centre are summarised in Table 4.2, which also lists the 13 SOS categories.

In addition to providing interesting information on the relative frequencies of the different social support behaviours of psychiatric hospital patients and ordinary people, this comparison also served as a validation

Table 4.1   Percentage of stylist responses observed to fall into each SOS speech category

Category	%
Prompting (acknowledging what is said, encouraging; agreeing)	30.7
Self disclosure (giving factual information about self, family or friends)	24.1
Positive social interaction (laugh; joke)	16.3
Nothing (no utterance during 10 s interval)	7.4
Request information (open and closed question)	7.0
Expression (voicing a personal opinion)	6.7
Reassurance (showing understanding; praising)	3.3
Information (providing general factual data)	2.2
Negative utterance (disagreement; complaining)	1.1
Advisement (suggesting action)	0.7
Tangible assistance (material help)	0.4
Request advice (seeking guidance)	0
Other (utterance not falling into above—e.g. singing)	0
	99.9

Table 4.2   Mean percentage client utterances in each speech category

	Mean %	
Category	Psychiatric hospital group ($N=20$)	High street group ($N=19$)
Requesting information**	5	10
Requesting Advice	2	1
Information	5	9
Advice	0	1
Tangible Assistance	0	0
Self Disclosure*	11	18
Expression**	6	10
Reassurance	1	2
Prompt*	7	13
Positive Interaction**	3	7
Negative Utterance	1	0
Other	1	0
Nothing***	58	29

Probability levels are indicated by one ($p < 0.05$), two ($p < 0.01$) or three ($p < 0.001$) stars. The definitions of these categories are provided in Table 4.1.
Reproduced from Milne and Netherwood (1997) by permission of Cambridge University Press, The Edinburgh Building, Shaftesbury Road, Cambridge CB2 2RU.

of the SOS. That is, if the SOS was indeed measuring the kinds of socially supportive behaviours that it purported to measure, then one would expect to find the kinds of differences that Winefield (1984) and others have noted in the psychiatric population. These include poor understanding of the norms regarding intimacy, showing little interest in others, and rarely reinforcing helping behaviour. Respectively, these were reflected in the SOS categories 'self-disclosure' and 'expression'; 'requesting information' and 'prompting'; and by 'reassurance' and 'positive social interaction'. The figures in Table 4.2 suggested that all three predictions were upheld, which indicated that the SOS was valid.

The SOS was also useful in examining whether there were clear patterns or contingencies linking the behaviour of the clients and the stylists. It was found that most stylist 'self-disclosure' was initiated by the client providing 'information', 'self-disclosure' or 'prompting'; in turn, when stylists were 'prompting' clients, this was preceded by the client providing 'information', 'self-disclosure' or 'positive social interaction'. These findings were similar for both the hospital and the High Street groups, indicating some stable, robust relationships between social support elicitation and provision.

The reliability of the SOS was demonstrated by having two observers independently code a video recorded sample of stylist:client interaction. This revealed complete agreement on the subject matter, 80% agreement for the clients' use of SOS categories and 88% agreement when the stylists were speaking. As a further check on the procedure, the impact of having a non-participant observer present ('reactivity') was evaluated by comparing data from the first and last observation sessions. If reactivity is present, it would be expected to reduce over time as people become accustomed to the observer ('habituation'). As there was no significant difference between these data, reactivity was assumed to be minimal, which was corroborated by informal reports from the stylists.

This study shows how careful observation of socially supportive interactions can be conducted, yielding interesting information regarding such issues as the relatively maladaptive profile of social speech in a sample of psychiatric inpatients (Table 4.2) and the salience of particular stylist speech categories (Table 4.1). Both are relevant to the work of mental health practitioners, as, for example, they highlight social skills needs in their clients and something of the style of the informal help that is likely to be available to their clients in hairdressing salons. The SOS is available from the author.

Alternative observation tools exist, such as the instrument employed by Dunn et al. (1990) to measure the social life of long-stay psychiatric patients, and there are also different ways to structure such observations. For instance, B.R. Sarason et al. (1992) had students and their parents engage in a supportive interaction in a laboratory context, in which a parent assisted the student to prepare a speech. Observers then rated a video-recording of the interaction, in order to assess how supportive and sensitive the parent had been. There was a clear relationship between the observers' ratings and the students' perceptions of the interaction, indicating that the observers could pick out important facets of a rather contrived social support interaction.

In summary, the functional or interactional approach to the measurement of social support has led to the development of numerous instruments, a sample of which have been outlined above. While each new study appears to create a new instrument, there is at least a fair degree of consensus on the main functions that should be measured in assessing social support. These are tangible assistance, emotional support, informational guidance and, to a lesser extent, positive social interaction. Such functions of social support are understood to arise as a transactional process between people, and several key supporter and support-recipient behaviours were identified as ingredients that were critical to the success of such supportive interactions (e.g. self-disclosure). This linked to the idea, more fully articulated in Chapter 3, that the elicitation and consequation of social support can usefully be viewed and assessed as coping responses, leading to the use of appropriate coping inventory scales.

However, it has been argued increasingly that this kind of functional analysis, although more useful than the network approach, is insufficient to analyse social support. Researchers such as B.R. Sarason *et al.* (1990) have argued that the social interaction approach omits the vital dimension of the perceived value of social support, i.e. the individual's emotional experience of the *adequacy* of a social interaction. It is necessary to measure this facet too, it is argued, if we are to properly understand how and why social support operates as it does. Therefore, the next section overviews some of the characteristic instruments that adopt this third approach to the assessment of social support.

MEASURING THE PERCEIVED ADEQUACY OF SOCIAL SUPPORT

This third and final focus in the assessment of social support relates to an individual's appraisal or perception of social support, a subjective judgement of the adequacy of the support that is available or received. Instruments designed to assess this aspect of social support will emphasise a person's belief that he or she is 'cared for and loved ... esteemed and valued ... and belongs to a network of communication and mutual obligations' (Cobb, 1976, p. 300). Such a belief arises from the individual's *appraisal* of social networks and interactions, including the attributions that are made. As touched on in Chapter 3, appraisals are evaluations of stressors, in terms of the degree of threat or challenge ('primary' appraisal), and in relation to the adequacy of one coping repertoire of resources to tackle this challenge ('secondary' appraisal) (Lazarus & Folkman, 1984). People who are distressed (e.g. anxious or depressed) tend to exaggerate the stressor and minimise their ability to cope, which then undermines efforts to cope (e.g. support elicitation). To illustrate, the way that carers of people with schizophrenia appraise the stressors entailed by their caring role (e.g. the signs and symptoms of schizophrenia) would be expected to influence how confidently and effectively they cope. And, in turn the level of distress that these social supporters feel in their caring role will have a bearing on their appraisal of the stressors and their capacity to cope. In order to examine this relationship, Barrowclough and Parle (1997) identified 85 patients with a diagnosis of schizophrenia, and then involved their relatives (parents, partners, children and siblings) as research participants. These relatives completed a measure of distress, the General Health Questionnaire (GHQ: Goldberg & Williams, 1988), an instrument assessing appraisal (the Family Questionnaire: Barrowclough & Tarrier, 1992) and an assessment of 49 possible stressors, in terms of their frequency, the concern they caused and their confidence in dealing with the problems. They indeed found that the relatives' appraisal processes (i.e. threat appraisal and coping efficacy) influenced how they reacted to the family member with schizophrenia and how distressed they felt. Those relatives who appraised the stressors as most threatening, who coped by means of high expressed emotion ('EE'—e.g. critical comments and hostility) and who were the most distressed were those at greatest risk of continued distress. This then tends to lead to the patient's readmission to hospital. By implication, Barrowclough and Parle (1997) suggest that mental health professionals should help such relatives to reduce their threat appraisal and to enhance their perception that they can cope successfully. From a theoretical standpoint, these findings also shed light on how social support is developed and maintained, again underlining the likely importance of the transactional stress model (see Chapter 3 for a full account). That is, instead of being a blameworthy personality trait, social support may best be regarded as resulting from a state of maladaptive coping.

Appraisal can be viewed as a 'personality' characteristic, influenced by such factors as an individual's expectation of control over stressors. An example is the Rotter (1966) Locus of Control Scale, which measures the extent to which someone feels personally in control of what happens in life (an 'internal' locus of control), as opposed to feeling that external factors (such as destiny or luck) are the cause of what happens (i.e. 'external' locus of control). To illustrate, in an interesting study of how social support protects relatively healthy people from distress (i.e. the 'main effect') Dalgard et al. (1995) administered a 12-item questionnaire to 269 people. This instrument asked the respondents to evaluate the adequacy of their social support (a parallel instrument measuring their social network had yielded only weak relationships to distress). In addition, Dalgard et al. (1995) assessed negative life events, distress and locus of control, finding an interesting pattern of results. People with an external locus of control ('externals') had a strong interaction between social support and stressors, but this effect was absent for 'internals'. When the 'externals' faced stressors and had weak social support, they tended to experience more distress. However, 'internals' showed no trend to increase symptoms (i.e. anxiety and depression) when exposed to stressors, regardless of the social support. Dalgard *et al.* (1995) concluded that good social support acts as a buffer between negative life events and distress (especially depression), but this effect is only present for those people in their sample who were 'externals'. By implication, those who have a high internal locus of control do not appear to need as much social support, most likely because they regard themselves as being able to cope with stressors. Conversely, 'externals' with poor social support are at risk of distress. This study illustrates how personality interacts with social support, whether measured as a network or in terms of its adequacy. The social support instrument used by Dalgard *et al.* (1995) is reproduced in Table 4.3.

Of course, locus of control is not by any means the only way in which an individual's personality may influence social support. Another example, considered earlier, was that of 'expressed emotion'. A third illustration is that of 'cognitive vulnerability', a style of thinking that makes an individual prone to misperceiving social support and consequently of being at higher risk of distress (especially depression). Therefore, this cognitive vulnerability parallels the social vulnerability as defined by Brown and Harris (1978: see Chapter 3). According to Champion and Power (1995), distress arises in part because of individuals' excessive expectations of social support, and partly because they have over-invested in a particular role or goal, which is essential to their sense of self-worth (i.e. giving meaning and purpose to life, particularly where the intrinsic belief in one's own value is weak). Social support fits into this model as a vulnerability factor, as it may interfere with an individuals' roles or goals or it may limit the options and flexibility they have for obtaining alternative sources of self-worth.

A key aspect of this cognitive vulnerability model is the discrepancy between ideal and actual levels of social support. Power *et al.* (1988) have designed the Significant Others Scale (SOS) in order to measure this perceived discrepancy in terms of a range of role relationships (e.g. partner). Up to six of these are generated by the client or by the practitioner, and then the client rates the relationships in terms of a seven-point frequency scale (from 'never' to 'always'). For example, in relation to each of the role relationships the respondents would rate how often they can 'trust, talk to frankly and share feelings' or 'get financial and practical help' from each identified person. The first of these items covers an emotional function of social support, the latter a practical purpose, representing the two dimensions that are covered by the SOS. Each set of relationships is evaluated in terms of these dimensions as they are

Table 4.3 An example of an instrument designed to measure the perceived adequacy of social support

1. How strongly do you feel attached to your *close* family?
   1 = very strongly ☐   2 = quite strongly ☐   3 = quite loosely ☐
   4 = not at all ☐
2. Do you find it difficult to know where you are with your *close* family, with respect to their points of view and opinions?
   1 = often ☐   2 = sometimes ☐   3 = never ☐
3. Do you feel that you, by and large, can be yourself in relation to your *close* family?
   1 = always ☐   2 = usually ☐   3 = seldom or never ☐
4. Do you feel that your *close* family puts reasonable weight upon your opinion?
   1 = always ☐   2 = usually ☐   3 = seldom or never ☐
5. Do you feel that you can count on your friends in the future?
   1 = very sure ☐   2 = quite sure ☐   3 = not sure ☐
6. Do you think you would be disappointed if you knew what your friends really thought about you?
   1 = yes ☐   2 = maybe ☐   3 = no ☐
7. Do you feel closely attached to your friends?
   1 = always ☐   2 = usually ☐   3 = seldom or never ☐
8. Do you feel that your friends put reasonable weight on your opinions?
   1 = always ☐   2 = usually ☐   3 = seldom or never ☐
9. Do you feel apart, even among friends?
   1 = often ☐   2 = sometimes ☐   3 = never ☐
10. Do you find it difficult to behave towards your neighbours, because you don't know what they expect from you?
    1 = yes ☐   2 = no ☐
11. Do you feel any closeness with people in your neighbourhood?
    1 = no closeness ☐   2 = some closeness ☐   3 = strong closeness ☐
12. Do you think that you, by and large, should be reserved about trusting your neighbours?
    1 = yes ☐   2 = no ☐

Reproduced by kind permission of Professor Dalgard of the National Institute of Public Health, Norway

currently (the 'actual' version of the SOS) and as respondents think things should have been (the 'ideal' version), which provides the discrepancy score (further details of the SOS, together with short and full versions, are to be found in Milne, 1992a).

I.G. Sarason *et al.* (1987) have developed a similarly brief measure of social support, also based on asking clients to judge their satisfaction with particular types of support in relation to up to nine people who provide particular types of emotional support (e.g. who accepts you totally, including both your worst and best points?). Respondents then rate their satisfaction with each identified person's support on a scale from 1 (very satisfied) to 7 (very dissatisfied). Again, the instrument is available in a ready to use form (Weinman *et al.*, 1995).

Another interesting approach to the assessment of perceived social support is based squarely on an interactional–cognitive model, a viewpoint that recognises that an individual's support is derived from several concurrent relationships, is multidimensional and is cognitive in the sense that relationships are regarded as being based on a person's 'general working model' of social interactions. Important premises in the model are that social support serves a communication function, as in indicating care or concern for another; and that such interactions are influenced by the nature of the relationship that exists between the participants (B.R. Sarason *et al.*, 1990). Amongst other things, the Quality of Relationships Inventory (QRI) instrument that was designed to measure this conception of social support notes that in addition to support one should also recognise the distinct dimensions of conflict and depth. Of 25 items in the QRI, seven are 'support' items (e.g. 'to what extent can you turn to this person for advice about problems?'), 12 are 'conflict' items (e.g. 'how much does this person make you feel guilty?') and the remaining six items tapped 'depth' (e.g. 'how significant is this person in your life?'). Each QRI item is rated on a four-point frequency scale, from 'not at all' to 'very much' in relation to respondents' perceived relationships with a key person (e.g. their mother, father or a best friend). Reliability and validity analyses indicate that the QRI is a psychometrically sound measure of close relationships (Pierce, 1994), making it a contender when practitioners want to assess social support from this kind of interactional cognitive perspective. Also, the QRI is set out fully as an appendix to the Pierce (1994) chapter, with the subscales of 'support', 'conflict' and 'depth' clearly marked. It is reproduced in Table 4.4.

In summary, the perceived adequacy or subjective approach to the measurement of social support taps an individual's feeling of being cared for, esteemed and loved by others. This is a more psychological approach than the social network or social interaction ones, stressing the role of the cognitive mediational processes of primary and secondary appraisal; and recognising the role of certain related personality characteristics in moderating one's perception of support (e.g. Locus of Control). These personality features can be regarded as creating in some people a 'cognitive vulnerability factor', to parallel the 'social vulnerability' factors identified by Brown and Harris (1978).

Given that the precise nature of social support is currently unresolved, it would be premature to advocate the use of instruments designed solely to assess the perceived adequacy of support. Unless there is good reason to restrict one's assessment in this way, a more appropriate strategy is to use one or more instruments to address the structure (social network),

Table 4.4   The Quality of Relationships Inventory (Pierce, 1984)
Please use the scale below to answer the following questions regarding your relationship with: (insert the name of a person with whom you have a relationship) _____

1	2	3	4
Not at all	A little	Quite a bit	Very much

1.[a] To what extent could you turn to this person for advice about problems?	1 2 3 4
2.[b] How often do you need to work hard to avoid conflict with this person?	1 2 3 4
3.[a] To what extent could you count on this person for help with a problem?	1 2 3 4
4.[b] How upset does this person sometimes make you feel?	1 2 3 4
5.[a] To what extent can you count on this person to give you honest feedback, even if you might not want to hear it?	1 2 3 4
6.[b] How much does this person make you feel guilty?	1 2 3 4
7.[b] How much do you have to 'give in' in this relationship?	1 2 3 4
8.[a] To what extent can you count on this person to help you if a family member very close to you died?	1 2 3 4
9.[b] How much does this person want you to change?	1 2 3 4
10.[c] How positive a role does this person play in your life?	1 2 3 4
11.[c] How significant is this relationship in your life?	1 2 3 4
12.[c] How close will your relationship be with this person in 10 years?	1 2 3 4
13.[c] How much would you miss this person if the two of you could not see or talk with each other for a month?	1 2 3 4
14.[b] How critical of you is this person?	1 2 3 4
15.[a] If you wanted to go out and do something this evening, how confident are you that this person would be willing to do something with you?	1 2 3 4
16.[c] How responsible do you feel for this person's wellbeing?	1 2 3 4
17.[c] How much do you depend on this person?	1 2 3 4
18.[a] To what extent can you count on this person to listen to you when you are very angry at someone else?	1 2 3 4
19.[b] How much would you like this person to change?	1 2 3 4
20.[b] How angry does this person make you feel?	1 2 3 4
21.[b] How much do you argue with this person?	1 2 3 4
22.[a] To what extent can you really count on this person to distract you from your worries when you feel under stress?	1 2 3 4
23.[b] How often does this person make you feel angry?	1 2 3 4
24.[b] How often does this person try to control or influence your life?	1 2 3 4
25.[b] How much more do you give than you get from this relationship	1 2 3 4

[a] Item included in the Support scale   [b] Item included in the Conflict scale   [c] Item included in the Depth scale
Reproduced from Burleson, B.R. *et al.* (1994) *The Communication of Social Support,* © 1984 Sage Publications Inc. Reprinted by permission of Sage Publications Inc.

function (social interaction) and experience (perceived adequacy) of social support. An example of an instrument that helpfully integrates these three dimensions is detailed in the next section of this chapter.

In addition to using multiple measures, it is good practice to do so by means of different assessment methods and from different perspectives (Roth & Fonagy, 1996), as in using a client self-report questionnaire, a structured interview with the client's carer, and direct observation of the client's interactions.

Conducting assessment of social support in this way should facilitate three major tasks that are undertaken by mental health practitioners, those of clinical assessment, problem formulation and service evaluation. These are discussed in Chapters 5–8, in relation to the kinds of measures that have been summarised above.

CRITERIA FOR A 'GOOD' SOCIAL SUPPORT MEASURE

Although not yet crystallised, the phenomenon of social support nonetheless appears to be *multidimensional*, incorporating structural, functional and interpersonal aspects. Therefore, efforts to measure social support should be based on multidimensional instruments. An example is the CORE questionnaire (Clinical Outcomes in Routine Evaluation: Barkham *et al.*, 1998). In addition to a very carefully selected group of 26 items that are designed to assess wellbeing, distress (including anxiety and depression), and risk, CORE also contains 8 items that cover the network, interactional and adequacy dimensions of social support functioning (e.g. 'I have felt I have someone to turn to for support when needed; 'I have felt criticised by other people' and 'I have felt warmth and affection for someone', respectively). Each of CORE's 34 items is scored on a five-point frequency scale, ranging from 'not at all' to 'most or all of the time', and the higher the score the more distressed the respondent is considered to be.

CORE has a number of outstandingly attractive features. In addition to providing clinicians and researchers with a set of items that are applicable to all therapy clients (i.e. valid across settings, clinical populations, presenting problems or mode of therapy), CORE has the advantages of incorporating a representative range of 'distress/wellbeing' items; of being linked to a computer scoring service; of relating to an unusually large sample of normative data for clients and for non-client populations; and of having excellent psychometric properties (Connell *et al.*, 1997). Because of these strengths, CORE will serve as an example under the headings that now follow.

A second criterion for a 'good' social support measure is that it should be capable of assessing *negative* as well as positive impacts. To again use

CORE as an illustration, in general terms CORE measures distress items (e.g. 'I have felt tense, anxious or nervous') alongside those tapping well-being (e.g. 'I have felt OK about myself'). Furthermore, as these two examples indicate, some CORE items are phrased negatively, others positively. That is, answering 'not at all' to a positive item like feeling OK about oneself scores 4, as does answering 'most of the time' to a negative item, like feeling tense. This allows the rule of 'the higher the score, the more distressed the respondent' to apply, as well as reducing response bias (e.g. ticking all the 'not at all' items).

Thirdly, as per any other instrument, those applied to the assessment of social support should have adequate levels of *reliability* and *validity*. In the case of CORE, early psychometric data indicate that it is a valid discriminator between clinical and non-clinical populations: highly significant differences between 124 clients and 253 non-clients were obtained across all four dimensions. Also, CORE was found to have good internal consistency (alphas ranging from 0.5 to 0.9) and acceptable test–retest reliability for a smaller sample ($n = 27$) assessed over a one week period ($r = 0.81$) (Connell *et al.*, 1997).

Other potential measurements problems with social support instruments arise because even content valid items sometimes appear under two headings, as when 'bereavement' is treated as both a life event and a loss of social support. Furthermore, such an event may also cause an alteration to the social support that others provide (Alloway & Bebbington, 1987). Another validity issue concerns the point in time to which the assessment refers, particularly where this is retrospective (e.g. 'in the past three months …') and starts from a time when the client is psychologically distressed. This is because, in addition to memory weaknesses, there is a 'black spectacles' effect in which both the range and the adequacy of social support are appraised more negatively, probably as a function of the distress and possibly because of clients' search for an explanation for their distress (Thoits, 1983).

Illustrations of reliability and validity assessments have already been provided in an outline fashion. Because of the importance of these psychometric criteria, a more detailed account of analysing the reliability and validity of two specific social support instruments is now provided, based on the work of Barrera *et al.* (1981), one of the earliest examples of a thorough check on a social support instrument's reliability and validity (i.e. the 'Inventory of Socially Supportive Behaviours'—ISSB). To assess the consistency or reliability of the scale, they asked 71 psychology students to complete the ISSB before and after a two-day interval. This interval was selected as an optimal balance between the students' remembering their responses and the occurrence of a number of social support events. Correlating the two sets of responses indicated that the ISSB had high test–

retest reliability ($r = 0.88$, $p < 0.001$), although the individual items ranged from 0.44 to 0.91. Barrera *et al.* (1981) then checked the internal consistency of the ISSB by applying the alpha statistic to both administrations of the scale. This analysis also indicated that the ISSB had good reliability (coefficient of 0.93 and 0.94 were obtained, respectively). These findings were replicated for a larger, international sample by Walkey *et al.* (1987).

In terms of assessing the validity of the ISSB, Barrera *et al.* (1981) related it to a structured interview, the Arizona Social Support Inventory Schedule (ASSIS). This consisted of six questions corresponding to six functions of social support, namely: material and physical assistance, intimate interaction, guidance, feedback and positive social interactions. Each of these six questions had one sub-part concerning the availability of these types of support and a second relating to the actual occurrence of each type of support. It transpired that the ISSB correlated significantly with both the available and the actual social support as measured by the ASSIS, suggesting that the ISSB had concurrent validity. Barrera *et al.* (1981) also compared the ISSB with the Family Environment Scale (Moos *et al.*, 1974), which amongst other things measures how individuals appraise the degree of social cohesion in a family. This refers to 'the extent to which family members are concerned and committed to the family and the degree to which family members are helpful and supportive of each other' (p. 4). Again, they found that the ISSB was significantly correlated to this scale, finding also that those students who reported the highest frequency of social support from family members were the ones who perceived their families as most cohesive. Barrera *et al.* (1981) concluded that the ISSB provided a reliable and valid way of assessing informal helping relationships, complementing measures of an individuals social network and perceived support.

More recently, Procidano (1992) reviewed the development of the Perceived Social Support Scale (PSSS: Procidano and Heller, 1983). The PSSS assesses perceived support from family and from friends by means of 20 declarative statements, each concerning the extent to which one believes that one's need for support, information and feedback are being met by family and friends (it also includes providing social support to others).

The reliability of the two PSSS instruments has been assessed by the internal consistency and test–retest methods. Samples of respondents, including students and multiple sclerosis patients, have participated in the internal consistency analysis, with statistical results indicative of reliability (Cronbach alphas ranging from 0.84 to 0.91). When the PSS has been administered twice over a 1 month period it has also provided reliable values between 0.75 to 0.82.

The validity of the PSS has also been examined carefully. Comparisons between the scores obtained by clinical (i.e. receiving psychological or psychiatric treatment) and non-clinical samples yielded highly significant differences for the family version ($T = 12.32$, $p < 0.001$). In addition to the above 'known (or contrasted) groups' methods for judging the validity of a social support instrument, Procidano (1992) also summarised the 'construct' validity findings. This was measured by comparing the PSS scales with the Social Network Questionnaire (Liem & Liem, 1977). As expected, there were only weak relationships between the scores obtained from both instruments (correlation range from $r = 30$ to $r = .01$), indicating that the PSS had discriminant validity. By contrast, correlations with similar instruments have been much higher (e.g. with the Social Support Questionnaire: I.G. Sarason et al., 1983).

Good instruments are also *sensitive* to the effects of a treatment or the level of impairment, yet wide-ranging enough to allow comparisons between subscales. The Social Functioning Scale (SFS: Birchwood et al., 1990) was designed with these criteria in mind (as well as those of providing UK norms and being available in self-report or key informant forms). The SFS assesses those areas of functioning that have been found to be critical to the community maintenance of people with schizophrenia, namely: social engagement, interpersonal behaviour (network size and nature; quality of communication), pro-social activities, recreation, independence and employment. The sensitivity of the SFS was determined by comparing the replies of 334 outpatients with schizophrenia against a sample of 100 'normal' people, nominated by the patients' relatives. This 'criterion groups' comparison revealed the expected differences to a highly significant extent, alongside the anticipated wide range of scores. Also, the sensitivity of the SFS to clinical change was indicated by a separate family intervention study which revealed a significant lowering of SFS scores following this treatment.

Finally, 'good' measures also meet a number of simple yet important *practical* criteria, as in being readily available, not too time consuming or complex to administer (e.g. not requiring special training) and straightforward to score and interpret. To illustrate, the 'Self Evaluation and Social Support Interview' (Brown & Bifulco, 1985) takes three hours to administer, while the Interview Schedule for Social Interaction (Henderson et al., 1980) required that interviewers received a week-long course of training. By contrast, CORE was derived from a careful scrutiny of instruments and was reduced to a user-friendly two-sided A4 self-report questionnaire, normally requiring only 5–10 minutes to complete. There are also two parallel short forms, each containing only 18 items (Barkham et al., 1998).

The information that one derives from the assessment of social support (by whichever method) needs to be processed if it is to serve its purpose. That is, even the most thorough assessment of social support model is only going to be useful if one has also taken steps to ensure that the information is properly communicated and put to good use. This has formed the 'treatment utility' of assessment (Hayes *et al.*, 1987) and is an important additional criterion for judging the practical worth of an instrument: 'good' tools make a useful contribution to assessment and can do so at the 'clinical' level (i.e. the individual client), the immediate 'proximal' environment, and the more pervasive 'distal' context for social support. However, at every level it is essential to maximise the utility of the assessment work, whether this entails engaging clients in a collaborative therapeutic alliance or involving service systems in participative evaluations (Papineau and Kiely, 1996).

CONCLUSIONS

In summary, there are a considerable number of instruments available to mental health practitioners who wish to measure social support, whether defined in terms of networks, interactions or perceived adequacy. Fortunately, some of the better-developed ones are highly accessible in portfolios and are helpfully combined with measures of stress and coping (e.g. the CRI), affording a pragmatic way to measure social support. The Clinical Outcomes in the Routine Evaluation (CORE) questionnaire also serves to assess all three social support dimensions, together with its other advantages. Unlike some of their predecessors, these new instruments minimise many of the old problems in social support measurement, as lamented over the years by reviewers such as Thoits (1982). Heitzmann and Kaplan (1988) have provided a helpful summary of these problems, together with a critical review of 23 instruments, emphasising their psychometric qualities and their unique attributes.

Although distinct progress has been made on the psychometric front, there remains a lack of conceptual consensus. Different researchers continue to define social support in distinct ways, resulting in findings that cannot be compared across studies. According to Tardy (1985), five different aspects of social support have been the focus of measurements. These are networks, functions (i.e. emotional, instrumental, etc.), perceived adequacy, 'dispositions' (i.e. whether social support is either available or utilised) and directions (received or provided). Tardy (1985) summarised instruments falling into each category, also providing a clarification of the uses for which they were most appropriate. However, there remains no agreement regarding which of these aspects should be measured. In the meantime, Heitzmann and Kaplan (1998) advised that practitioners and researchers can either choose to focus on the specific social support operationalisation that is most relevant to their work (e.g. networks), or they can utilise multiple instruments if they seek a broader understanding.

On the subject of a broader formulation of social support, it is worth mentioning a dimension that I have ignored so far but which is part of the model presented in Chapter 3. This is the habitat or 'behaviour setting' within which social support takes place. Early thinking on environments led to a theory of behaviour settings that related specific actions to their physical contexts (Barker, 1968). A behaviour setting was defined as a place having a stable time and space within which people interacted, such as a restaurant or a church. The most important conclusion of the theory was that the way people behaved in such settings appeared to be reliable (i.e. people were 'interchangeable'), indicating the importance of assessing settings as a context for the other social support dimensions. Barker (1968) presented a 'k-21' scale in order to identify behaviour settings within a community. This scale defines settings in terms of their physical and temporal boundaries, the patterns of specific and molar behaviour that predictably occur within them, the inanimate objects that make up the settings, plus the human occupants of the setting, classed into six 'zones' depending upon the degree to which individuals exercise leadership (e.g. zone 1 represents onlookers, zone 6 single persons with the power to influence what happened in the setting). For example, Barker & Wright (1955) provided a behaviour settings account of a mid-western USA town.

The link between behaviour settings and mental health will be discussed more thoroughly in Chapter 7, but an example at this stage may help to underline the important interaction between the two. In studying why the mothers of 'oppositional' children failed to maintain their use of successful and behavioural methods, Wahler (1980) showed a link between the setting (e.g. visiting a friend's home) and the social support of others (e.g. criticism for using these methods). In particular, parents experiencing very limited and aversive social interactions (the 'insular' sample) were the least likely to use the behavioural methods, even though when applied they were successful in reducing their childs oppositional behaviours (e.g. hitting and throwing). It appeared that, as a result of being insular, these mothers tended to use more coercive child management techniques (e.g. yelling), when contrasted with those with a higher frequency of 'friendship days'.

PART 3

Implementing social support interventions

It is argued that the phenomenon of social support occurs across a spectrum of professional activities, starting with its embeddedness in traditional, face-to-face clinical therapy and ending with significant opportunities for community work (e.g. health education). The next three chapters detail the options and the evidence across this spectrum, with the aim of fostering an evidence-based approach to social therapy.

Chapter 5

CLINICAL INTERVENTIONS

INTRODUCTION: SOCIAL SUPPORT IS SEAMLESS

The potential scope of social support work for mental health practitioners extends from the outer fringes of therapy to prevention programmes in the community. However, as summarised earlier (see, for example, Table 2.1), the conventional social support role of practitioners has been to stay firmly within this fringe, at best liaising with those who form a central part of clients' social networks and assisting client's social support efforts within their networks (e.g. skills in eliciting support), or in trying to extend their network. In short, there has tended to be a rather dichotomous view of social support, founded on the idea that social support is by definition what goes on outside therapy sessions and therefore something also resting outside the sphere of normal professional activity. An elaboration of this dichotomy is the parallel view that those mental health practitioners who do engage in social support interventions that go beyond the fringe (as summarised in Table 2.1, such as developing support groups or enhancing the quality of working life) are a breed apart, to be appropriately redesignated not as therapists but as 'community workers', 'neighbourhood health practitioners', 'politicians' or whatever.

In this chapter I will attempt to replace this misleadingly dichotomous view with a seamless perspective that sees social support as inextricably bound up with even the most formal versions of therapy. Indeed, step one is for mental health practitioners to realise that this is the case, so as to avoid causing unintended harm. In the social ecology of therapeutic relationships, we are bound to influence support directly and indirectly, whether we realise it or not. Step two then entails a deeper awareness of the forms and functions of help, on a continuum from formal individual therapy to informal helping transactions. This should heighten sensitivity to the ecology of social support, as well as raising fresh possibilities for clinical interventions.

The heart of the chapter is a careful scrutiny of the various ways in which practitioners can foster social support within the normal limits of formal therapy. I consider how our assessment of client needs, the formulation of clinical problems, and the therapeutic interventions themselves may contribute directly and indirectly to a client's social support.

Given that the above approach is something of a challenge to the traditional, dichotomous view of social support and the conventional role of the mental health professional, it is important to detail the existing evidence. The chapter closes with some of the problems and issues associated with this account of social therapy.

NEVER DO HARM!

Clients with mental health problems tend to have frequent crises, challenging presentations and a resultant need for formal help. As they approach such groups as mental health practitioners, they are entitled to expect concern and competence. But this expectation may not always be fulfilled, as an early study by Weiss (1972) illustrated. He taped regular structured interviews with 13 single, low income mothers over a six month period. During this time most of them made approaches for help to physicians (re pregnancy; child's ill health), teachers (re poor grades achieved by child), social workers (re financial aid), lawyers (re divorce proceedings), police officers (re son's bicycle stolen), probation officers (re dealing with husband) court clerks (re support for child), priests (re a religious survey) and an undertaker (re an infant daughter died)! Weiss (1972) distinguished between two kinds of requests for help to this diverse range of helpers, namely seeking the provision of a specialist service, or accessing support and guidance. The first encompassed the performance of some activity or the delivery of some resource, controlled by the specialist (e.g. treatment or financial aid); the second consisted of help in imposing structure on a confusing situation, deciding on a course of action and gaining the confidence to carry through the action. A poignant example of the latter type of help (i.e. support and guidance), quoted by Weiss (1972), concerned a mother's perception of a favourite social worker:

> 'I don't know how I can stand it. I'm going to end up at the state insane asylum. My nerves are shot. I don't know where to turn. I'm going nuts, just nuts. If only Miss Fahey was there, I could call on her. She always had a solution.' (p. 321)

More to the point, Weiss (1972) was concerned to report the problems that those mothers had in obtaining formal help, problems of access, having to 'bargain' for services and having to jeopardise their self-esteem. Regarding access to help, the typical procedure was a stressful one for the mothers of trying to convince a non-specialist 'gatekeeper' of their eligibility for the specialist's service. Often this eligibility depended upon the possession of a statement from another agency (e.g. access to a dentist was dependent upon a doctor's certificate) and could entail considerable effort. Even when a mother had successfully accessed a service there was often an inconvenient wait, stretching from an hour to the best part of a day in a waiting room (bear in mind that these mothers usually also carried sole responsibility for the care of their young children).

A second kind of harm that formal services can cause is to engage clients in a demeaning form of pleading or bargaining for help. The mothers in Weiss' (1972) study were often refused assistance, and in a manner that questioned their mental health. For example, one mother requested that her social worker move her son from group therapy to individual counselling, which the social worker interpreted as the mother's displacement on to her son of her own competitive feelings! Other examples led the mothers to feel trapped, cheated, devalued and generally helpless in the face of large bureaucracies, since if they attempted to object or 'bargain' for services they were often treated by specialists as 'uncooperative' or 'unreasonable'.

The third and final form of harm identified by Weiss (1972) was damage to the mothers' self-esteem. As already mentioned, questioning someone's eligibility for a public service or keeping an anxious person waiting for a considerable period of time can communicate their relative unimportance (or even 'invisibility'), by comparison with the seemingly all-important procedures of the organisation. The general tenor of these contacts with formal helpers was adversarial, including cynicism, disapproval and the condemning of a particular way of life.

There are also those who believe that even if clients receive a sympathetic reception, the provision of therapy inevitably diminishes their dignity, autonomy and freedom (Masson, 1989). This revolves around the abuse of power, the use of therapists' authority and special knowledge to manipulate, control and humiliate their clients. Like the techniques employed in religion and royalty, the therapist can control contact and can question the client on any topic, but the reverse is not true. Therapists are fundamentally regarded as abusing power, believes Masson, because they are convinced that they posses a kind of truth or definition of reality that prevails over the client's. Although Masson's critique focuses on the more mystical aspects of psychodynamic psychotherapy, power is an aspect of all therapeutic relationships and should be recognised (e.g. controlling 'homework assignments' or 'behavioural tasks' in cognitive–behavioural therapy, or discharging a client who is 'non-compliant').

Returning to the more mundane examples cited by Weiss (1972), thankfully there was evidence that the mothers in his study used their own power to get what they could out of the organisations with which they struggled to access help. In order to cope, the mothers learnt to 'manage the system' as best they could, from a mixture of personal experience and social support. To illustrate, they would exchange information and accounts of experiences, developing a better grasp of their rights and how to access them. They also seemed to learn to persist until they located a helpful professional. Weiss (1972) concluded pessimistically that new rules, improved attitudes, the introduction of advocates and extra resources (e.g. to employ staff to child mind or to offer non-specialist support) were probably all necessary before the help that they provided exceeded the psychological harm that they caused. In summary, although the general quality of clinical services has probably improved since 1972, it is worth remembering the importance of initial contacts with the client. As the Hippocratic Oath put it 'never do harm to anyone'.

Enabling clients to access help

A more topical illustration of some of these psychologically harmful practices concerns clients' equity of access to mental health services. It has been asserted that these services fail to acknowledge the significance of social inequalities, resulting in dissatisfaction and anger amongst the service users (Williams, 1996). In particular, those providing a mental health service should be careful not to replicate wider social injustices (as above), which render users powerless or marginalised.

An everyday example for those providing a clinical service is the need to ensure that socially deprived groups have equal access to therapy. This was checked in relation to the clinical psychology service provided at GP surgeries to adults with mental health problems in Dundee (McPherson and Murphy, 1997). They used a simple index of deprivation and applied it to two years' worth of referred clients ($N = 1152$), finding that they were significantly more likely to have come from the more socially deprived parts of the city. Therefore, McPherson and Murphy (1997) concluded that the psychology service was equitable, at least in terms of the relative numbers of clients that were drawn from a range of social backgrounds. As they noted, this left unanswered the question of relative need, in that those living in social deprivation may well have an exceptional call on mental health services, since such deprivation is associated with a range of health problems (Townsend et al., 1992).

Accessibility of mental health services covers much more than attendance at a mental health practitioners clinic. According to Huxley (1990), acceptable services are geographically accessible (e.g. physically near patients' homes and utilised by all groups in the neighbourhood), bureaucratically accessible (e.g. easy to gain entry to and maximally available for use around the clock), cognitively accessible (e.g. whereabouts and services well known to those in need) and psychologically accessible (including being appealing, non-threatening and friendly).

Thus, even those mental health practitioners who regard their practice as traditionally intrapersonal (i.e. focusing on how an individual's thoughts, feelings and behaviours interact) may recognise that there is an interface with the interpersonal domain. By running a service that shows respect, empowers individuals, is accessible and provides concern and competent assistance, such practitioners are probably also indirectly providing social support and influencing their clients' subsequent social support. This represents one end of the social support spectrum, the end featuring little awareness of or attention to social support. These have been referred to as 'latent functions' by Merton (1968) i.e. consequences of interactions that are not clearly recognised by the participants. Next, I detail other important points on this spectrum.

THE SPECTRUM OF SOCIAL SUPPORT

There is reason to believe that the functions that are served by social support, whether latent or manifest, are remarkably similar across the range of formal and informal help providers. Rather, what distinguishes these helpers are such things as the degree of family ties, the intimacy of the help and the role of mutual obligations. Caplan (1974) believed that the overlap between formal and informal helpers was such that a continuum of support systems could be defined, with the formal helpers distinguished most clearly by their interest in promoting the health of the whole population (not just family and friends), by occupying a job that requires them to provide support, and by belonging to organisations whose purpose is to systematically foster wellbeing (e.g. the NHS). However, Caplan (1974) did not actually test this belief.

Commonalities in the form of social support

Cauce and Srebnik (1990) carried out a belated study to assess Caplan's theory. They asked a sample of students to judge how alike or different a list of people were in making them feel supported (e.g. parents, University staff, doctor). The students were given 15 adjective rating scales, such as flexible, loving, warm and comforting. Their replies indicated that there were essentially two dimensions along which the supporters could be plotted. One they called 'intimacy' which featured kith and kin, and the other was labelled 'relevance to daily life', which was most strongly associated with support from peers and friends. Figure 5.1 displays graphically these relationships, which shows how formal supporters were mainly characterised by the students as relatively non-intimate but nonetheless as relevant to daily life. However, it can be seen that there are marked differences amongst both the formal and informal supporters, creating a noticeable continuum. Cauce and Srebnik (1990) concluded that their findings did support Caplan's (1974) theory, indicating a differentiation between the two clusters of supporters.

Commonalities in the function of social support

Whether or not the form of social support is similar across formal and informal helpers, there is a more fundamental issue of the existence of a functional overlap: can mental health practitioners in a sense replace informal social supporters, even if they tend to be less intimate or relevant

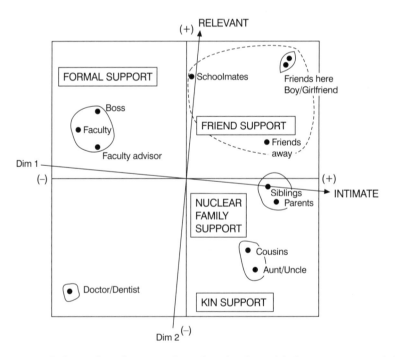

Figure 5.1   Relationships between formal and informal helpers, in terms of the dimensions 'relevance to daily life' ('Dim2') and 'intimacy' ('Dim1'). From a study by Cauce and Srebnik (1990). Copyright © 1990 by the American Psychological Association. Reproduced with permission.

to their clients' daily life? Barnes and Duck (1994) seem to think so, in that the 'everyday talk' that formal and informal helpers engage in shares six important functions, as set out in Table 5.1.

Table 5.1 Six functions served by everyday talk (Barnes & Duck, 1994)

Social support categories	Social support functions
1. Information	Talk provides information which automatically creates impressions about the degree of similarity between the ways conversing individuals perceive the world and the qualities of a potential supporter (e.g. a capacity to help others to solve problems or to remain calm).
2. Detection	Conversation also provides people with an opportunity to monitor and notice fluctuations in how others are coping (e.g. a normally cheerful and optimistic individual becoming self-absorbed and cynical). This may allow for the early detection of problems as the affected individual may not even notice fully the signs of their distress.
3. Ventilation	Hassles, setbacks, grumbles and physical complaints can all be expressed through everyday talk, relieving negative feelings, such as frustration or bewilderment. Airing these minor hassles can also help to reduce the risk of their becoming major life events, since others may provide helpful information (e.g. alternative interpretations, coping strategies) or demonstrate more adaptive coping (e.g. defusing the situation or cheering up the speaker).
4. Distraction	As everyday talk may not focus on a specific stressor it may serve to distract or distance people from stressors, creating at least temporary relief. Amidst this kind of conversation a distressed individual might also support or nurture others, exercising a relatively effective part of their coping repertoire and benefiting through enhanced self-esteem. Therefore, the characteristically trivial, humorous and playful quality of everyday talk is more than simply an 'escape' from stressors.
5. Perpetuation	The history that typically underlies a relationship brings continuity and cohesion—people recollect and reconstruct, so as to obtain comfort (e.g. the conversation provides a haven or recalls a success, making the interaction helpful in maintaining morale and in maintaining access to potentially valuable information on past coping efforts). This perpetuation also provides the framework for more explicit social support.
6. Regulation	Conversations tell the participants whether it is safe to raise certain topics and help them to judge the appropriate level and timing of self-disclosures—i.e. these talks are at times a prologue or scene-setter to mobilising social support. This serves to reduce the risks associated with support seeking (or to do with facing stressors) for both parties (e.g. giving the helper time to prepare a response).

There is reason to believe that this is only a partial list, since the related literature on the 'patient requests' expressed by clients when they attend clinics for formal help also includes a need for such things as succour, reality contract and confession (Burgoyne et al., 1979). When these authors asked 325 consecutive users of an outpatient psychiatric clinic (and the psychiatrists who helped them) to rate the importance of 14 categories of 'patient requests' there was a major mismatch: the psychiatrists significantly underestimated the perceived importance that clients gave to 10 of these 14 forms of help. For example, whereas the psychiatrists tended to assume that the clients sought medication or practical help, the clients themselves were primarily interested in having their emotional needs met (e.g. 'getting help to control my feelings', 'to have a place where I can discuss things of which I feel ashamed and guilty and can tell no one else'). A more recent UK analysis of patients' requests found that a sample of 292 new psychotic clients attending an acute psychiatric unit also rated the same range of social support-type help above physical treatments (Whalan & Mushet, 1990). They labelled the clients' need for control, succour and advice as 'non-specific psychotherapy', distinguishing it from more formal approaches. When clients were asked on discharge to rate how well their needs had been met, the high-priority needs (including that for non-specific psychotherapy) were judged as least adequately provided for.

Given these findings, the functions in Table 5.1 can be seen to apply also to formal helpers, such as therapists. Either they occur as per other informal helpers, as in a relatively casual conversation on the way to and from the waiting room (that nonetheless communicates information about the therapists' capacity to help on a particular day); or they can be thought to occur at a different level, as in the detection of a client's functioning against their own particular history of coping.

Another difference may be that requests for the formal or informal aspects of support become more direct, in relation to therapists, because of the clearer mutual obligations. For instance, clients may regulate less, feeling that the therapeutic relationship encourages them to minimise the normally cautious matter of raising distressing topics. This kind of variation as a function of the nature of the relationship has been reported for married couples, whose responsiveness to such appeals for help from one another are thought to play a significant role in protecting individuals against depression (Cutrona, 1996). The relative provision of social support signals critical information to the partner concerning the degree of trust, care, interdependence and commitment that exists in the relationship. This is thought by Cutrona (1996) to then accumulate into a deeply held belief or schema about support. In a similarly profound sense, Barnes and Duck (1994) were of the opinion that 'social support is any set of behaviours that communicates to a person the knowledge that she or he is valued and cared for by others' (p. 191). It follows from this definition that social support can be provided by anyone, whether in a formal or informal role.

Therefore, it would appear that, despite the traditional emphasis on differences between therapists and social supporters, in practice there are important areas of continuity and possibly also of overlap. This can arise in a manifest way that therapists consciously employ in a deliberate attempt to foster their clients' functioning (e.g. encouraging ventilation), but if not then it is likely that social support processes and functions will nonetheless occur at a latent level. Such a continuum of formal and informal help was anticipated in Tables 1.3 and 1.4, which elaborate some of the additional areas of overlap.

On the belief that it is adaptive for therapists to be more aware of these manifest and latent support processes, the next section summarises relevant research, followed by a small and practical 'case study' detailing how nurse practitioners, intent upon physical care, nonetheless provided more valued emotional care.

Illustrations from research

One way to study the spectrum of social support is to conduct naturalistic analyses of formal and informal helpers, an approach that has provided several fascinating accounts of helping behaviours. My own introduction to this research came from listening to Jim Orford recount the work of Emory Cowen at a conference (see Orford, 1992). Cowen (1982) had summarised how hairdressers, divorce lawyers, work supervisors and bartenders dealt with the moderate to serious personal problems that others raised with them, noting how some of the methods that they used were like those used by mental health practitioners. In one study, Cowen and his colleagues (1979) interviewed 90 hairdressers about their responses to these personal problems, finding that they reported utilising support and sympathy, listening, presenting alternatives and asking questions. These are strategies that therapists would use too, but Cowen's stylists deviated from therapists in also utilising lightheartedness, explaining to clients that they should count their blessings, and giving (premature) advice.

A less subjective approach to the issue of social support and therapy was provided by Toro (1986) who observed 14 mental health professionals, 14 divorce lawyers and 14 leaders of mutual help groups (the mental health professionals were psychologists and social workers). He audio taped individual contacts between three female 'helpees' that he asked to portray a woman considering divorce, and then coded the conversations that they had with the three types of helper, using a counsellor rating system. It transpired that the lawyers focused more on providing information, asking questions and generally talked more. By contrast, the mental health professionals and group leaders were more similar, being less talkative, focusing more on feelings, asking more open questions and providing more interpretive comments. The only clear distinction between these latter two groups of helpers was that the leaders were more inclined to self-disclose and tended to use a narrower range of helping behaviours. Overall, there were clear similarities between the approaches used by two of the three groups, which not surprisingly were perceived to be equally helpful by the 'helpees'. Toro (1986) argued that this overlap between the mental health practitioners and the mutual help group leaders might help to improve professionals' attitudes towards social supporters, leading to greater contact and collaboration.

In what appeared to be a re-analysis of the same data, Tracey and Toro (1989) looked more closely at the timing with which the different counselling behaviours were used by the three groups of helpers. They found some clear differences in how the helpers responded to the 'helpees', leading to differential outcomes. For example, the more successful professionals tended to use complex responses (e.g. interpretation or reflection) only after the 'helpees' provided a problem description, whereas the successful group leaders tended to respond more to emotional material by questioning the 'helpee'. They concluded that simple frequency counts of helper behaviours may provide a misleading impression of overlap between formal and informal helpers, but when the pattern of help is analysed as a more complex sequence of interactions then differences emerge.

Inspired by these analyses and by the desire to find out more about the spectrum of helping relationships, I conducted a series of small projects with my colleagues (Milne et al., 1992a), each of which compared formal and informal helpers. The first of these extended the above studies by conducting naturalistic observations of hairdressing clients drawn from a psychiatric hospital and from the High Street, and by using a broader instrument with which to code what the stylists said to these clients (i.e. the Helper Behaviour Rating Scale: HBRS, Hardy & Shapiro, 1985). When related to the HBRS data as previously published from 'prescriptive' and 'exploratory' therapy, non-significant correlations were obtained, being strongest with the 'prescriptive' approach ($r = 0.35$). In keeping with Cowen's (1982) results, our sample of six stylists gave more information, asked more questions and reflected less of their clients' speech than did the therapists, who also gave much more reassurance and engaged in more interpretation and exploration, in keeping with Tracey and Toro's (1989) results.

In the second related study (Milne et al., 1992) 40 clinical psychology clients participated in a postal survey concerning the support that they received from their psychologist, relative to that provided by friends, relatives and their hairdresser. They reported that all four groups provided the four identified types of social support (i.e. informational, emotional, practical and positive social interaction). However, the respective helping profiles differed, in that the psychologists were perceived by their clients as providing more informational and emotional support, with a significantly different helping profile overall. Also, as per Tracey and Toro (1989), the help of these professionals was judged by the clients to be significantly more adequate, even though relatives were reported to provide more frequent help. A meta-analysis of the value of specialist mental health interventions (as compared to 'usual GP treatment') reached a similar conclusion (Balestrieri *et al.*, 1988).

These two sets of findings led us to the view that the form and function of the help provided by social supporters and psychologists showed overlaps, but also reflected important differences. We interpreted this as suggesting distinctive and complementary helping roles for the two groups, with mental health practitioners providing training in information-giving and counselling skills to social supporters. In relation to therapy, it was also noted that professionals could assess the adequacy of their clients' social support, for example in relation to clients' support elicitation skills or to resettling clients from hospital to the community.

Towards the middle of this social support spectrum, research has examined how non-specialist health professionals handle emotional problems. For example Cape (1996) interviewed 88 patients of GPs about their experiences of consultations for emotional problems. Historically, GPs have been encouraged to attend to the psychological aspects of their work with clients, not just those who present with an overt emotional complaint (Balint, 1964). Listening, concern and empathy were regarded as the principal methods for what was termed 'GP psychotherapy'. Therefore, Cape (1996) analysed the interview data to determine the extent to which such semi-specialist help was actually provided by a group of nine experienced GPs with an interest in psychological problems and methods, as well as assessing the extent to which it was therapeutic. The 88 patients were selected on the basis of a high score on the 30-item General Health Questionnaire (Goldberg & Williams, 1988). The impact of their consultations with the GPs was assessed by means of a semi-structured interview and questionnaire, completed up to five days post-consultation in the patient's own home. The interview probed the ease of the consultation (e.g. 'to what extent did you feel you could say what you wanted to the doctor?'), understanding, concern, warmth, explanation, advice and helpfulness. The *ad hoc* questionnaire covered the same issues. In addition, audio-taped recordings of the consultations were coded using four different systems. These addressed the extent to which the consultations were psychological in content (e.g. attending to causes of stress or emotional complaints); the types of GP speech, using a similar system to the HBRS; the GP's interactional style (i.e. doctor or patient-centred); and ratings of empathic understanding, concern and warmth. From these measures, Cape (1996) found that, in the discussion of psychological problems, the GPs focused mostly on social stressors and social adjustment (32% of doctor/patient utterances), with the patients' feelings and emotions less pronounced (11%). Amongst these stressors were family, marital and other intimate relationships (16%), followed by work and housing (both 2%). During these interactions the GPs mostly listened encouragingly (43% of speech), gave explanations (18%) and asked closed questions in order to elicit information from the patients. The style of the consultations was patient-centred and they were perceived by patients as conveying considerable concern, empathy and warmth. Most of these patients (78%) reported the consultations to have been a positive experience, and those consultations that featured higher proportions of empathy, listening and more discussion of psychological problems tended to receive the most positive evaluations.

Overall, Cape (1996) noted that less than half of the average consultations comprised attention to emotional problems, despite the deliberate selection of patients who presented such difficulties to doctors interested in providing a psychological response. Moreover, this response consisted of listening, discussion and simple counselling, rather than the 'GP psychotherapy' recommended by Balint (1964) and even taught to other doctors by some of these participating GPs.

Closer still to the informal end of the social support spectrum, Kitson (1987) has described how general nursing overlaps with what she called 'lay caring', sharing the same attributes of commitment, competence and respect. However, she thought that they differed when nurses set up a specialist service and dealt with the care needs of those who could not care for themselves or others in an acceptable manner. Two case studies were provided to illustrate nursing care that featured the above attributes, including providing in-patient care over a two-year period, using skills to encourage personal self-care, and having a respectful concern for the patient, reflected in a positive attitude towards recovery and in providing informational and emotional support (e.g. spending time discussing the day's events on the ward).

Just as GPs and general nurses have been encouraged to play a psychotherapeutic role, so therapists have attempted to engage those in the client's social support network as co-therapists. In a seminal example, J.P. Cobb *et al.* (1984) involved the spouses of clients with agoraphobia in their home-based behavioural therapy. Ten of these clients were treated without spouse involvement, while the remaining nine had the spouse as a co-therapist. In the latter approach, both client and spouse were provided with self-help manuals, both attended therapy sessions, and the spouse was instructed to help the client to undertake the therapeutic homework assignments (e.g. graded exposure). Although all clients improved, these authors found little evidence that those clients in the co-therapy group did any better than those receiving the traditional individual approach. One of the few differences favouring the co-therapy group was a greater improvement in the client's sex life, which the authors attributed to feeling physically closer because of the shared problem-solving effort. On the negative side, however, spouses involved as co-therapists reported significantly more anxiety by the end of the programme, suggesting a sensitisation or reverse-buffer effect (see Chapter 3), possibly as a result of a raised level of uncertainty and responsibility, produced by the relatively sudden and major changes in their spouse.

In an extension of this kind of social network analysis, Brody and Farber (1989) investigated how 20 significant others were affected by their partner's therapy. By means of interview and questionnaire assessment they established that most of these significant others harboured conflict feelings about their partner's therapy (e.g. feeling excluded or inadequate), but that they themselves had become more introspective and better able to understand their partners, who were in turn perceived as more empathic, open and communicative. This, then, represented a point on the continuum mirroring the therapist's latent social support activity: just as therapists may not fully recognise how they provide social support to their clients, so they may not realise how this social support impacts 'ecologically' on significant others. It would appear that this impact is less than that achieved with their clients, placing it closer to the informal end of the social support spectrum.

A final step away from formal help are the strategies that people in the High Street use to cope and to seek help. Latching on to one of the regular public surveys conducted by the BBC, C. Barker et al. (1990) interviewed a representative sample of 1040 adults to ascertain the presence of psychological symptoms, coping strategies and sources of help when faced with a psychological problem. The sample reported few psychological symptoms, and would most frequently turn to kith and kin for help. The highest rated formal helper was the GP (41% of interviewees endorsed this source of help), followed by priest (17%), mental health worker (16%) and self-help group (15%). Returning to the issue of the spectrum of social support and its implications for therapy, it was found that cognitive and behavioural coping strategies were most popular (e.g. 88% of respondents endorsed the item 'think about ways of overcoming the problem' and the same proportion said they would 'keep busy'). If nothing else, these data suggest that, when consulted, therapists can build on and refine the more popular adaptive coping strategies (i.e. the cognitive and behavioural ones) while reducing dependence on the generally less helpful avoidance methods. As noted by Barker *et al.* (1990) this information may also help clinicians to see the broader context of how people generally cope and seek help, which one can imagine will interact with the transfer of any therapeutic effects. That is, if the coping strategies promoted by therapists run counter to those advocated and practised by their clients' social supporters, then one would anticipate poor transfer and even some adverse consequences for the client (e.g. being stigmatised or ostracised).

To summarise this section, the sample of research studies outlined above can be viewed along a social support spectrum that ranges from the latent provision of informal help by therapists to the manifest accessing of formal helpers by the general public. Each point that was illustrated along this continuum carries some implications for mental health practitioners, even if they operate as an intrapersonally focused therapists. They include:

1. Social support is an inextricable dimension of human interactions, including formal therapy (Frank & Frank, 1991, referred to it as 'thoroughly enmeshed'). Therefore, therapists can probably be more successful if they become more aware of the latent ways in which they provide social support (e.g. by offering an accessible service that treats clients with dignity).
2. Therapy can re-value and incorporate more of the manifest aspects of social support, such as warmth, mutual respect and concern regarding non-clinical topics.
3. In a related way, therapists should try to recognise and build on the popular strategies that people in general use to cope, including accessing social support. Clinical assessments, for instance, can extend to the kind of interview content covered by C. Barker *et al.* (1990).
4. Greater awareness and incorporation of a client's social support strategy into treatment can impact on significant others. Positive impacts include improved communication, openness and empathy; while negative consequences have included a feeling of inadequacy (relative to the therapist) and heightened anxiety.
5. Considerable common ground exists between therapists and informal helpers, including the nature of the problems faced, the helping processes and the therapeutic outcomes. However, it appears that professionals have a distinctive profile in all three respects. This can be construed as the basis for complementary roles, in which, for instance, therapists can encourage their clients to make more appropriate use of informal help.

If nothing else, heightened awareness of these implications may help therapists to 'never do harm'. In the next major section more detailed accounts of how to 'do good' are specified.

Case study: Emotional support and district nursing

A small observational study of formal social support was carried out with four local colleagues in the District Nursing Service (Milne et al. 1992). Their official, manifest role was to assist clients with physical complaints (e.g. changing dressings), but the focus of the study was on the latent psychological care that they provided as they visited people in their own homes. The emotional, informational and practical support that the nurses offered was observed for 19 home visits, and the emotional support was found to be the most frequent form of social support. This included sharing personal experiences as a consequence of the client's disclosure (e.g. 'that can be awful, it once happened to me'), verbal expression of caring (e.g. 'I hope that doesn't happen again') as well as non-verbal ones (e.g. hugging). The clients were highly satisfied with the service, which appeared to meet physical as well as psychological needs through the mechanism of social support. Not surprisingly, the nurses also reported high job satisfaction.

This example illustrates how informal emotional help can be inter-twined with formal medical assistance, and where the kind of clear awareness that these nurses had of their social support role can contribute to a mutually satisfying 'social therapy' interaction.

'DOING GOOD': COMBINING THERAPY AND SUPPORT

In some important respects formal therapy has always been known to incorporate certain elements of social support, labelled typically as 'non-specific' or 'placebo' factors. By contrast, the 'specific' factors (e.g. dream interpretation, guided discovery) were regarded as the vital essence of effective therapy. Naturally, therapists attributed their success to these specific factors, coming as they did from impressive theory, sophisticated research and intensive postgraduate training. However, analyses of the relative importance of the specific and non-specific factors tend not to support this tempting perspective. In a review, Oei and Shuttlewood (1996) recorded how different theorists over time have attempted to explain the influence of non-specific factors, including the provision of a relationship that provides inspiration and the expectation of help (Frank & Frank, 1991), warm involvement including concern and friendliness (Stiles *et al.*, 1986), and the opportunity for catharsis (Grencavage &

Norcross, 1990). Perhaps the handiest conventional phrase for this 'non-specific' dimension is the 'therapeutic alliance', which includes the degree to which client and therapist are emotionally bonded and are agreed on the purpose and methods of therapy. This definition accords with the provision of emotional, informational and practical social support. Oei and Shuttlewood (1996) concluded that both the specific and the non-specific factors contributed to outcome in psychotherapy, and argued that it was time to analyse how the non-specific factors related to given therapies. From the mini-literature review in the previous section we can begin to understand why this might be the case: the so-called non-specific and rather mundane ingredients of therapy (such as social support) may actually play a powerful part in promoting clinical outcomes.

Having outlined how therapists can optimise these non-specifics within therapy, in this section I proceed to detail how therapists can, through conventional one-to-one therapy, harness some of the non-specifics that occur at the interface between the client and his or her social world. This is done by discussing a social support orientation to problem assessment, formulation and therapy.

A social support approach to clinical assessment

In broad diagnostic terms, problems directly related to social support are classified as 'Axis IV' in the *Diagnostic and Statistical Manual of Mental Disorders* (DSM IV: American Psychiatric Association, 1994). These include problems associated with the client's primary support group (e.g. bereavement, divorce, sexual abuse) or social environment (e.g. inadequate social support, adjustment to life-cycle transitions, such as retirement). Other categories include problems over education, occupation, housing, economics, accessing help, interaction with the criminal system (e.g. being arrested or incarcerated) and exposure to psychosocial and environmental stressors (e.g. disasters or war). Reference to DSM IV allows one to diagnose and code such social environmental problems and to note their relationship to the various clinical disorders that make up 'axis I' (e.g. anxiety; eating disorders) in terms of the 'principal' diagnosis.

While such a well-established diagnostic approach may help to frame the general nature of the problem, it is insufficient as a clinical assessment in the psychological tradition. This requires a detailed and systematic statement of the identified problem, typically expressed in terms of its frequency, duration or intensity, which is then related to those factors that appear to have caused and maintained the problem. (Of course, the ways in which clinicians assess, analyse or formulate these factors will vary significantly as a function of their therapeutic model, to which we will turn in the next section.) Clinicians will often make use of assessment instruments in order to complete these tasks, including structured interviews, questionnaires and direct observations, as illustrated earlier in this chapter and especially as detailed in Chapter 4. Given the theoretical differences between the various models of psychopathology, the present example assumes the fairly pan-theoretical approach as outlined in Chapter 3, namely the transactional stress model.

Clinical assessment according to this approach would typically begin with an attempt to specify the nature of the client's distress (i.e. the 'presenting problem'). Of especial relevance to social support are such symptoms as depression or anger. For instance, Lane and Hobfoll (1992) administered the Recent Anger Scale and the Anger Expression Scale to 85 patients with chronic breathing problems. These two scales comprise questionnaire items from Spielberger et al.'s (1983) State-Trait Anger Scale. Other questionnaires assess depression in a way that subsumes anger, such as the Inventory of Depressive Symptomatology (IDS: Rush et al., 1986) which asks about the clients' irritation and interpersonal sensitivity, alongside the usual depressive features (e.g. suicidal ideation and sleep disturbance: the IDS is reproduced in Milne (1992a), as part of a portfolio of assessment methods. Key interpersonal aspects of depression can also be noted in the clinical interview, as in deficiencies in initiating, maintaining or encouraging social interactions. These tend to be associated with mumbling, poor eye contact, and inexpressive or incongruent body language (Winefield, 1984). At a more fundamental level, there is considerable evidence attesting to how people with depression are less likely to use problem-solving skills and are more likely to use emotion-focused coping strategies (e.g. Billings et al., 1983). These authors utilised a collection of self-report instruments, such as a social network analysis, the quality of significant relationships and support at work and from the family.

Another characteristic of depressed clients is that they may well report loneliness and dissatisfaction with such social support as they do experience, characteristically expressing excessive (idealistic) expectations for support and perceiving their actual support as less frequent than it is in reality (Champion & Power, 1995). Power et al. (1988) developed an instrument (The Significant Others Scale—SOS) in order to measure this characteristic discrepancy between the real and ideal levels of social support. The SOS and other instruments with which to quantify social support itself have been detailed in Chapter 4. For example, the Inventory of Socially Supportive Behaviours (Barrera et al., 1981) is a popular and straightforward way to assess the nature of the informal help that they receive.

Perhaps a final aspect to touch on regarding the assessment of social support concerns the environmental rather than personal domain. A focus on this sphere would enquire into such issues as the client's social activities and interactions. For example, Murray *et al.* (1996) assessed eight social domains of client functioning, including social activity. They gave a score out of 20 for each of a range of activities in relation to adults with a major mental illness (e.g. a score of six for structured daytime activity and a further three for involvement in a social stimulation programme). Together with assessment of seven clinical domains (e.g. psychosis) this provided a problem definition. Interestingly, such problems were further classed as 'cardinal' (i.e. a problem requiring action) when the client was uncooperative, the care giver was reporting severe distress or inconvenience, or where there was a risk to the client or others.

As I hope this brief section has indicated, therapists can incorporate some of the critical aspects of social functioning within a routine assessment process, preferably based on a combination of interview, clinical observation and self-report measures (a fuller account of such assessment methods and instruments was provided in Chapter 4, from where the interested reader may be able to select alternative approaches). Whatever the methods used in the clinical assessment phase, they should feed in to a problem formulation: i.e. *why* is a particular client distressed in a particular way (e.g. depression) at this particular time, and what implications are there for therapy?

Problem formulation, with a social support orientation

The transactional stress model that underpins much of the thinking in this book necessitates a fairly complex explanation for a client's distress. As per Figure 3.4, the therapist needs to gather relevant information about stressors, coping strategies and social support in order to make sense of the situation. As detailed in Chapter 4, instruments such as the Coping Responses Inventory (CRI: Moos, 1997: in Milne, 1992a) can be employed in order to provide a straightforward assessment of these variables. This has been illustrated by Moos (1997) in relation to a 23 year old woman whose focal stressor was an ongoing verbally and physically abusive relationship with her alcoholic father. The stress intensified when he lost his job and became more abusive. Completion of the CRI at this stage indicated this woman's actual coping efforts, together with a profile representing how she would prefer to deal with her father (the 'ideal' profile). This is reproduced in Figure 5.2, and indicates that, at assessment, she relied heavily upon the coping strategies of cognitive avoidance and emotional discharge. More adaptive methods, such as reappraisal and gaining more social support, were infrequently used. Such a coping and support profile affords an explanation for distress (e.g. depression) and the fluctuation in the focal stressor suggests why this distress is pronounced at this time point.

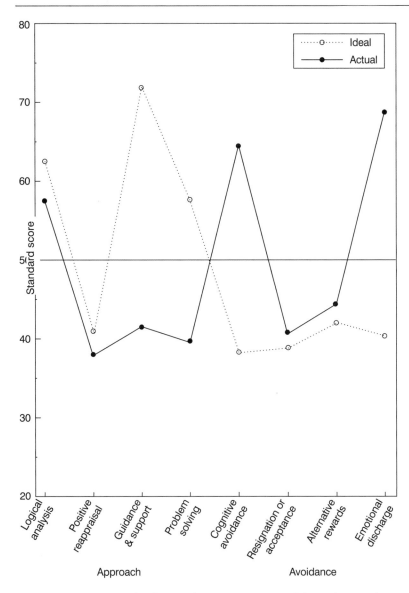

Figure 5.2 An example of a social-support-orientated formulation of a woman's actual and ideal coping with an alcoholic parent. Reproduced from C.P. Zalaquett and R.J. Woods (eds) (1997): *Evaluating Stress: A Book of Resources*, copyright © 1997, with permission from Scarecrow Publishers, Lanham, MD, USA.

Helpfully, the CRI 'ideal' profile in Figure 5.2 also indicates what the therapist might focus on in therapy, including the customary 'specific' targets in therapy (e.g. cognitive approaches to reappraise the stress or how she coped with it) as well the glaring need to improve the clients' social functioning. At least initially, the latter might be tackled by encouraging her to engage in a fresh cycle of more positive and logical problem-solving in therapy, leading to some graded attempts to improve her social support between the therapy sessions.

Additional assessment instruments might be used to refine or extend the formulation that the CRI provided. For instance, it could be that this client, although recognising the need for more social support, is unclear about how social support operates. The therapist could then use the clinical interview to probe this area in some depth, attending in particular to such key factors as the extent to which she reciprocates social support (Heller, 1990) and how flexibly and appropriately she deploys her other coping strategies (Moos & Schaefer, 1993). A further, more specific and personal assessment of her social support could then be undertaken, based for instance on the sociogram approach of 'power mapping' (Hagan & Smail, 1997). This would help to assess the social support 'terrain', clarifying the nature of the problem and indicating possible solutions. Power was defined by these authors as an individual's ability to involve and influence others, in order to foster 'solidarity' with them. This makes a map of a client's power relations of especial relevance to a social support formulation, including the degree to which clients feel able to exercise control over the material and personal resources that relate to their power (e.g. the attitudes one has to others represent a form of personal resource).

Not only might a power map help to formulate a client's distress, it can also reveal a client's predicament more clearly. As Hagan and Smail (1997) emphasise, being explicit about social support and its relations to personal and material resources may indicate to the therapist that the client is not so much 'deficient' as 'damaged'. They suggest that such demystification can itself provide significant relief of distress, indicating both how good assessment can also be therapeutic (the 'baseline cure') and how the kind of 'non-specific' factors outlined earlier can operate (e.g. the ventilation and succour that would naturally follow from a therapist and client completing a power map in a collaborative way). As a consequence, therapist and client may be better placed to understand distress and the wider social factors that contribute to it, which takes us neatly into a discussion of the features of socially sensitive therapy.

Social sensitive therapy

According to Smail (1993), therapists who are being sensitive to their clients' social and material worlds have three roles. The first of these is to provide 'comfort', characterised by a non-directive counselling style that signals solidarity through the provision of social support (featuring companionship, kindness and sympathy). This is not significantly different from the points already made in this chapter and labelled as 'GP psychotherapy', 'non-specific factors', 'social alliance', etc. The second role is to help the clients to clarify the basis for their distress, so as to achieve an accurate view of how they came to be trapped by fate and fortune in a 'power field'. This role Smail refers to as 'demystification', namely removing from the clients the usual burden of being entirely responsible for their condition, not to mention the task of overcoming it. Demystifying requires the therapist to patiently and persistently work towards an understanding of distress in terms of its origins in the social and physical environment. This demonstrates to clients that the reasons for their distress may be beyond their capacity to influence, which Smail asserts has always been accompanied by relief. As such, demystification shifts the onus away from the traditional emphasis upon clients to 'pull their socks up', 'take responsibility' or to 'act on therapeutic insights', all of which Smail (1995) suggests represent a kind of psychological manipulation or exhortation to tap supposed intrapersonal resources (e.g. optimism or 'will-power'). To illustrate, he provided a case study of a client who presented with agoraphobia, including panic attacks. By providing the first companionship element of social therapy, the client was encouraged to recount her childhood, which, the age of 10, featured looking after her smaller brother because her parents had to work virtually non-stop in unskilled jobs to make ends meet. There was little time for this client to go to school or to develop her personal resources, just an onerous responsibility that was formulated as the origin of her panic attacks.

Having provided companionship and demystification, the third role for the social therapist is to encourage clients by directing them towards the power and resources that they need to exert counter-influence on those proximal and distal factors that are the cause of the distress. This includes working towards social and material advantage, such as by acquiring more powerful friends or financial capital. Smail (1995) recognises that these forces may not be amenable to change, and also that therapists would have difficulty encouraging a counter-influence approach. However, he believes that ultimately the emphasis has to be placed upon the wider environment rather than upon the individual client, so that even if encouragement and counter-influence is impossible at least the client is not put under yet another powerful influence, that of a therapist placing a moral burden to be different and to take responsibility for adjusting to an unacceptable environment (the traditional 'blaming the victim' stance).

Smail (1994) is therefore critical of the 'empowerment' movement because it can be diametrically opposed to social therapy. However, it need not necessarily be so, since empowerment can also assist individuals to access more power. Rappaport (1994) gives examples of how the introduction of informed consent and participative decision-making into proximal environments (e.g. hospital or school) can help empower individuals. Smail himself (1993) recognised that social therapy needs to 'encourage patients to develop ... enduring sources of solidarity in their lives, thereby rendering therapeutic comfort redundant' (p. 169). These sources of solidarity are social supporters, including family, friends and lovers.

To what extent do therapists already engage in demystification? Is Smail's (1993; 1995) rhetoric based on a flawed perception of therapy? This is discussed in Chapter 8, indicating some support for Smail's assertions. Next we turn to a second and more orthodox way to provide social therapy, the enhancement of the client's social skills as they relate to the elicitation and reinforcement of social support, a way of 'rendering therapeutic comfort redundant'.

Social skills training

Early attempts to empower clients by developing their social skills had only limited success, attributed to the use of standard packages designed to improve eye contact, conversational skills, assertiveness and so forth for groups of clients. Winefield (1984) noted the need for a more subtle, ecologically sound approach, one that incorporated work on improving the client's understanding of social norms (e.g. concerning intimacy), and more attention to others, leading to the provision of more positive reinforcement for those who offer social support. For example, part of the coping skills enhancement programme is to encourage clients with schizophrenia to increase their social activity by initiating social engagement (Tarrier et al., 1993). However, although this resulted in a greater use of the targeted coping skills and to symptomatic improvement, it did not lead to improved social functioning.

A review by T.F. Smith et al. (1996) notes that the successful generalisation of social skills training remains a major challenge. They suggest that to meet this challenge the training should be personalised for specific clients and based on an analysis of the tasks that they face. It should also recognise three interacting processes that underlie social skills, starting with the receiving of social information (social perception), the processing of this information (e.g. problem-solving) and the selection and enactment of the relevant verbal and non-verbal social skills. Furthermore, these skills should be distinguished from 'social competence' (an individual's ability to be socially effective) and from 'social adjustment' (the meeting of instrumental and affiliative needs). In this sense, clients with schizophrenia may be socially skilled but may have limited competence, due to environmental factors (e.g. high expressed emotion) that interfere with the execution or results of the skills. Likewise, even if socially competent, clients may experience poor social adjustment in that they may not be able to meet the task requirements of a worker or a student. In short, more subtle, ecologically sensitive approaches to social skills training are required if we are to empower clients sufficiently for them to access successfully the 'enduring sources of solidarity' identified by Smail (1993).

One practical way forward is to combine social skills training with other necessary interventions, such as family education and therapy that addresses the poor social competence (Hogarty *et al.*, 1991). A fascinating and appropriately subtle analysis of such a therapy package approach has been detailed by Longabaugh *et al.* (1995). They evaluated a therapy designed to enhance the social conditions thought to be conducive to success, called 'relationship enhancement'. By means of enlisting the involvement of significant others in therapy, the clients' affiliative investment in their social network can be modified. Four of the eighteen therapy sessions are devoted to relationship enhancement, where the client's selected significant other (e.g. a partner or a friend) is involved in improving mutual communication, problem-solving and social reinforcement. Other sessions are devoted to one-to-one cognitive behavioural therapy (e.g. addressing stimulus control, restructuring cognitions and assertiveness training). The value of this approach was assessed by measures of social functioning (covering network size and the adequacy of social support), alcohol abuse, and the support (or otherwise) of others for the use of alcohol. Longabaugh *et al.* (1995) found that extended relationship enhancement was the most effective therapy package (i.e. compared to brief relationship enhancement in a broad spectrum approach and extended cognitive behavioural therapy) in increasing abstinence for those clients who began therapy with a problematic social network (i.e. that was either not supportive of abstinence or in which the client had little involvement). Further illustrating the important role of social support in relation to therapy outcome, they found that clients in the cognitive behavioural group who already had appropriate support also gained significantly from the programme. Longabaugh *et al.* (1995) concluded that therapists (and researchers) should assess the clients' social support and calibrate their interventions accordingly. If there is little investment in supportive relationships or high investment in unsupportive relationships then relationship enhancement is called for. This assessment allows social skills training to be matched to the needs of clients and better recognises and addresses systematically the additional challenges of social competence and social adjustment. Here, then, is another kind of subtle, ecologically valid social therapy which can be used by therapists who wish to restrict their social support work to the clinic.

Case study: Professional befriending of people with a dementia

On the margins between the clinic and the neighbourhood are such forms of social therapy as setting up, supporting and evaluating befriending schemes for the patients who are dementia sufferers. This can be illustrated by a local project in which care attendants from a voluntary sector organisation (Crossroads) were trained in befriending skills by mental health practitioners (Kalsy & McDonnell, 1997). This training covered information on dementia, relationship-building, reminiscence and validation, all following the approach of Stokes and Goudie (1990).

Befrienders used this training in an effort to improve the twelve participating clients' quality of life through social contact, friendship and community integration. Objectives included enabling the clients to participate in a valued pastime (e.g. resuming a hobby) providing regular social support, maintaining valued relationships, and fostering emotional wellbeing.

The evaluation of this befriending scheme was based on a wide range of assessments and perspectives, including a challenging behaviour checklist, a befriender log book and satisfaction interviews. The latter indicated that all carers were satisfied with the scheme, as were over 80% of clients and the great majority of mental health practitioners (keyworkers). Other findings were also generally favourable, and the report concluded that important changes to professional practices had occurred, resulting in an enriched social life for their patients.

CONCLUSIONS

To summarise, in this chapter I have argued that social support is inextricably intertwined with formal therapy and so is best regarded along such dimensions as intimacy and utility. Therefore, informal helpers are at times most appropriately located alongside therapists, while on other occasions the therapist is more of a social supporter. However, although there is significant overlap, the therapist tends to have a distinctive helping profile. This is analogous to friendship, which has been found to range along a continuum from strangers and acquaintances to close friends and best friends (Fehr, 1996). All such relationships differ with regard to the degree of physical proximity, emotional expression and breadth of self-disclosure. The 'best friend' is defined because of greater amounts of these kinds of relationship qualities, rather than because of differences in the ingredients or the type of relationship quality. For instance, while one might share some personal information with an acquaintance, a best friend is someone who can be trusted and depended upon with all information. In a striking parallel to the building of the working alliance in therapy, Fehr (1996) described friendship as:

the process of achieving closeness which involves becoming more fully engaged, affective and prosocial in one's interactions with another person. It also involves gradually revealing more intimate information about oneself in an increasing number of domains. People who are close also are similar to one another in important, psychological ways. (pp. 111–112)

The therapist–client interaction cannot be construed adequately in a social vacuum, since therapy can impact on the clients' social support network and vice versa. Therefore, it follows that therapists play a helping role that is complementary to that fulfilled by the clients' significant others, and that the coping strategies that clients use to influence their social world is a highly relevant focus for assessment and intervention. Examples of such socially attuned clinical assessment and formulation were provided, reflecting the transactional stress model that underpins this book. This model explicitly recognises the interactions between clients' coping strategies and their social support, and in turn between these efforts at adaptation and the physical/social environment. Such formulations provide a unique and subtle account of a client's distress, offering an explanation of why this should be occurring at this stage and indicating therapy options. A major outcome of clinical formulation is that the therapist comes to understand that clients are not simply 'deficient' but are also to some extent 'damaged' by a stressful environment in which they can exercise little power.

Two forms of 'socially sensitive therapy' were then outlined: Smail's (1993) version, almost lost beneath his powerful rhetoric, and the more conventional approach of social skills training. Smail's social therapy emphasises social support ('solidarity'), demystification of the causes of distress and supporting the clients' attempts to exercise counter-influence. Although opposed to the traditional therapeutic approach to client empowerment, helping clients to acquire skills or resources that promote their access to power (rather than encouraging them to adapt to a powerless role) may be acceptable, including fostering social support skills. The second version of social therapy that was presented was social skills training. This has a 20-year history, during which time it has gone from the regimented provision of standard programmes of skills to groups of clients to more individualised and socially subtle therapy packages. These can include the clients' significant others and match their needs to a tailored intervention, promising greater success.

Of course, in this book the term 'social therapy' is also used to refer generally to the ways that mental health professionals can intervene to foster social support processes, including acting as therapists for those who provide social support (e.g. carers of people with a severe mental illness) and trying to alter social environments (see the Preface).

Although this chapter has detailed several latent and manifest ways in which conventional therapy can better address clients' social support needs, it is recognised that this is not without its difficulties. For one thing, therapists are loath to accept the repeated finding that the general, non-specific factors (i.e. such as the therapeutic alliance, which equates with social support) are a major determinant of treatment outcome. This is understandable, given the heavy investment that they make in extensive professional training, their need to offer a distinctive service, and their involvement in research trials designed to examine the latest technical (i.e. specific) treatment factors. A second and perhaps more profound consideration is the commitment to a rationale for therapy that assumes that it is appropriate for clients to be helped to adapt to their world, rather than adapting an excessively stressful world to the needs of clients. As Smail (1995) puts it, therapists are wedded to the idea that human agency (e.g. 'will power') can alter the necessary intrapersonal variables (e.g. states of mind or feeling states, such as unhappiness), perhaps because such a rationale enables therapists to access and maintain considerable power.

We should not underestimate the influence that these personal and situational factors exert on therapists. Indeed, like Smail's (1993) version of social therapy, perhaps all we can hope to achieve through devices such as this book is to support a process of demystifying some part of the therapy business. However, always optimistic, in the next two chapters I hope to additionally encourage therapists to engage in the kinds of proximal and distal social support interventions that afford them ways of empowering those with mental health needs to gain sufficient personal power to strike a better balance between deficiency and damage.

Chapter 6

PROXIMAL INTERVENTIONS

INTRODUCTION

In comparison with direct or one-to-one clinical work, 'proximal' mental health interventions target those who provide the immediate social support for our clients, including partners, families and groups. The larger context, that of the 'distal' environment, is the subject of the next chapter. These distinctions are inevitably blurred, but do provide three coherent chunks of research and practice on the social support continuum.

Proximal contexts provide the most clear-cut examples of the kinds of social support interventions that mental health professionals have carried out, and a representative sample of these projects have been selected for scrutiny in this chapter. They include work with couples, caring for carers, family-based programmes and facilitating self-help groups. The chapter closes with a look at the fascinating, social-support-like role of companion pets. The underlying themes remain those of highlighting the importance of social support and identifying how mental health practitioners can play a greater role in fostering social support. As summarised in Chapters 1 and 2, as a group we have rarely taken up the long-standing challenge to move away from our unnecessarily limited clinical role in order to create a more 'just society' for our clients (Albee, 1986) through what has previously been labelled as 'social network therapy' and 'social system psychotherapy'. The present chapter paves part of the way to this 'just society'.

RECONNECTING COUPLES

Social support, based as it is in acts that communicate caring, is especially evident in close relationships such as those between partners. Most social support occurs in this context, as indicated in the finding that the partner was the most highly endorsed source of help for a large national sample of UK adults (C. Barker *et al.*, 1990). Furthermore, a close confiding relationship with a friend does not compensate for the absence of a partner

(Brown & Harris, 1978). A key element in this relationship with a partner is the mutual responsiveness that exists to one another's needs. Arising from a responsive relationship that meets caregiving needs is an attitude of trust—an expectation that a partner or carer can be relied on both to validate one's worth over time and to facilitate coping with short-term stressors, the heart of social support. And as a result of experiencing trust in others, individuals develop a sense of confidence that protects against depression and other forms of distress (Cutrona, 1996).

Conversely, when the expectation of social support is not fulfilled, especially of responsive emotional support, then a fundamental 'relationship rule' is broken and the bond is threatened. Feeling emotionally supported, and belief in a partner's responsivity in a time of need, has been found to rank as one of the most basic expectations of an intimate relationship (Baxter, 1986). Evidence of responding to another's needs by providing caring creates and maintains a feeling of being loved in that individual.

It appears that, while emotional responsivity is critical to relationships, men and women are affected differently, at least in the context of marriage. Researchers' findings suggest that marriage is more strongly associated for men with happiness, satisfaction with home life and measures of mental health. Men rely on marriage more for social support, but it seems that it is the quality of the relationship, rather than the marital status *per se*, that is most important for women. The strongest relationship for women is that between relationship quality and mental health. It appears that while women depend on friends, relatives and others for their social support, men turn to their partners. Cutrona's (1996) research programme has indicated that this social support imbalance is a result of differential socialisation processes, one encouraging men to appear in control while facilitating women's articulation of their emotional state. Compounded by parallel differences in their respective work and social environments, it follows that men are more dependent upon their partners for social support. For example, it was found from a survey in the USA that 82% of married men compared to 63% of married women reported that they confided in their partner when upset (Antonucci & Akiyama, 1987). A less striking difference was obtained from a UK sample—i.e. 71% versus 64%, respectively (C. Barker *et al.*, 1990). A further manifestation of this socialisation process is that men and women are thought to have different social support needs and social support styles. While women seek respect, affirmation and tangible assistance from their husbands, men seek affirmation and intimacy (defined as being able to talk, receiving affection and evaluating their spouse as a good sexual partner). Recent research has attempted to isolate two fundamental needs in relation to marital adjustment, those of 'enhancement' and 'verification'. Both are assumed to underpin self-evaluation, which in turn supports self-esteem. Enhancement refers to information that promotes a positive self-image or protects individuals from negative information (e.g. 'my spouse thinks highly of me or finds me interesting'); verification concerns efforts to confirm self-conceptions (e.g 'my spouse brings out my best qualities, or lets me know I am appreciated just as I am'). Katz *et al.*, (1996) included these terms in a self-esteem scale as part of a test of the enhancement and verification hypotheses. A community sample of 265 married individuals provided additional questionnaire data on the perceived social support of their spouse and their marital adjustment. The results indicated strong associations between marital quality and both enhancement and verification, suggesting that these two processes combined to produce greater social support from the partner. However, increases in these two forms of social support were connected with improved marital quality only up to the point that they verified or matched an individual's self-esteem. That is, social support that is consistent with someone's view of themselves is helpful, but ceases to be so when it indicates exaggerated or diminished individual value or worth. Katz *et al.*, (1996) provided the example of partners who perceived their spouses as shy, noting that this does not necessarily imply a negative evaluation and may well be consistent with the self-perceptions, making such an exchange supportive. By contrast, equally negative interactions between spouses that do not match or verify the self-perceptions do not fulfil a supportive function. This carries implications for clinical work, which will be considered in the next section, on couple therapy.

As regards their respective helping styles, women emerge from research analyses as better at social support than men; they are judged as more skilful by observers, being more attentive and more effective at alleviating loneliness and fostering wellbeing. Cutrona (1996) attributes this superiority to a lifetime of training in helping and nurturing others, making women in general an excellent source of emotional, esteem-enhancing and tangible support. By contrast, men have generally been socialised to conceal their own needs and their struggles to cope, and so lack support elicitation skills. They also tend to be less sophisticated at self-disclosure and emotional expression of support.

These broad generalisations about gender differences provide a seductively straightforward explanation for the social support imbalance in couples: as men marry women, they get a net benefit in social support, enough to take them above a threshold of emotional need and hence minimising their dependence upon others for support. By comparison, when women marry men they tend to suffer a net loss in social support, leaving them below the required threshold and therefore in need of support from family, friends and others (Cutrona, 1996). This is a sweeping conclusion, and obviously there can be equally large differences within the gender groups.

Whether or not these gender differences are due to distinctive socialisation processes, mental health practitioners will no doubt recognise these relationship ingredients as important, as they bear a close resemblance to the 'core conditions' for effective therapy. According to the influential work of C.R. Rogers (1957), the fundamental qualities of a therapeutic relationship are empathy, warmth (acceptance) and genuineness, qualities that were later recognised as featuring in successful marriages (Rogers, 1975). In a study of partners' social support to their spouses who had breast cancer, Pistrang and Barker (1995) administered a structured interview and several psychological distress questionnaires to a sample of 113 heterosexual women in order to assess the role of these relationship qualities. The interview was designed to tap aspects of the womens' social support relationship with their partners, including the women's level of disclosure, and the partners' helpfulness, empathy, criticism and withdrawal (disengaging). The results indicated that women who found talking to their partner to be more helpful reported less distress, and confirmed that poor social support from a partner was a risk factor in womens' psychological response to breast cancer. Informal help from other relationships did not compensate for the lack of a confiding relationship with the partner. Good communication with the partner featured high empathy, a good level of understanding, and less withdrawal. And, reflecting Cutrona's (1996) observations, Pistrang and Barker (1995) found evidence of a social support threshold or 'ceiling effect', in that beyond an adequate level of satisfaction with the help that was received there were few additional benefits. They concluded that there was something unique about the social support that is provided by a partner. This is elaborated shortly.

Couple therapy: the rationale

While partners can and usually do provide a profound form of help to one another, they can also contribute disproportionately to one another's distress. In one survey it was found that being married and getting along with one's spouse provided some protection against depression, whereas being married and not getting along with one's spouse provided a 25-fold increase in the risk of depression (Weissman, 1987). In this sense, it has been observed that the benefits that tend to be associated with a good marriage may be viewed more accurately as the absence of detrimental effects arising from a poor but vital relationship.

Given the seeming primacy of dysfunctional couples as the cause of one another's distress, mental health practitioners can play a major role in fostering helpful support by rectifying marital disharmony. Given the unique and powerful nature of the relationship between partners, interventions at this point may prove more important than the provision of individual therapy or of efforts to foster social support to individuals from friends, family or others. However, these levels of interaction are likely to influence each other, and therefore couple therapy can also bring primary and secondary social support benefits. For instance, Moos (1991) reported that successful therapy for one partner's depression was related to improvements in the spouse's social activities, family cohesion and to a more positive home environment. Similarly, Brody and Farber (1989) assessed 20 partners of individuals in therapy and reported that the therapy had resulted in greater empathy, openness, and improved communication in the clients, related to more introspection and understanding from their partners. However, successful therapy can also lead partners to feel excluded, resentful or inadequate (Brody & Farber, 1989), or undervalued and dissatisfied (Katz *et al.*, 1996). In short, as per Chapter 3, social support has to be viewed as part of a transactional system, one that can help or hinder, depending on the sometimes subtle aspects of couple relationships. Because of the complex interrelationship amongst the stress, coping, social support and distress variables in this system, conceptually and practically different interventions can have similar effects. It follows that they may also have compound effects, such that concurrent interventions at several levels may produce the best outcomes (Moos, 1991).

Couple therapy: some methods

An early illustration of combining individual and couples work was provided by Cobb *et al.* (1984) who involved spouses as cotherapists for 19 married clients with agoraphobia, although to no significant effect. This may have been because the cotherapy consisted simply of shared access to a therapy manual, attendance at the therapy sessions and encouraging the clients' efforts at self-help. The intervention did not address the social transactions between the couples, unlike more recent programmes that seek to directly mobilise relationship factors. To illustrate, Longabaugh *et al.*'s (1995) relationship enhancement approach devotes four sessions to the partners' therapy, focusing on strengthening the couple's communication, problem-solving and mutual reinforcement. When linked to cognitive behavioural therapy for the client, significantly better results were obtained. A second possible reason for Cobb *et al.*'s (1984) negative results was that this finding held true only when the clients invested in their wider social network (e.g. regarded their friends etc. as important to them) and when these people were supportive of the change (i.e. abstinence from alcohol), variables not assessed by Cobb *et al.* (1984). Longabaugh *et al.* (1995) concluded that therapists should match the therapeutic emphasis on relationships enhancement (RE) to client need: where there are moderate levels of difficulty in a couple then RE is indicated, otherwise individual cognitive behavioural therapy yielded the best results.

In addition to strengthening effective forms of communication between partners, such as problem solving and mutual reinforcement, traditional marital therapy has attempted to decrease aversive interactions, such as criticism and sarcasm, and to foster joint social activities (Schmaling *et al.*, 1989). But these efforts to tune communication and social patterns may need to be preceded by work on resolving basic conflicts between couples, as in the loss of mutual goodwill, trust or even love. Table 6.1 summarises some of Cutrona's (1996) suggestions for work with couples, while Crowe *et al.* (1990) have provided a practical guide to behavioural therapy with couples.

The methods listed in Table 6.1 are best regarded as general guidelines, since research suggests that we need to recognise large individual differences in terms of what is helpful to specific couples. This is illustrated by some research conducted by Pistrang *et al.* (1997), who employed an inter-

Table 6.1   Ways to help couples to improve their mutual social support (based on Cutrona, 1996).

	Objective	Method
1.	Recognising the importance of social support	Education by the therapist; encourage mutual recall of supportive and unsupportive exchanges, highlighting the feeling consequences and the importance of consistent, everyday emotional support.
2.	Improving communication	Openness (e.g. sharing feelings) and specificity about required changes; develop ways for the couple to signal approval and validation to one another; self-disclosures should be treated with particular care: help the couple to listen, empathise and value it.
3.	Identifying helpful forms of support	Enhance mutual understanding of the different ways that the couple seek and provide social support, perhaps fostered by tape-assisted recall (see text).
4.	Working as a team	In times of adversity, encourage the couple to support each other more than ever, especially emotionally (e.g. suffering and fighting it together). They should share thoughts and feelings, rather than withdrawing; cooperate on a coping strategy; balance out the stressors and the effort that is needed to handle them; negotiate, compromise and above all be compassionate with one another.

esting procedure called 'tape-assisted recall' to encourage partners to describe the personal meanings of their interactions. The procedure entails making an audio recording of couples' interactions during a semi-structured communication task in which one member of the couple is asked to help the other. The tape is then played back immediately to each of the participants, who are asked to say what they experienced in the exchange and to rate its helpfulness. A standard questionnaire was used to facilitate recall, namely 'how did this response make you feel?', which was followed by a list of positive and negative impacts (e.g. reassured, accepted, confused and not listened to). Pistrang *et al.* (1997) found that these tape-assisted recall sessions yielded insights about the personal meanings of the interactions, in the context of the couple's relationship. These insights were necessary to understand which responses were helpful and which were not, although certain well-established responses transcended these personal histories (e.g. lack of empathy and change of focus were judged to be unhelpful; responding to the essence of a concern and self-disclosure were perceived as helpful).

To elaborate these points, Pistrang *et al* (1997) provided several verbatim 'talking turns', of which the following is an example. In this episode the patient (P) explains to her husband (H) why she felt it necessary to stay with her niece after each treatment:

P (15):   Well, as I had it explained to me [by the breast care counsellor], I just felt I had to do that, do something, um, not on a surface level, but subconsciously I had to do that because I needed to be looked after, I needed to be mothered.

H (16):   Well why didn't you go to your mother's?

P (17):   (Laughs). You know exactly why I didn't go to my mother's. Um, and as I was at home, if I was at home I was mothering you and I couldn't ask you to reverse your role because I wanted everything to be as normal. I tried to keep everything as normal.

H (18):   Going away for the weekend is abnormal, weren't it?

P (19):   No. But I needed to do that. I sorted you out during the week, I tried to, I juggled everything so that I knew everything was fine for you and then at the weekends I needed to do everything fine for me. I needed someone looking after me.

H (20):   Oh, I thought it was some weird thing like you never liked me.

P (21):   (Laughs). Well, that's why I went to [breast care counsellor] because, this is why I had a problem, I didn't know why I was doing it …

Pistrang *et al.* (1997) interpreted this episode as follows:
The patient rated turn 16 as moderately unhelpful (rating of 2, where 0 = very unhelpful and 6 = very helpful). She said that her partner's response

made her feel misunderstood (empathy rating of 2): 'That isn't what I was trying to say. I said I needed mothering—he ignored the deeper part of that.' She thought his intention was to throw her off completely. 'By injecting a little bit of humour in there, he was trying to throw me off completely.' She said that she would have liked him to have responded by saying 'If you'd have told me what you needed then, I'd have tried my best to give you that.'

The husband rated turn 16 as very unhelpful (1). He said that his intention was to try to lighten the conversation: 'Knowing the sort of relationship my wife has with her mother … It would not have been very helpful for her to go to her mother.' (In the recall addressing his partner's statement in turn 15, the husband said he had felt very uncomfortable and shocked at what his wife was saying.)

The patient rated turn 18 as moderately unhelpful (2) and felt not at all understood (1). She said she felt angry and criticised by her partner at that point: 'He was trying to reprimand me for going away for the weekend.' She also felt he was taking the focus away from herself: 'I was trying to talk about *me*, and he was turning it around to talk about himself and what he wanted.'

At the same turn 18, the husband felt that he had been very unhelpful (1). 'I was just trying to let her know how I felt at the time, when she was going away at the weekend. I'd have liked to have seen her at the weekend after she had treatment, rather than somebody else …' He said that he didn't know how to be helpful to her at that point in the conversation.

At turn 20, the husband disclosed what he imagined was his wife's reason for going away at the weekends following treatment (i.e. that she was rejecting him personally). The wife rated this response as very helpful (6) and felt very understood (6): 'We were talking about what we should be talking about—why I was going away.' She indicated that the impact of this response included compassion, sympathy and some remorse, although she had felt momentarily annoyed ('Initially, it made me feel, "Cor I've just been talking care of my own feelings, I don't want to talk about *him*" '). She thought his intention was to try and make sense of the situation: 'He was trying to understand why I was going away, he was confused.'

In contrast, the husband thought that his response was very unhelpful (1). He said that he was thinking of himself, which got in the way of his being helpful. The intention behind his response was to 'try to get her to open up, to explain herself'.

Finally, Pistrang *et al.* (1997) offered a summary of this episode. The trough, at turns 16 and 18, seems to be characterised by a lack of helper empathy (i.e. the husband). At turn 16, the helper's intention of lightening the conversation had the impact of distracting the patient and making her feel misunderstood. Turn 18 was characterised (within the context of the couple's relationship) by criticism from the husband, plus a lack of focus on the patient's needs and feelings. The peak was at the next response from the husband, turn 20. Although he still focused on himself (his response took the form of a self-disclosure) he now felt that he was engaged and responded seriously to her, in that he was trying to make sense of what she was saying. However, there was a disparity of perceptions about this response: the helper rated it as very unhelpful.

This illustration underlines the contention that social support can be a highly subtle and personal matter, having meanings for the participants that are founded on a long-term relationship and which transcend the more superficial ways of assessing or classifying social support. Also, the method of tape-assisted recall helps us to understand how attempts at providing social support can succeed and fail.

In summary, the relationship between partners provides mental health practitioners with particularly important information about unique and critical social support functions in their context. Although there appear to be clear gender differences in the nature and adequacy of their mutual help, one that favours men, at least two functions deserve attention, namely how partners enhance one-another's self-esteem and how they verify the other's self-evaluation. Other relationship qualities, (especially empathy, acceptance and engagement in mutual problem-solving) support these functions. It was noted that, while mental health practitioners could restrict their work to one-to-one therapy and still influence the client's close relationships, the benefits of creating better communication connections between partners (especially the reduction of aversive exchanges) made it an especially efficient focus for an intervention. This might comprise traditional cognitive–behavioural marital therapy, one-to-one therapy linked to relationship enhancement sessions (e.g. developing problem-solving skills), or some more general social support enhancement work (see Table 6.1). These might usefully be preceded by the 'tape-assisted recall' of specific interactions, as a basis for assessing the nature and adequacy of social support in specific couples (following Pistrang et al., 1997).

Thus far we have considered social support between couples under relatively 'normal' circumstances. Next we turn to a major example of social support under particularly stressful conditions, namely caring for a relative with mental health problems, and to the implications for mental health practitioners, one group who might care for these carers.

CARING FOR THE CARERS

Perhaps the clearest example of social support at the proximal level is that of family carers who help their elderly relatives with a dementia to stay at home. There is a large research literature on this form of support, most of it detailing the considerable burdens of caring and its implications on carers' social, leisure and work activities, not to mention how it can create psychological problems for them (Zarit and Edwards, 1996; Kuipers, 1998). The existence of burden signifies a collapse to the reciprocal arrangements that characterise social support under more normal circumstances, a 'loss of mutuality' or relationship breakdown. It is this that may be viewed as the critical component of the carer's distress (McKee et al., 1997). Similarly, carers of people with schizophrenia experience disruption of their social and family relationships, as well as significant stress from the dependent (e.g. recklessness, trouble with the police and destructiveness) (Winefield and Harvey, 1993).

Although the stress of caring is considerable, as per the transactional model (outlined in Chapter 3) there are recurring demonstrations that this is usually moderated by the carer's appraisal, coping strategies and social support. For instance, Barrowclough and Parle (1997) administered the Family Questionnaire (Barrowclough and Tarrier, 1992) to 85 carers of people with schizophrenia, a tool that amongst other things assesses how they appraise 49 possible problems, in terms of threat appraisal and control appraisal (i.e. perceived ability to cope with the problem). Barrowclough and Parle (1997) found that these two appraisal variables underlay relatives' reactions to caring and were associated with distress. They noted that assessment of carers' appraisals would help mental health practitioners to better identify those carers who were at risk, as well as to define a focus for therapy (i.e. challenge unduly negative appraisals and increasing confidence in coping).

The role of carers' coping strategies is also recognised repeatedly in the literature. For example, in the McKee et al. (1997) study a sample of 228 family supporters of community-resident older adults (50% with a dementia, 50% without) were assessed by means of the Ways of Coping Survey (WOCS: Lazarus and Folkman, 1984: see Chapter 4 for a summary). They found that most of the carers noted themselves as coping well with the stress of caregiving. Interestingly, these carers mostly utilised emotion-focused coping strategies, such as 'suppression' (keeping feelings to oneself; ignoring the problem; and just getting on with things), 'expression' (shout at others, pray or joke), and 'displacement' (physical activity, eating or drinking). McKee et al. (1997) had predicted this bias, based on the widely held view that, although problem-focused coping is normally associated with better outcomes (e.g. higher morale and improved health), it can be counterproductive when nothing useful can be done to buffer or remove the stressor (as is the case in dementia, a progressive, irreversible disease). However, even under these very difficult circumstances more of the carers felt that they were coping well when they used problem-based methods (i.e. 89%; e.g. talk about the problem with someone; make use of formal and informal support), compared to 70% in the case of emotion-based coping. Rating of the carers' coping by the interviewers further exaggerated the difference attributed to these two types of coping (i.e. 64% versus 31%, respectively). Overall, the coping analysis was exceptionally powerful, explaining 70% of the variance in the findings. McKee *et al.* (1997) conjectured that the remaining 30% of the explanation as to how the carers coped may be due to their other personality characteristics, as an enduring disposition (e.g. 'hardiness'), in conjunction with the blow-by-blow coping in the care-giving situation that was assessed by the WOCS instrument. Another plausible part of the explanation is the prior relationship between carer and sufferer, for which McKee *et al.* (1997) found some evidence, and then of course there is also social support. McKee *et al.* (1997) noted that mental health practitioners need to understand such variables if they are to be successful in their work.

As a result of effective coping, carers can feel surprisingly good psychologically. For example, O'Connor *et al.* (1990) reported that their sample of carers of 120 older adults with a dementia derived some satisfaction from their role. Grant and Nolan (1993) summarised some of the rewards reported by a minority of those ($N = 726$) who cared for dependents with a range of handicaps and disabilities (physical, mental, and both). These included a correspondence with their religious convictions, altruism and meeting needs to nurture. However, although positive interpretations of the situation are very important for many caregivers, most carers' coping strategies and social support are insufficient for the task and they tend to experience significant strain (e.g. depression) (Haley *et al.* 1987; Zarit and Edwards, 1996).

Social support is inextricably interwoven with the coping process, for better and for worse. To illustrate, weak social support is one of the risk factors for carers (Morris *et al.*, 1988) and a study by Bledin *et al.* (1990) sheds some light on its interaction with coping. They studied the role of 'expressed emotion' (EE, i.e., emotional aspects of verbal behaviour, such as the tone of a carer's voice, or the presence of hostility), finding that those carers of older adults who had low EE scores (i.e. made fewer critical comments and made more positive remarks) experienced less distress. In turn, having a lower EE profile was associated significantly with the availability of social support for the carers. Similarly, in relation to carers of people with schizophrenia, Winefield and Harvey (1993) surveyed 134 members of The Schizophrenia Fellowship (a self-help group for those affected by schizophrenia) and reported that the majority of respondents did not always act in a supportive manner towards them (e.g. not listening and not offering practical assistance) although 43% of the carers felt that the social support that they received was 'just right'. Similarly negative ratings were provided for formal helpers (e.g. only 35% found their doctor supportive). As noted by Zarit and Edwards (1996), 'social support is perhaps the most important modifying variable for family care givers' (p. 349), so mental health practitioners need to attend to it.

Case study: Social support in an older adults carer support scheme

This case study illustrates how social support is provided and how it influences the clients' (carers and their dependants) satisfaction with a voluntary sector respite care service. This project was the undergraduate dissertation of Fiona MacDonald while she was a psychology student at Newcastle University, and it was supervised by the author. The respite care service was run by Age Concern (Northumberland).

Age Concern set up the Carer Support Scheme in Northumberland to provide respite care to the carers of elderly, physically handicapped and sick people, so complementing other formal and informal services. The service employed care attendants to provide carers with temporary periods of relief away from the dependant.

In a previous evaluation of this scheme, Milne, et al. (1989b) found that the use of the scheme led to reduced strain in carers, associated with less use of formal and informal support services.

It was decided to follow the above study with an evaluation of the process of caring, the rationale being to try to explain the favourable outcomes noted by the previous evaluation. It was expected that there would be differences between the most noticeable function of the care attendants (i.e. providing practical support) and what is actually perceived to be valuable by the carers. Nolan and Grant (1989) found that 'the objective circumstances of caring contribute only a small part to carer stress and that emotional elements are more significant' (p. 957).

Based on this reasoning, it was hypothesised that the support given to carers and their dependants by the care attendants would include practical and informational components; that emotional support would take up more of the contact time and be perceived as more important than the other types of support, (by both carers and care attendants); and that satisfaction with the service would be as high as in the previous evaluation.

Method

A diary was completed on carers and their dependants by the care attendants over a two-month period of routine activity (N = 106). In addition, an interview was administered to 18 pairs of carers and care attendants, the carers having been chosen by the care attendants as people who would be willing and interested in taking part. The diary was used to collect demographic information and ratings for the time spent providing social support and the importance of each of the forms of social support (i.e. informational, practical and emotional support), each rated on a five-point scale. It was felt that ratings for both the time spent providing support and the importance of support were needed, because care attendants had found in a pilot study that even short amounts of time may make an important contribution to the visit.

The interview was aimed at complementing the information gained from the diary, and was conducted in a semi-structured format. Participants were interviewed in their own homes.

A satisfaction questionnaire was completed by carers who took part in the interview (N = 18), developed from the satisfaction questionnaire used in the previous evaluation of this scheme (Milne et al. 1989b).

Results

The reliability of the diary, interview and questionnaire were assessed by the test–retest method, in which clients were reassessed a few hours later. All three instruments were found to be reliable.

The mean diary ratings for informational, practical and emotional support were in the expected direction, in that they increased from informational through practical to emotional support. Table 6.2 presents these data, which lend support to the prediction that emotional support occupies more time and is perceived as more important than the other two types of support. These differences between informational and emotional support were statistically significant, although practical support ran emotional support a close second, and did not differ from it significantly.

In terms of client satisfaction with the scheme, all responders indicated that the scheme provided the right type of help. The overall quality of the scheme was said to be 'very good' by 88% of respondents, and 72% of the users said they were 'very satisfied' with the help that they had received. These results suggested that satisfaction with the scheme was, if anything, higher than in the previous evaluation (Milne et al. 1989b), providing support for the third and final hypothesis.

Concluding remarks

The support given to carers and their dependants was found to consist of the three predicted types of support, as a fourth response category ('other') was only used in 9 out of the 106 diaries.

The trend in the results pointed towards emotional support as the most highly valued part of the help given to carers and dependants in this scheme, and it can be suggested that a reason for the high level of satisfaction in carers is the emotional support that they received. This finding concurs with the view that emotional support 'is probably the least well defined but the most important need to meet for carers' (Kuipers, 1998, p. 203).

Table 6.2 Mean ratings of the social support provided by Age Concern's carer support scheme (Northumberland), from the perspective of both the care attendants and the carers

		Mean scores		
Diary: care attendant ratings		I	P	E
Carer	TS	1.96	2.69	2.56
	IMP	2.47	2.85	3.20
Dependant	TS	1.88	3.52	3.62
	IMP	2.20	3.75	3.82
Interview: carer ratings		I	P	E
Carer	TS	1.50	2.39	2.56
	IMP	3.11	3.44	4.00
Dependant	TS	1.40	2.20	2.80
	IMP	3.20	3.33	3.87
Interview: care attendant ratings		I	P	E
Carer	TS	1.70	2.17	3.11
	IMP	2.78	2.72	4.00
Dependant	TS	1.61	2.50	3.89
	IMP	2.17	3.72	4.33

Key to table
I = Informational support
P = Practical support
E = Emotional support
TS = Time spent
IMP = Importance

Role of professionals

By comparison with the above case study, the behaviour of mental health practitioners towards carers has tended to receive poor evaluations, dating from a study by Deasy and Quinn (1995). They analysed the requests made of psychiatrists by carers for information (e.g. on prognosis) and advice in coping, reporting that nearly two-thirds were dissatisfied. When the psychiatrists who were involved with these carers ($N = 23$) were interviewed, they stated that the 'bad' carer showed signs of distress, tried to thwart the hospital, and took up a great deal of their time. Latterly, Winefield and Burnett (1996) have noted that carers 'still frequently express considerable frustrations with available mental health services' (p. 223).

More helpful roles for professionals include strategies to promote coping and social support, such as family and systems interventions (e.g. improving care practices in residential care) and therapy designed to alter high EE (Whitehead, 1991); coping strategy enhancement training allied to memory training for suffers with a dementia (Brodaty & Gresham, 1989); counselling and support groups (Zarit *et al.*, 1987); education and developing problem-solving skills (Lovett & Gallagher, 1988); as well as improving practical services, such as providing respite carers and domiciliary help. Not least, practitioners should themselves find ways to transcend the unsympathetic approach noted above (Deasy & Quinn, 1955) in order to offer emotional and informational support. They can also play a significant role in addressing the personal barriers that some carers erect between themselves and both formal and informal support. In offering this suggestion, Zarit and Edwards (1996) proposed that mental health practitioners could use cognitive therapy methods to dismantle irrational beliefs about social support (e.g. 'reality testing' the feared reactions of significant others, such as disapproval for a particular approach to caring).

Some of the options for family work are elaborated next, but in closing this section it is worth noting some of the factors that contribute to the frustration of carers. Winefield and Burnett's (1996) survey of 134 members of the Schizophrenia Fellowship in Australia indicated that there were four times as many spontaneous negative comments on the service provided by mental health practitioners as there were positive ones (e.g. lack of information or acknowledgement of the carer's understanding of the dependent person). Winefield and Burnett (1996) presented these and other data to multidisciplinary groups of mental health practitioners, clarifying six barriers to successful collaboration with carers (see Table 6.3).

Complementing the above emphasis by Zarit and Edwards (1996), Winefield and Burnett (1996) suggest that to overcome these barriers it is necessary for mental health practitioners to continue to work on improving their communication (since carers and dependents can be 'exquisitely sensitive' to negative feelings), to participate in training addressing the role conflict and low self-confidence they experience, to lobby jointly with carers for better resources, and to respect the efforts of carers while more fully involving them in the management of their dependents. As regards training, this could borrow from the methods employed with carers. Brodaty *et al.* (1997), for example, provided a successful 10-day course consisting of topics on reducing distress, combating isolation, coping skills, fitness and diet, and social and leisure activities. Kuipers (1998) has stressed the need for ongoing supervision, so that staff can be helped to focus on the positives and be offered a safe place to ventilate negative emotions (e.g. anger and distress).

FACILITATING FAMILIES

As already touched on, work with families can focus on such areas as education, individual stress management (for the carer or the dependent

Table 6.3   Barriers to an alliance between carers and mental health practitioners (Winefield & Burnett, 1996)

1. *Conflicting relationships.*	Practitioners can be torn between therapeutic, supportive, educative and collaborative roles, as well as between the needs of the carer and the dependent person.
2. *Responsibility for the problem.*	Professionals' hopelessness about effecting change can trigger attributions of a family cause for the problem.
3. *Lack of gratitude.*	Because there is no 'cure', and as blame, ignoring or dismissing may be present on the practitioner's part, carers may only rarely express their appreciation.
4. *Power conflicts.*	Sharing information with carers can cause staff to fear losing some of their expert power; practitioners may limit collaboration so as to limit the carer's awareness of the shortcuts or errors they commit.
5. *Deficient training.*	Inadequate training of professionals in group and family skills may mean that the 'dynamics' of collaboration with carers are avoided.
6. *Insufficient resources.*	Practitioners, such as psychiatrists, may see up to 20 clients in succession for 15 minutes each. This limits attention to collaborative decision-making. Treatment facilities are designed for one-to-one work. Funding in mental health is inadequate.

person), crisis intervention, self-help, advocacy and social support. The advent of major tranquillisers (such as Chlorpromazine that made possible effective community-based treatment) provided a new impetus for mental health practitioners to collaborate with families who were caring for dependents with such difficulties as a dementia or schizophrenia.

Family education

The education of families with or without the client present has been examined in some detail, with such positive results as increased family knowledge about the problem and improved family belief systems (for example more optimism about the future and less self blame) (Roth and Fonagy 1996). To illustrate, Solomon *et al.* (1996) provided 183 relatives of people with schizophrenia with brief psycho-education designed to improve the family members' sense of confidence regarding their relatives. The intervention, provided either individually or in groups of between 6 and 12 individuals, included a definite emphasis on social support. The staff informed family members about community resources that might help them to meet their needs and even occasionally accompanied the family members to meetings with other agencies to help them to get appropriate services for their relatives. In the group format it was possible to help families to realise that others in their situation have similar feelings and experiences. It was also possible to provide guidelines for coping more effectively with both the dependent person and the mental health system. Information was of course provided about schizophrenia and its treatment. Interestingly, homework was usually assigned at the end of each group session to help the relatives apply what they had learnt to their interactions with the dependent person. In addition to measuring family burden, Solomon et al. (1996) used a social support questionnaire to measure practical assistance, emotional support and social networks, finding that the family members' self confidence had improved significantly following the intervention. This included improvement in the social support domain, such as being able to locate needed resources and gaining acceptance of the dependent person from other family members. Both the individual and the group formats produced similarly desirable outcomes amongst the family members. The authors noted that in designing future group meetings better results might follow from adapting the meetings so that the mental health practitioners running the groups provided more empathy and support for participants' descriptions of their caring predicaments. This echos the observation by Winefield and Burnett (1996). Subsequently, meetings could then focus on helping members to develop ways of managing their personal situations. This phase would provide explicit social support and enable group members to learn such skills as problem definition and prioritisation.

A related study by Leff et al. (1990) evaluated the effectiveness of family therapy versus a relatives group for families of people with schizophrenia. Of particular interest was the attention to and measurement of expressed emotion (EE) before and after the family therapy sessions. Leff et al. found that both forms of intervention (i.e. family sessions in the home or a relatives group that excluded patients) resulted in important improvements in EE (i.e. relatives over-involvement reduced steadily) and both groups had similar relapse rates (33% and 36% respectively at a 2-year follow-up point). This indicated that both treatments were similarly effective, but that the relatives group approach was the more efficient option, requiring as it did fewer mental health practitioners. Relapse rate was significantly lower than the 75% that is realistic for patients whose families receive no formal help. Positive changes in social functioning amongst those in the study with schizophrenia were noted and were thought to confer long-term benefits (for example four of the clients in the study moved out of the parental home to live independently and had succeeded independently at the follow-up assessment).

Educational interventions of the above kind are a feature of a whole range of validated models of family intervention for schizophrenia, as summarised by Mueser (1996). Common features of these programmes include (in addition to education about the nature and management of severe mental illness):

- showing concern, sympathy and empathy to family members;
- avoiding blaming family members or pathologising their efforts to cope;
- improving communication and problem-solving skills in the family members;
- encouraging family members to develop social supports outside their family network.

Therefore, social support is a recognised element at both the level of the mental health practitioner's interaction with the family (for example, by recognising the difficulties family members face and by showing genuine concern and empathy for the trials they have endured) and in terms of the family's own social support interactions. Indeed, Mueser (1996) suggested that empathic understanding is perhaps the first and most important quality that practitioners can bring to their working relationship with the family. As regards encouraging family members to develop their social support, it is noted that families often feel isolated and have constricted social support networks. For example, family members may stop seeing old friends as they become overwhelmed by coping with a family member who has mental health problems. Mueser (1996) noted that it is helpful to encourage family members to re-establish old friendships or to expand their social networks by reaching out to others who are trying to cope with similar experiences.

Therapeutic interventions

Turning to family-based interventions that focus on various forms of therapy or stress management, Kane and McGlashan (1995) noted that communication skills are an integral part of effective collaboration with families (such as listening, clarifying needs and providing clear feedback). Other interventions include social skills training for clients or for families as a whole. However, of much greater interest latterly has been the introduction of cognitive behavioural treatments (CBT) that target positive psychotic symptoms (Birchwood and Tarrier, 1994). Two major treatments have been evaluated, namely coping strategy enhancement and problem-solving interventions. As per the family education studies above, these various forms of psychological intervention with families appear to result in important improvements in both the family environment (for example in improved EE) and clinical improvement in the client group (Roth & Fonagy 1996).

Coping strategy enhancement (CSE) is designed to develop the individual's coping repertoire, including the ability to formulate and tackle symptoms (e.g. by means of cognitive therapy techniques designed to restructure and re-evaluate negative assumptions about oneself). Problem-solving has been evaluated alongside CSE, consisting of goal setting, option appraisal and evaluation of progress. Whereas clients receiving CSE improved in their problem-solving skills, the reverse was not found (Tarrier *et al.*, 1993).

Crisis interventions

The third category of work with families with a member who has schizophrenia is called crisis or early intervention. This involves a combination of medical and psychosocial interventions targeted primarily at young vulnerable people, with the intention of limiting or even preventing some of the social psychological deteriorations that normally occur (Birchwood & Tarrier, 1994). These authors present evidence to indicate that the first five years of schizophrenic illness are a critical period in which vigorous interventions designed around recognising early symptoms of relapse can play a critical part in this new approach to care (compare this with reacting to relapse and the long-term rehabilitation that is required following failures to deal with relapse). To illustrate, Falloon *et al.* (1996) described the Buckingham project, a model of community-based mental health care that commenced in 1984 and served a semi-rural population in England. Part of their programme was to enhance the screening skills of members of the family practitioner service (GPs and general health nurses). This included developing a ten-item screening interview questionnaire similar to the General Health Questionnaire which was designed to detect possibly serious mental health problems (for example 'have you ever had the experience of hearing people's voices speaking when nobody seems to be around?'). A further aspect of the care system was the rigorous training of mental health practitioners, so that they could provide interventions such as family therapy. The early interventions strategies, triggered when somebody was considered to be experiencing the early phase of schizophrenia, included an integrated crisis management programme which was initiated without delay. Within the programme were components covering education, stress management and medication compliance. Stress management approaches included the key care giver helping the client to identify stressors and to generate ways of coping with these problems.

Although crisis intervention, based around work with families, has yielded some impressive outcomes, the willingness of families to enter this sort of treatment is limited. Not only do some refuse to accept this form of intervention, but there is also a moderate level of attrition from therapy (Roth & Fonagy, 1996). The refusal rate has been quoted as reaching over 20%, while withdrawal from treatment may be as high as 40% (Atkinson & Coia, 1995). It follows that the very positive results obtained may be from an unrepresentative sample of families.

HELPING SELF-HELP GROUPS

Self-help, advocacy and social support

The final category of work with families outlined by Kane and McGlashan (1995) was encouraging self-help, providing advocacy and offering social support. Encouraging self-help amongst families and dependent members with mental health problems is an integral part of most therapeutic interventions, and is therefore the focus of this section. For example cognitive behavioural approaches, including social skills training, encourage the learning or relearning of critical skills in eliciting and providing positive consequences for social support. As regards advocacy, mental health practitioners can help families to define and articulate their needs in terms of both formal and informal support. They may also assist families to advocate politically, as health care consumers. This could include assisting organisations such as the Schizophrenia Fellowship or Age Concern to agitate for greater resources to be devolved to the mental health field. Lastly, in terms of social support mental health practitioners are both direct providers of support (through the way that they signal valuing and caring for families) and indirectly in the way that they help families to access informational, practical and emotional support from others in the social network.

Self-help groups

Self-help groups may exist either to assist relatives to cope with a dependent individual or to assist such individuals directly. As a rule, self-help groups of both kinds tend to have the following purposes:

1. to support members in dealing with problems and in improving their coping skills;

2. to provide help through peer support and the belief that personal participation and face-to-face interaction are extremely important;
3. to share a common problem and to develop a general consensus on the best course of action;
4. to retain control of the group, although some advice or involvement may be sought from mental health practitioners;
5. to provide a reference point through which the members are able to identify with each other and agree common stressors and possible coping strategies (Atkinson and Coia, 1995).

While self-help groups appear to have evolved because of a distrust or dissatisfaction with formal help, latterly there are signs that groups wish to include professionals for at least the educational aspects of their functioning. Reciprocally, professionals and local and central government are increasingly consulting self help groups about the services they receive, so as to ensure that they are as equitable as possible. An account of various self help groups, such as the National Schizophrenia Fellowship in the UK, is provided by Atkinson and Coia (1995). Wilson (1994) has also described the vital but problematic relationship between self-help groups and mental health practitioners. He noted that while professionals' attitudes are generally favourable towards collaborating with self-help groups, there remains confusion about partnerships. This may be due to an underlying tension, one which revolves around the experiential knowledge base of the carers and sufferers, as juxtaposed with the formal knowledge base of professionals. Wilson (1994) summarised the important contribution that self-help groups can make in terms of informational and emotional support, a preventative role, the opportunities they give to get feedback and opinions from users and carers, and for the personal development and growth that individual members experience.

It is important to note that an emphasis on fostering self-help groups on the part of professionals, as advocated by the Community Care Act (1991), represents an important restructuring of the way that society helps people. Reissman (1990) noted that the receipt of formal help is often problematic, either because of the stigma associated with mental health problems or because it tends to underline personal inadequacy. Thus, formal help casts the person with a mental health need in a dependent role, which is made even more asymmetrical because of the higher status of the practitioner. In this relationship the client is automatically deprived of the benefits that accrue to the practitioner, such as self-esteem enhancement and being helped by helping others. Reissman (1990) noted that on this argument, if help giving is so beneficial and the receipt of help so problematic, practitioners should restructure the helping process so that more people play the helping role. This new emphasis would amount to empowering those who normally receive help to function more frequently as helpers. As a result, the new helpers (who for example may facilitate self-help groups) will be in a position to gain the self-esteem enhancement that normally accrues to professionals. In order to make this logic more concrete, the following sections detail how mental health professionals can help those in self-help groups by the following means: setting up group environments; providing assessment assistance; offering to support or even provide interventions that bolster self-help; and providing evaluation and corrective feedback that assists the group to develop in the future.

Helping to set up self-help groups

Atkinson and Coia (1995) note that as self-help groups become more legitimate and formalised the role of mental health professionals will shift accordingly. This will include active involvement in facilitating the emergence of appropriate self-help organisations, including establishing a venue and other practical resources to allow the group to operate successfully. They note that the practitioners may also help in other ways, such as acting as a consultant to a group leader and in providing up-to-date information for use within the group.

A case in point from my own experience (Milne *et al.*, 1989a) was one of helping some clients who had successfully completed individual therapy to set up a community support group for others who were experiencing anxiety. Working closely with social services and the local branch of MIND, a suitably accessible and non-stigmatised venue for these ex-clients to convene their anxiety management groups was secured. In addition, we agreed that our role would include advertising and recruiting group members from the community by the dissemination of posters and by writing articles in the local newspaper.

Assessment assistance

In addition to helping the ex-clients to set up a self-help group, we also screened those who responded to the posters and articles for inclusion in the self-help group. This included assessment of motivation and symptomatology, resulting in a whittling down of 24 applicants to 14. In a larger-scale analysis by Meissen *et al.* (1991) the problems and concerns of the participating groups were assessed by a standardised personal interview. This indicated that the most important problems faced by self-help groups were involving members, improving attendance and recruitment, increasing public awareness and establishing better financial support. There was also a need for greater public education. Meissen *et al.* (1991) believed that these findings provided important feedback to mental health practitioners concerning the kind of support that they can provide for groups. Interestingly, these findings were contrary to prior assumptions that had been made, which included an expectation that groups would ask for workshops to help group leaders, that a library of self-help material for groups would be useful, and that the group leaders would wish to network with other groups. The authors assumed that a 'self-help clearing house' would have been able to address these latter needs. They conceded that the data from this needs assessment allowed them to overcome a natural tendency to generalise from limited contact with those leaders who actually sought professionals and requested their assistance.

Another way in which mental health practitioners can help within the assessment domain is by conducting observations of what goes on in self-help groups and feeding this information back. For example Roberts *et al.* (1991) developed a behavioural observation system for mutual help settings. This recorded some crucial behaviours such as helping, questioning, task orientation, help seeking, disclosure, and affective responses. Of particular interest in relation to this book, key helping behaviours were the provision of social support. Examples included raising or enhancing another group member's status, nurturing, encouraging or approving of another group member, offering tangible assistance (such as offering information and guidance about possible courses of action) encouraging self-disclosure of personal information normally not revealed in public, and providing constructive and supportive feedback. These authors worked with a group called GROW, a mutual help organisation for individuals with a history of emotional and psychological problems. The results indicated that all of the categories in the observation instrument were observed and as few as 2% of them were negative. In general, the results of this analysis highlighted a central assumption of mutual help, namely that members tend to be supportive of one another during meetings. In the GROW groups, those observed categories that indicated positive supportive climate were seven times more frequent than their negative counterparts. This consisted of a substantial number of comments made by members which were direct efforts to help one another. The results also indicated that the overwhelming majority of the conversation occurring in the GROW meetings was related to members' concerns, since only 4% of observed comments were classified as 'small talk'. Such assessments of groups can help leaders to develop their helping styles and can encourage professionals to contribute to groups by providing clear evidence on the appropriateness of group processes.

To return to my own related experience (Milne *et al.* 1989a) a parallel outcome analysis was conducted of the anxiety management groups run by our ex-clients. This complements the analysis by Roberts *et al.* (1991) of the process side of self-help groups. We administered self-report questionnaires assessing the group members' stress, coping and strain, and were able to establish by means of before and after assessments with these instruments that clinically significant improvements were obtained on our questionnaires by the end of the ten-session group for 14 group members. This provides valuable evidence that professional time was associated with successful group outcomes, ones that bore a respectable resemblance to those achieved by mental health practitioners in individual work with clients of this kind.

Promoting self-help interventions

Turning to intervention options, practitioners have been involved in consultation and training efforts to promote the success of self-help groups. For example, in connection with religious systems, Pargament et al. (1988) described how professionals can consult to foster organisational change in churches and synagogues. The consultation can consist of dealing with conflict between members or members and leaders; a lack of clear congregational mission; and to establish better contact with the local neighbourhood.

In terms of training, my own work with the leaders of self-help groups (Milne et al. 1989a) entailed training ex-clients over a 15-hour period to set up and run groups, and to provide counselling, carry out assessments and use limited therapy skills in relation to anxiety management. Each of these four topics was carefully addressed using a structured learning format in which each topic was briefly described. A more detailed demonstration and behavioural rehearsal phase followed, so that as consultants the professionals were able to guide skill development amongst the group leaders ($N = 6$). A manual was also provided to the leaders, to summarise the knowledge base for their activity. Once the self-help groups were under way, the group leaders met regularly with the supervising professionals for support and to discuss and plan sessions. The effectiveness of this training was evaluated using multiple measures, including the group leaders ability to formulate anxiety problems, to manage them (including competence in relaxation training) and also an assessment of their proficiency in relation to ten counselling skills. Post training assessments on these dimensions indicated statistically significant improvements over the baseline scores, indicating that the course did indeed enhance relevant skills and knowledge amongst the group leaders. As already indicated above, there was additionally the evidence that the clients who attended these groups improved clinically by the end of the programme.

In a similar vein, Silver et al. (1997) developed a parent-to-parent network for mothers of children with ongoing health problems, provided a 40-hour training programme to ten women focusing on listening, reflection and communication skills, as well as information relevant to the mothers. Some of these mothers went on to accept jobs as lay therapists, working approximately 20 hours a week and receiving supervision from a psychologist and a social worker. The groups that these specially trained mothers provided ran over a 12-month period and provided at least three group activities for families and six face-to-face meetings in families' own homes. The main goal was to improve the mother's psychological wellbeing by increasing her social support and access to relevant information, services and knowledgable advisors. As a result, it was hoped that mothers would feel more empowered and active participants in their childrens' health care. The trained mothers ('interveners') attempted to link families with existing community resources, encouraged them to talk with the child's health care providers, and shared information about child health, parenting and the coping strategies used by other mothers in the programme. The interveners also provided a source of emotional support by being available to listen, by showing sympathy and understanding, and by helping mothers to identify sources of support within their own naturally occurring network of family and friends. Positive results included reductions in the mothers anxiety, anger and general cognitive disturbance. However, overall the results were disappointing to the authors, who speculated that, although the interveners tried throughout the year to help mothers develop their social support, in a number of cases the mothers did not have adequate support systems available and therefore they had little hope of recruiting the required support. Interestingly, amongst those mothers who reported having adequate support, a unique kind of relationship was established with the interveners, who became a 'one-sided friend' i.e. providing emotional sharing but not asking for reciprocation. This is typical of the kind of social support that mental health practitioners provide.

Evaluating self-help groups

As these training interventions indicate, another role that mental health practitioners can play in helping to foster self-help groups is to assist them in evaluating the success of their work. Not only can they select, administer and score assessment instruments such as the ones used in Silver *et al.* (1997) and Milne *et al.* (1989a), but they can also engage the group and its leader in interpreting the data, particularly with regard to improving future groups. This role might be equated best with the kind of practical support that enables groups to develop as described by Wilson (1994). Ideally, to be truly enabling and empowering, evaluation work of this kind would gradually be handed over to the group leaders.

PROVIDING PETS

Companion pets play a fascinating role in the social support sphere. Consider a case study reported by McCullagh and Rich (1996) in which a relatively young woman who suffered from multiple sclerosis had been abandoned by her husband, and as a substitute her family had given her a dog for company. A church-based 'good neighbour scheme' provided a visitor for this woman, someone who could share some of her interests. The group also supplied someone to take the dog for occasional walks and to take the woman to dog-training classes. As this case study indicates, companion pets can play a critical role in meeting the emotional needs of a lonely individual and can also provide a form of bridge to the local community, thus facilitating access to social support. A parallel case study has been provided by a clinical psychologist (Howells, 1993) who started taking her own dog to work to keep her company, while alone in a community team building. She was surprised to note the reactions of her clients, who would frequently stroke the dog during periods of stressful disclosure. The dog, an affectionate golden retriever, always responded by placing her head in the clients' laps while gazing up at them. The clients would then talk about something quite distressing, while continuing to stroke the dog. The psychologist was also surprised to note that re-attendance rates improved remarkably (from 67% up to 91%). She conjectured that the presence of the dog in the room was at least partly responsible for the improved attendance rates and also that its presence led to clients feeling generally more relaxed and positive. The dog seemed to provide not only an ice-breaker at the start of some sessions but also a support when clients wanted to disclose sensitive or traumatic information.

Anecdotal accounts of just how important pets are to people are legendary. They include legal disputes over the custody of pets, through to a dog being designated best man at a wedding. More commonplace examples include the vast amount of affection, time and money that people (at least in the West) lavish on their pets, including offering rewards when they are lost, paying for grooming and health care, buying them presents and especially feeding them. The psychological bond that explains this behaviour is thought to be that of attachment, a concept very close to that of social support. To illustrate, Lago et al. (1988) developed a pet relationship scale which assessed aspects of attachment, particularly what was termed 'affectionate companionship'.

Companion pets (as well as other animal relationships) can serve three sorts of human needs. Psychologically they provide unconditional positive regard, they allow humans to care for and control an animal, and they offer solace, security, devotion and protection. In terms of social needs, a pet can provide a form of infantile dependence, companionship and a relaxed friendly atmosphere. In addition, as discussed shortly, they may facilitate social interaction. Lastly, pets can meet a physical need as in providing tactile stimulation. Closer to mental health concerns, studies have been conducted that indicate that animals soften children's hostility and reserve towards their child psychiatrists, that pet owning adolescents are more popular than non-pet owners, and even that pet owners have a better chance of surviving a heart attack. During counselling, unhappily married couples display fewer negative emotions when accompanied by their dogs (J.B. Smith, 1989).

How can mental health practitioners facilitate the role of pets in relation to their clients? One pragmatic option is to collaborate with organisations that try to provide pet companions for people with mental health problems, such as Pro-dog Active Therapy (PAT). Over 200 British hospitals and hospices and hundreds of nursing homes are visited on a regular basis by PAT. And a parallel organisation, Society for Companion Animals Studies (SCAS) aims to study the formation and nature of the relationship between people and companion animals, and their effects on the emotional and physical wellbeing of both parties.

Case study: Teaming up with companion pets

In an illustration of how mental health practitioners can team up with the PAT dog scheme, Elliott and Milne (1991) arranged for a local PAT dog scheme member to visit two psychiatric hospital wards (for older adults with a dementia or a depressive disorder). The owner brought to the wards her Wheaton Terrier for weekly hour long visits, during which she took the dog around each of the residents and engaged in some conversation, encouraging the residents to stroke the dog. Observations of the residences during periods when the dog was present or absent indicated that there was a marked improvement in the residents' behaviour when the dog was present (up to tenfold increases in positive interaction). In addition, nurses working on the wards rated the dog's visits very positively, regarding the impact on their residents as decidedly favourable, including prompting more appropriate speech, raising mood and morale, and creating a better atmosphere in the ward. A subsequent study with the same PAT organisation (Haughie et al., 1992) tidied up the issue as to whether it was simply the presence of a visitor as opposed to the presence of a dog that led to these positive impacts on residents. To do this, they compared a baseline condition (no dog, owner or photograph of the dog) against the dog plus owner, and against a phase of the owner plus photograph of the dog. Careful observation over all three phases of the study indicated that the dog plus owner condition was the most successful in improving the levels of social interaction amongst the residents, with the photograph coming second above the baseline condition. It was concluded that the data added support to the idea that pet therapy was a valuable adjunct to care systems in hospitals, providing a more normalised environment with better opportunities for social interaction. In addition, the dog actually provides a 'social bridge' between the hospital community and the local neighbourhood, promoting involvement between the two groups.

Losing a pet

Another illustration of the importance of companion pets to human beings comes from a study of bereavement reactions following the death of a pet (Archer & Winchester, 1994). In their introduction, these authors noted that a grief-like reaction following the death of a cherished pet had been noted anecdotally over many years and indeed there were recorded reports that practitioners have counselled people who are bereaved through the loss of a pet. The matter has sometimes been so serious that people have been noted to commit suicide following their pet's death, and some clients have been reported as saying that they would rather lose their husband or wife than their pet!

In their study, Archer and Winchester (1994) surveyed 88 people regarding their reactions to the loss of their pet. They found support for the bereavement hypothesis, in that the participants indicated all the phases of a bereavement reaction, including initial numbness or disbelief, preoccupation with the loss, perceiving the loss as part of themselves, in addition to urges to search, avoid or mitigate a problem, accompanied by feelings of anxiety and depression. They concluded that the findings indicated a parallel reaction to the one that follows human bereavement, albeit with a lower frequency of emotional distress. Those who regarded their pet as something of a baby, child or loved one experienced greatest grief. Those who regarded the pet as a friend experienced only moderate distress, as one would again expect from human reactions to relationships of this kind. Archer and Winchester (1994) noted that one particular way in which the grief was accentuated was where the pet served as the main form of social support for the owner. In this sense, Lago *et al.* (1983) noted that those who enjoy an adequate social support network may obtain limited benefit from animal companionship, whereas widowed persons and others who live alone seem to derive a great benefit from this form of support.

SUMMARY AND CONCLUSIONS

This chapter has sampled some of the diverse ways in which mental health practitioners may engage in social support interventions at the proximal level. The first such way is orthodox clinical work with couples, albeit with an emphasis on the social support aspects of affirmation and validation. A second well-recognised area of professional activity lies in supporting those who care for dependent people. The social support dimension of this activity was particularly pronounced, as clearly recognised by most mental health practitioners. While such caring is normally accompanied by considerable burden and psychological distress for the carer, the transactional stress model (as set out in Chapter 3) provides a basis for understanding how carers may nonetheless cope and at times even feel positive about a caring role. It follows that professionals have a significant part to play in educating carers about the problems that their dependants are experiencing, and in supporting them. Methods include fostering social support and coping strategy enhancement. Of particular importance to the present book is the evidence that social support plays a critical role in influencing the carers' use of coping strategies. For instance, it was noted that carers in receipt of adequate social support had lower levels of expressed emotion in their exchanges with the dependent person, resulting in better outcomes for both parties.

Another well-accepted area of professional activity is in supporting families to care for dependants, as documented in the literature on supporting people with schizophrenia in the community. Research on the role of social support in relation to families again bears out its central role, which is recognised by professionals in their incorporation of social support within their packages of care (for example facilitating social reintegration for both the carers and the clients).

However, the involvement of mental health practitioners in supporting self-help groups is less well established and indeed (as per some of the interactions with families) has traditionally been characterised by significant levels of mutual antipathy. The barriers to an alliance were listed in Table 6.3, including the need for better training and resources to enable practitioners to play a more facilitating role in supporting self-help groups. This can be based on applying the usual assessment, intervention and evaluation skills that they use in face-to-face work, as indicated by some clear demonstration projects.

Finally, on a lighter note it was observed that companion pets play a fascinating and under-recognised role in fostering social support. Pets have always played a significant role in our society, so it is not surprising to find evidence that involving them not only provides individuals with important forms of companionship, closely approximating to human relationships, but also provides a 'social bridge' to the community, opening up other opportunities for support which would not be there in the absence of a pet.

In conclusion, mental health practitioners can participate in proximal social support interventions across a diverse and fascinating range of options, participating in what has previously been called social network therapy and social system psychotherapy. Encouragingly, the skills required for work at the proximal level are fundamentally those that are required at the clinical level, including basic problem-solving skills such as assessment to define the nature of the problem, identification of options, intervention and evaluation. While it is recognised that there are obstacles to what would be an extended role for most mental health practitioners, the major benefits and efficient use of service resource that can follow from this work surely justify a proportion of every mental health practitioner's time being dedicated to analyses and interventions in the proximal environment. Progress in this direction will move us closer to the inspirational work of Albee (1986) and to his call for a 'just society', in which we move away from blaming the victims to creating the kind of social environments that allow our clients to function more effectively and to be recognised as grappling with unreasonable and at times unbearable proximal stressors.

Chapter 7

DISTAL INTERVENTIONS

INTRODUCTION

'Distal' interventions address the important factors, settings and people that encompass the couples, groups, families, etc. as discussed in the last chapter. Examples include housing and the general physical environment, material resources, health education, social deprivation, the workplace and other social settings (e.g. schools, churches, playgrounds, high streets). Attention to such domains reflects a community orientation to mental health practice, one that builds on the idea that our wellbeing cannot meaningfully be separated out from the diverse range of settings and people with whom we interact. This has been termed 'social field theory' and 'social system psychotherapy' (Pattison, 1973), and Smail (1991) used the phrase 'distal influences' to define this field in terms of some pervasive and inescapable forms of power, such as culture (e.g. consumerism), ideology, and social class. In practice, these influence the individual through what Smail refers to as 'proximal' units, such as schools, workplaces and housing. As he stresses, attention to such influences does not mean that mental health practitioners need to become political activists or 'social engineers'. Rather, the onus is on recognising the forces that tend to bear down upon our clients, at times working to alter or 'improve' them and regularly reviewing our conventional services, so that they accommodate more compassionately to our clients' experience of their distal environment.

Many other conceptions of the nature and dimensions of the work we should do in our communities exist, emphasising also such targets as pollution control, policy development and crime reduction (Humphreys, 1996). However, in this chapter a course will be steered so as to maximise the relevance of the summarised material to mental health practitioners. Following Shinn (1987), the focus will partly be on schools, workplaces and religious settings, because these interact with our client's lives and because they are amenable to intervention. Also, in keeping with Smail (1991), influences that in turn impinge upon schools, workplaces etc. are discussed, such as health education and material deprivation. It is recognised that this blurs somewhat arbitrarily the boundary between the 'proximal' and 'distal' levels of social support activity, but such a division is adopted because it probably makes more sense to the work of mental health practitioners.

The chapter is organised 'from the outside in', that is, it starts with the most widely influential dimensions (physical environments and social deprivation) before examining the slightly narrower domain of health education. Within these nested community layers some relevant settings are discussed, namely schools and workplaces (religious settings have been covered in the previous chapter). Finally, the chapter dwells on social support as provided in the high street, taking an imaginary trip from the park at one end through to the florists, the cafe, the hairdressers, along to the vets and finally to the town square. This journey serves to indicate how social support is an inescapable influence on our mental health, as well as to highlight some realistic ways in which mental health practitioners can intervene at this distal level.

PHYSICAL ENVIRONMENTS

The idea that the buildings within which we live, play and work are more than bricks and mortar is not widely accepted in the mental health field, as indicated by the contents of textbooks and training courses. Yet there is compelling reason to attribute at least physical ill-health to the built environment, dating from Engels' vivid account in his book, *The Condition of the Working Class in England* (1844):

> There is ample proof that the dwellings of the workers who live in the slums, combined with other adverse factors, give rise to many illness (*sic*). (p. 111: cited in Halpern, 1995).

Poor housing conditions eventually led to slum clearance programmes and other associated improvements to the built environment (inc. clean water supplies, sanitation and the reduction of pollution). As a result, the link between poor housing and physical health is much weaker today than in the past. This has led to greater attention to the relationship between the built environment and mental health. In the mental health field there has been a considerable interest in the interaction between the physical environment and such variables as quality of life (e.g. Perry & Felce, 1995), psychological and physical functioning (e.g. Moos & Lemke, 1980), and behaviour.

Initial studies of these variables indicated that the pattern of psychiatric disorders was not random: admissions were least common from the outer suburbs, and most common from the inner city. This led to the interpreta-tion that the stress and social isolation of the inner city caused mental health problems amongst its inhabitants. However, research suggests that this pattern is probably due to a 'social drift' phenomenon, rather than to social causation. The social drift explanation proposes that there is a ten-dency for the more able, successful and mentally healthy individuals to selectively move out to the suburbs or to the new towns; whereas others with poorer mental health are less successful economically and tend to drift into the cities (e.g. as they become less able to maintain stable social relationships or hold down employment), ending up living in the least pleasant environments. As such, these correlational studies of city dwelling have been unable to illuminate the cause of mental health prob-lems, and the general conclusion has been that if there is a causal link it is unlikely to be a strong one (Halpern, 1995).

An alternative way to study the link between buildings and wellbeing has therefore been to try and isolate important variables within urban environments, such as density and noise, and to analyse their link to health. Based on interviews with 7500 Britons and objective measurement of the built environment, Halpern (1995) has summarised the effects of various environmental stressors on wellbeing. Surprisingly, he reported that noise, although annoying to many people, only exerted a very limit-ed effect on wellbeing (measured by the Hospital Anxiety-Depression Scale). However, this effect grew when noise-related stressors were taken into account, such as danger from traffic and the absence of areas for chil-dren to play in. Similarly, excessive heat, the absence of daylight and high-er levels of air pollution were found to have a small effect on mental health. Other important stressful features of the environment include lit-ter, graffiti, vandalism, urinary/faecal pollution, inability to see or control approaches to dwellings, infestation by vermin and water penetration (damp) and toxicity (Lundberg, 1998). For example, damp and mouldy housing is associated with respiratory/bronchial symptoms, headaches and diarrhoea (Townsend et al., 1988). The psychological stressors include security and fear of eviction, which has been related to depression (Brown & Harris, 1978). Accessible play areas are also an opportunity for social support between parents.

As some of these examples indicate, the built environment tends to interact with the social environment (e.g. places to play). Other combina-tions of variables that have mental health implications include better street lighting and maintenance (cleanliness) to reduce fear: passers-by perceive well-lit streets as reducing the risk of being molested and as increasing the likelihood of being helped. But neighbourhoods in which there is good social support seem to minimise the importance of objective differences in housing or the built environment: involvement in supportive neighbourly contacts and the local community tends to promote satisfaction with the physical environment, regardless of the physical quality of the homes (Halpern, 1995). Environments designed to bring together groups who have something in common (e.g. the retired older adults) are generally thought to foster such neighbourliness, but there are well-recognised dangers in designing neighbourhoods that are too divisive or socially homogeneous (e.g. ethnic segregation tends to increase inter-group conflicts).

The physical environment and social support

The link between the built environment and social support is mediated by such factors as proximity: within reasonable bounds of compatibility, the closer people live (and work) together, the more likely they are to form friendships and supportive groups. An interesting example has been provided with professionals by Hewstone *et al.* (1994), who analysed the impact of a 'shared' learning workshop on the attitudes of the participating social workers and medical personnel. In keeping with the 'contact' hypothesis, they found reductions in hostility, dislike and mutual misunderstanding following shared learning.

In addition to contact, other important factors include the privacy and autonomy that some form of built or symbolic enclosure can provide, which is associated with group cohesion and other psychological benefits. An example is a psychiatric ward or sheltered housing environment, which, if designed and organised appropriately, can facilitate peer support and enhance the 'ward atmosphere'. By measuring staff's and clients' perceptions of the way the ward is and the way that they'd like it to be (the 'real' and 'ideal' ward atmosphere) and utilising this information to facilitate discussion of desired changes, significant improvements can be obtained in both the respective perceptions of the environment and in the patients' clinical status (e.g. see Milne, 1986).

The design of the built environment so as to incorporate U-shaped courts, shared access stairs, smaller numbers of dwellings, narrower and cul-de-sac streets, common play areas, and so forth tends to be associated with greater attachment or 'belonging' to the neighbourhood. It also fosters supportive relationships with neighbours (e.g. practical help with shopping or emotional support over traffic pollution). There are, of course, limits to these relationships, as in excessive proximity or 'density' accompanied by little choice or 'regulation' of social contact and by heterogeneous groupings. These may promote social antipathy, tension and social isolation, that seems to be associated with limited and passive levels of social support (Halpern, 1995). Density, or crowding, has been found to impair cognitive functioning and to produce a variety of negative physical and psychological effects, thought to be due to such factors as information overload, unpredictability and privacy interference (Nagar & Paulus, 1997). These authors developed a Crowding Experience Scale to measure these variables, including such items as 'how often are you disturbed by the playing of radios, TV, or other such activities?'; 'how often are you disturbed by outside noise?'; and 'how often do others in your home make it difficult for you to carry out your daily routine?' The scale also includes several social support items (e.g. 'how often do other residents of your home provide emotional support when you need it?'), and Nagar and Paulus (1997) found that these and the other items that recorded the participants' subjective perceptions of their dwelling were better predictors of physical and psychological wellbeing than were the objective indicators of crowding.

In keeping with these findings, it appears that the provision of semi-private, informally regulated space in neighbourhoods or estates does seem to foster social support and with it improved mental health. For instance, the erection of a fence around a high rise flat complex can lead to reduced vandalism and increased maintenance of the area by the residents (e.g. sweeping hallways and picking up litter). Similarly, breaking up long dormitory corridors into smaller units can reduce withdrawal and hostility. Such alterations set the scene for people to meet and for various forms of social support to take place. The same effect has been noted in relation to shops placed on residential streets, which encourages strangers into the previously relatively private zone and reduces the local group's control, contact and cohesion.

To illustrate the latter point in the context of mental health services, Fairbanks et al. (1977) observed four psychiatric wards in order to ascertain the relationship between their social, behavioural and physical features, finding that 'deviant' resident behaviours increased as a function of decreased numbers in the same room (i.e. it was most likely to occur when residents were alone or nearly alone). They noted that there were large regularities in these relationships between environments and behaviours, concluding that 'To look at one ward is, in effect, to look at them all' (p. 206).

In all four wards there was spatial segregation between patients and staff, with the latter spending most of their time in the office, while the residents were dispersed throughout the remainder of the ward, resulting in low levels of interaction. However, they noted that small architectural changes, such as creating small circles of comfortable chairs, could influence these patterns. Thirteen thoroughly detailed examples of such environmental manipulations have been described in Cherulnik (1993), covering hospitals, housing, offices, parks, neighbourhoods and city centres. Usually, the designs featured in these case studies all drew on psychological and other research, so as to maximise human benefits (e.g. clarifying the behavioural goals for a design, then asking residents/users to evaluate whether they had been attained, such as promoting territoriality and contact between neighbours). Together with two introductory chapters on design, this book is a useful resource to mental health practitioners with an interest in the interplay between the physical environment and behaviour.

From his review of the literature and the evidence from the 7500 interviews, Halpern (1995) concluded that:

> There is substantial evidence to suggest that the physical environment can have real and significant effects on group and friendship formation, and on patterns of neighbour behaviour. (p. 133).

Therefore, this parallels the perception of Engels in 1844 on the relation between the built environment and physical wellbeing, but the emphasis on the moderating role of social support is apparent in Halpern's conclusion and in the other material summarised in this section. A further example and extension of the role of social support has been provided by C.A. Smith *et al.* (1993), who related it to housing stressors (including physical condition and crowding) and to psychological distress for samples of over 200 poorer people in the cities of Auckland and Christchurch. They found a strong association between the housing stressors and psychological distress, and an indication that living in a substandard dwelling represents an independent and additive source of stress to that of poverty. But social support appeared to act as a buffer against the housing stressor, at least when this is at a low or medium level.

As regards the 'social drift' hypothesis, in keeping with the findings from the four psychiatric wards studied by Fairbanks *et al.* (1977), more recent research has indicated that alterations to the physical environment can improve mental health. Dalgard and Tambs (1997) undertook a rare longitudinal study of a naturalistic environmental change, the creation of a 'new town', by carrying out a 10-year follow-up to test out the 'drift' and 'stress' hypotheses. They found that only in the area where substantial physical improvements were introduced (including extended playground, new sports facilities and shopping centre) were there significant improvements in the mental health of the residents who continued to live in the area, which supported the 'stress' interpretation: the 'enriched' neighbourhood had an impact on mental health. They noted that amongst the clinical implications were the need to attend to the opportunities for social contact and participation amongst the residents of recently established neighbourhoods, and the need to empower residents so that they can play an active part in the solution of environmental problems (e.g. youth activities, traffic, public transport).

Housing and homelessness

Environmental stressors such as noise not only annoy people, they can even lead to attacks and shootings between noisy neighbours. Part of the problem is insufficient sound proofing in poor quality housing (A. Walker, 1996). In terms of people with recognised mental health needs, another problem is the lack of effective inter-agency collaboration. A special issue of the *Journal of Inter-professional Care* (1996, volume 10, no 3) highlighted this amongst numerous other barriers to healthy housing, as listed in Table 7.1.

In the UK, homelessness tripled during the period 1978–92, and in 1996 stood at a third of a million people. This includes those who sleep rough, those in hostels, squats, bed and breakfast accommodation or overcrowded housing. Serious mental health problems have long been associated with homelessness, especially amongst those who sleep rough. Even amongst the bed-and-breakfast group it has been found that 31% report psychological problems (depression and anxiety), and not surprisingly they make greater use of GP, inpatient and casualty departments than do the local

Table 7.1 Some of the issues associated with poor housing, alongside possible actions

Barriers to healthy housing	Possible ways forward
Limited inter-agency working (inc. different priorities, levels of resource and different planning cycles in social services and housing organisations)	Government level coordination to ensure consistent priorities across services; local alignment of planning; improving mutual understanding by job swaps, secondments, shadowing and joint projects.
Ignoring the user agenda	Developing a customer-led vision, based on surveys of their wishes (one such survey indicated that users wanted to remain in control through the receipt of support at home, in contrast to the 'managed dependence and risk' that prevails).
Inadequate services	Provide better information about services (from home care, aids and adaptations to leisure options); improve practical support (e.g. security, safety checks and cleaning); designing appropriate housing.
Lack of information about the homeless	Official statistics underestimate the number of homeless people, so there is a need for better data, including information on health care needs.

residents. However, lack of information about the extent or nature of their mental health makes it difficult to develop appropriate services.

One strategy in London has been to set up a drop-in centre, with facilities for inpatient care, social rehabilitation, and support provided by a team of GPs, chiropodists, dentists, opticians, social workers and psychiatrists. As part of a programme to get users back into decent housing, this team attempts to build up the users' coping strategies (including social skills) and to provide social support. Other interventions relating to homelessness have included semi-formal social support arrangements for people discharged from psychiatric hospital to community housing (including non-professional workers providing support and advice, mediating conflicts and negotiating ground rules for relationships); very formal arrangements for the police to transport homeless mentally ill people from the streets of New York to a special clinic; encouraging citizens to provide supervised social support; compassionate care for homeless people attending an accident and emergency department; improving service systems in other ways and preventing homelessness (see, for example, Shinn, 1992). If homelessness does occur, it has been found that an experienced worker who supports psychiatric clients to locate suitable accommodation in cases of failed resettlement can make a valuable impact (Susser et al., 1997).

In summary, having a home is fundamental to human wellbeing, even if it brings with it many stressors. The links between housing (or lack of it) and social support are numerous, as in the ways that the physical environment shapes attitudes and relationships. Although rarely recognised as a significant aspect of mental health, and relatively difficult for mental health practitioners to address, the physical environment should at least figure in our efforts to understand our clients.

MATERIAL AND SOCIAL DEPRIVATION

Economic and social forces in our society lead to inequalities in health, most typically associated with social class differences. Social class has been defined as 'segments of the population sharing broadly similar types and levels of resources, with broadly similar styles of living and some shared perception of their collective condition' (Townsend et al. 1988, p. 39). Other factors are also important, such as occupation, income, wealth, type of housing, tenure, education, styles of consumption, mode of behaviour, social origins and family connections. These dimensions are interrelated, of course, and so the research tradition has been to treat a few as indicators of social class, principally occupation. The five most commonly used categories of social class are summarised in Table 7.2.

Table 7.2   Occupation as the basis for social class: the Registrar General's categories. The percentages are of the total number of economically active and retired males.

I	Professional (for example accountant, doctor, lawyer) (5%)
II	Intermediate (for example manager, nurse, schoolteacher) (18%)
IIIN	Skilled non-manual (for example clerical worker, secretary, shop assistant) (12%)
IIIM	Skilled manual (for example bus driver, butcher, carpenter, coal face worker) (38%)
IV	Partly skilled (for example agricultural worker, bus conductor, postman (18%)
V	Unskilled (for example cleaner, dock worker, labourer) (9%).

As the 'Black Report' indicated (Townsend *et al.*, 1988), there are marked inequalities in health in the UK between the social classes, typically measured by mortality rates. These rates tend to rise inversely with falling occupational class for both sexes and at all ages, providing a class gradient for health. The Report, named after the working group chairperson Sir Douglas Black, included recommendations to develop health and social indicators for areas, for use in resource allocation, and to research how social factors interact with health (e.g. working class people make more use of GP services, but may receive less good care). The Report also recommended that professionals should accept responsibility for making improvements in the quality and geographical coverage of their service, especially in areas of high prevalence of ill health and poor social conditions. However, the emphasis was on a united attack on inequalities from a wide spectrum of agencies, inside and outside health. Another emphasis was to advocate that resources be allocated on the basis of need, linked to imaginative approaches to health care. The Report concluded that differences in the material conditions of life and social inequalities were best understood in terms of specific and general features of the socio-economic environment, including working conditions, overcrowding, cigarette-smoking, use of health services, poverty, and class structure. Although health inequalities were acknowledged to be multi-causal, the 'inequalities in the material conditions of living loom large' (p. 199).

The measurement of these material conditions has been based on relatively simple deprivation indexes. The Townsend one, used in the Health Divide, assesses unemployment, lack of a car, overcrowding and living in a house that is not owner occupied. Other indexes also weight low social class, being a single parent, a lone pensioner, or an immigrant in the last year (see Morris & Carstairs, 1991, for a summary which suggested that the Townsend index was one of two 'best buys').

The Black Report stimulated considerable research, and the vast amount of evidence that resulted was considered to need a special report, which was called *The Health Divide* (Townsend *et al.*, 1988). This report confirmed much of the Black Report, extending it to note that women have higher levels of morbidity and that the gap between the health of the rich and the poor is greatest in the north of the UK. Income impacts on health through such variables as diet, in that people in low income households tend to eat less fruit, vegetables and high fibre foods, and more fat and sugar, than people from high income households; other financially related factors are the kind of housing and heating that can be afforded, and access to one's own transport. Similar findings have been reported in the USA, where the inverse health gradient has also become more pronounced during the past 25 years. Despite rises in the average US person's income, greater social security payments, improved housing and more consumer goods, the number of poor people in America rose for the third consecutive year in 1992, an increase that was three times the rate of growth for the general population. As the editorial from which these figures were drawn noted, poverty is inextricably tied to class, and both of these factors influence patterns of behaviour that determine health. (Editorial, *The Lancet*, **342**, 1373–1374, 1993). It was noted, as per *The Health Divide*, that to improve matters professionals need to form partnerships with politicians and the public in order to reform the institutions that serve these communities. Doctors, for example, should be encouraged to work in these poorer areas (e.g. President Clinton proposed a 20% bonus for those professionals who choose to work in such areas).

But such individual or small-scale group efforts need to be placed in the context of increasing material inequalities and the profound effect this has on health. For example, under Prime Minister Thatcher, the UK Government enacted social policies that gave the richest 10% of the population an extra £87 a week from tax cuts, while the poorest 10% lost £1 a week. When housing costs are taken into account, the group receiving the lowest 10% of income suffered a 14% loss between 1979 and 1991 (G.D. Smith & Egger, 1993). Under Prime Minister Blair, by contrast, the 'new labour' government has stressed a more collaborative approach, the 'third way'. The central ethic of the third way has been described as cooperative self-help—i.e. the government's job is to help people to get together to help themselves. In this vision, self-help, self-reliance and self-improvement are pivotal to fostering individuality, within an interdependent community (Leadbetter, 1998). The distal influences of such policies can have a definite impact on economic security and social inclusion (see, e.g., special issue of the *Journal of Community and Applied Social Psychology*, **8**, 75–178, 1998).

The place of social support

According to the transactional stress model (see Chapter 3), the stress that is represented by low income and other facets of material deprivation may be moderated (or exacerbated) by individuals' personal coping strategies and by social support. A personal sense of social coherence and of belonging is an important dimension that can, for example, buffer people against adversity. In one large survey, high social integration was strongly associated with good health (Baxter, 1986), as measured by such variables as frequency of contact with family and friends, having children and surviving parents, attending a place of worship, involvement in community work and feeling 'part of the community'. In particular, Baxter reported that mental health showed a marked decline (across sexes and classes) as social integration and perceived support declined. She concluded that:

> Social and economic resources are importantly related to health ... this analysis ... has pointed to particular dimensions of ill health to which particular groups appear to be vulnerable, and has demonstrated what the protective mechanisms may be—not only resources such as income or a favourable environment, but also personal and social resources such as feelings of social support and integration. (p. 112)

The idea that personal and situational factors work jointly to produce ill-health is now gaining acceptance, since there is evidence from detailed longitudinal research that the latter, referred to as 'ecological' or 'community' affects, have their most pronounced impact when deprivation is severe (e.g. a concentration of disadvantaged men living in the same area). However, socio-economic personal factors (e.g. employed, higher social class and presence of a spouse) appear influential, regardless of where one lives (Sloggett & Joshi, 1994), although one would assume that personal behaviours that influence wellbeing (especially eating, smoking, drinking and exercising) do not occur in a social vacuum. For example, in poorer areas less healthy food is available and under such circumstances smoking may serve as a coping strategy (G.D. Smith & Morris, 1994).

In summary, social and material deprivation can be seen as providing a significant context for personal coping and social support. The transactional stress model recognises them as stressors that can be buffered by social support, but it is apparent that responsibility for ill-health (mental or physical), should not rest solely at the feet of individuals. Rather, an environmental and political initiative is required to shift the balance towards equalities in health, one in which mental health practitioners can play a vital part. They can assist individuals to cope more adaptively, recognise that some seemingly 'maladaptive' coping makes ecological sense, and they can provide more accessible services to disadvantaged areas, services which in part empower their clients to work collectively to improve their physical and social environment.

An illustration of the complex interactions between some of these variables is presented in Figure 7.1. This shows the strength of the relationships (or 'paths') between variables in the transactional stress model, in relation to a study of 166 mothers caring for a child with a severe learning disability (Quine & Pahl, 1991). It shows that all variables have a direct effect on maternal distress (labelled 'stress' in the figure), with age and social class as original causes, but are mediated by various personal factors (academic skills, finances and coping, including social support). In essence, having a stressful child affects a mother's ability to cope, which can impact on the social and domestic aspects of her life, creating further stress and distress. Together, the nine variables provide a powerful explanation for distress (i.e. they accounted for 56% of the variance in this analysis).

One implication that Quine and Pahl (1991) drew from these data is that, since these variables were so clearly interrelated, a single doorway to mental health services was appropriate. This would enable one worker to provide information and coordinated access to various social, educational and health services. Similarly, there was an implication that professionals

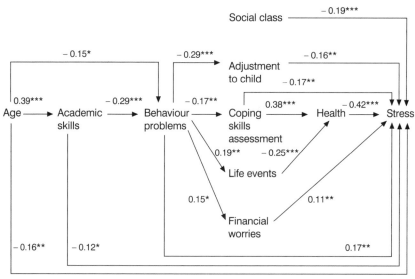

N.B. These variables explain 56% of the variance in stress scores

Figure 7.1   A path analysis of the complex relationship between social class and the transactional stress model. The numbers express the correlations between variables and the asterisks indicate statistical significance (* means $p < 0.05$; ** means $p < 0.01$; *** means $p < 0.001$). From Quirne & Pahl (1991). Reproduced by permission of John Wiley & Sons Ltd.

should assess the variables listed in Figure 7.1, in order to best identify needs and target resources, such as financial help.

HEALTH EDUCATION

Just as social support is bound up with therapy so therapy is intertwined with health education. Mental health practitioners tend to teach, inform, advise and counsel their clients as regards healthy living. But health education is also a profession in its own right, targeting various facets of health and lifestyle, and drawing on epidemiology, environmental health (as in the previous section on material and social deprivation), sociology and psychology. It aims to raise awareness and knowledge of health-related matters in the general public, leading to attitude and behaviour change. Health education may also lead to social change, for example by encouraging politicians to use taxation to increase the cost of unhealthy behaviours (e.g. consuming excessive alcohol or smoking) and to decrease the cost of following a healthy lifestyle (e.g. more accessible, inexpensive sports facilities). Health education uses a range of methods to foster these changes, as listed in Table 7.3 (the goals and methods are drawn from Ewles & Simnett, 1987).

Health education has developed markedly in the past three decades, most conspicuously in schools. In the 1970s health education was restricted mainly to hygiene and sex education, but by the 1980s approximately 68% of secondary schools had a planned approach (e.g. a designated co-ordinator), one that had broadened and become more positive to embrace self-esteem, mental health and relationships. In the wider community, however, progress has been more piecemeal, with, for example, some community health councils employing a health worker to support isolated older adults, and health education officers working for the NHS in order to help residents of severely deprived areas to set up and run a food cooperative to provide reasonably priced fresh fruit and vegetables (Townsend et al., 1988).

Closer to the routine role of the mental health practitioner are such activities as dispensing information and self-help materials to their clients. This is included in Table 7.3, which will now be detailed by reference to the research literature.

Raising awareness

Providing information can be a simple yet powerful way to educate and support individuals, and most mental health professionals will use leaflets at some stage in their work. For example, the British Association for

Table 7.3   Health education methods, designed to achieve individual, group and social goals, with illustrations from the mental health field (see text for details)

Health education goals	Methods	Mental health examples
Health awareness	• Displays leaflets at exhibitions • Campaigns	• Distributing an 'emotions questionnaire' at an exhibition
Health knowledge	• Talks and presentations • Booklets and pamphlets • Mass media	• Self-help information for depression • Telephone/TV/radio counselling
Attitude change	• Group work • Individual therapy	• Providing information on property values • Violence, in relation to community care for the mentally ill
Behaviour change	• Teaching practical skills • Self-help groups	• Self-help therapy—tape—booklet packages
Social change	• Lobbying parliament/ politicians • Pressure groups and collective action	• Voluntary sector lobbying for better understanding, more resources and for compassion (e.g. Age Concern; Schizophrenia Fellowship)

Behavioural and Cognitive Psychotherapy* has disseminated simple and attractive A4 size leaflets on the range of common mental health problems. The one on schizophrenia has paragraphs on:

• the extent of the problem;
• what is schizophrenia? positive symptoms/negative symptoms;
• course;
• causes;
• treatment and care;
• what are behavioural and cognitive psychotherapies?

More difficult routes to raising the public's awareness of mental health issues or services include exhibitions. A case in point was described by Collerton *et al.* (1991) who set up a stand to promote clinical psychology at a large garden festival in the north-east. Their stand, called 'Mindworld',

---

* Leaflets may be obtained from: BACBCP, The Old Church Hall, 89a Quicks Road, Wimbledon, London SW19 1EX (tel: 0181 715 1725)

was run for a week within a section of the festival called 'Bodyworld', which was organised by the local Health Authority. The Mindworld stand included stickers, posters, leaflets, a computer programme (giving the flavour of memory retraining) and an emotions questionnaire, all designed to increase public awareness of psychology. A rota of local psychologists continuously staffed the stand. During the week, some 7000 members of the public visited the stand and 83% of a sample of those who were interviewed stated that they had enjoyed it and 35% said that they had learnt something from it.

Promoting knowledge

While stands at exhibitions can help people to be aware of mental health matters, if the objective is to promote behaviour change then it is usually necessary to provide a more powerful message. Traditionally, this has included self-help booklets which can be used instead of or in addition to formal therapy. These will be discussed shortly, under the 'behaviour change' section. A more recent development has been the emergence of a variety of regular mass media programmes, magazines and newspaper columns, ranging from serious accounts of mental health that are based on the participation of experts, to the TV soaps and the agony aunts.

Mental health practitioners can contribute in such ways as setting up telephone counselling services, or supporting voluntary groups (e.g. Samaritans). An early illustration (O'Donnell & George, 1977) involved the setting up of a 'crisis line' in a community mental health centre (CMHC). The line was founded and operated by 60 volunteers and was intended to improve coordination of local mental health crisis services, increase consumer involvement in the CMHC and provide social support to callers. In turn, the mental health practitioners who were involved provided support and training for the volunteers. An evaluation of the help line suggested that the volunteers were as helpful as professionals, both of whom did better than a control group on measures of counselling.

A more recent example is the provision of counselling on TV (Burns, 1997). A TV series ('A problem aired') presenting live assessment and formulation of emotional problems by psychiatrists, was broadcast for 5 years in London, tackling the mental health problems of a total of 105 people. Half of these people had problems that were sufficiently serious to merit intervention by a GP or a mental health professional (relationship problems, bereavement and eating disorders). Viewer feedback indicated that direct interventions by the therapist were more appreciated (e.g. exposure techniques for compulsions were sometimes used live), but the participants valued most the feeling that they had been listened to attentively and understood. Being taken seriously was enough—it did not matter that the problem was still there.

Attitude change

The growing presence of mental health issues in the mass media contributes to changing perceptions. Burns (1997a) reported that the TV counselling programme 'suggests a significant change in public attitudes towards self-disclosure and stigma' (p. 381). However, public attitudes towards what may be judged to be weightier mental health matters are more intransigent. Sussman (1997) summarised attitudes towards the community care initiative by noting that, while studies in the UK, USA and Australia all revealed that it was preferred by patients and relatives, the initial response from the rest of the community is rejecting (the 'not in my back yard' (NIMBY) response). The NIMBY reaction is fuelled by such things as fears for one's own or one's family's safety, fears that the value of one's property will decline, and more mundane matters like increased noise and traffic congestion (for a review, see the special issue of the *British Journal of Psychiatry*, **168**, 1996). Sussman (1997) noted that public education campaigning had helped to reduce fears, incorporating information that property values do not deteriorate and that violence is not a major problem among treated patients in the community.

Behaviour change

The role of self-help groups in fostering behavioural changes to alleviate mental health difficulties has already been addressed (e.g. see Chapter 6) and will be touched on again under 'social support in the high street'. Therefore, the focus here is on the use of self-help booklets as a way to provide health education.

Books designed to offer advice to the public have been available for years, becoming increasingly popular latterly. Most book shops now have attractive stands displaying accessible and inexpensive guides dealing with anxiety, depression, shyness, phobias, weight loss, insomnia, sexual and marital problems, stress, smoking, etc. Often, these books are written by sufferers, rather than by those with any formal qualification. Mental health professionals have increasingly joined in at the booklet end of this 'DIY' or 'bibliotherapy' market. Some examples and accounts of the value of this work now follow.

Savage *et al.* (1990) developed a self-help manual for problem drinkers, administered under conditions of minimal therapist contact. The manual consisted of basic information on drinking (e.g. defining 'alcoholism' and its effects) and provided guidelines for controlled drinking, together with a self-monitoring diary. Therapist support consisted of four 10-minute structured telephone interviews over a 12-week period, and together with the manual was effective in reducing the alcohol consumption of a media-recruited sample of volunteers. This positive outcome is typical: a meta analysis of 40 self-help programmes concluded that they were reliably more effective than no treatment (Scogin *et al.*, 1990).

Variations on the focused self-help booklet include ones designed for co-morbid presentations (e.g. anxiety and depression—Holdsworth *et al.*, 1994), booklet and audio tape packages (Donnan *et al.*, 1990) and the combination of handouts with public lectures (White & Ross, 1997). The Donnan *et al.* example (1990) consisted of a 55-minute audiotape and a printed, illustrated booklet (approximately 4000 words) on managing anxiety. It included information on anxiety and promoted behaviour change by outlining relaxation and other adaptive coping strategies (e.g. dealing with panic). The booklet was analysed for its 'readability', and found to be of a level that 80% of the population would find understandable. Also, it resulted in lowered anxiety (and an even larger effect on depression!).

White (1995) has developed 'stresspac' as a general self-help treatment for a range of stress-related problems. 'Stresspac' contains a 79-page booklet and a double-sided relaxation tape (for deep and rapid approaches). Results indicated that 'stresspac' was successful, in that clients randomly allocated to receiving it ($N = 21$) improved significantly more during a three-month waiting list period than did control or advice only groups. Indeed, almost 40% of the 'stresspac' group no longer required individual therapy when their turn arrived. Those that did receive therapy improved more than clients in the other two groups, and they required fewer appointments.

Social change

It is more difficult to locate examples in the empirical literature of health education creating social change, although we are all familiar with poster campaigns and the like that are designed to influence the public and the politicians. A recent illustration in the UK has been the Chancellor of the Exchequer's budget statement (March 1998), in which 'public pressure' was an acknowledged source of influence in areas such as reducing smoking in public places and cutting road tax on smaller, fuel-efficient cars. A browse through professional journals will provide examples of other forms of public pressure. For instance, in the *British Medical Journal*, Sussman (1997) (a Director of Social Services in Canada) made the familiar comment that community care was inadequately funded.

In summary, it is hard to think of a way in which mental health practitioners could operate effectively without the use of health education. Raising clients' awareness and knowledge of their mental health conditions and options is part and parcel of a comprehensive approach. In addition, practitioners have tended to develop and add written and audio-visual tapes to information that they provide verbally. Less commonly, they have contributed to the more distal methods that are summarised in Table 7.3, such as help lines and radio counselling.

SCHOOL AND WORK

Schools have been a major example of community psychology work since the 1950s, with interventions directed at empowering teachers (e.g. disseminating interpersonal problem-solving skills to prevent maladjustment in their pupils), empowering parents (e.g. increasing their involvement) and empowering the pupils themselves (e.g. handling the stressors associated with transitions to high school). In the case of the latter, schools' environments have been restructured to increase social support and reduce confusion by keeping a group of students together and by modifying the role of the main teacher. Research has indicated that classrooms that are perceived as high on order, organisation and affiliation are likely to be those that encourage sociability and liking amongst the pupils. Similarly, schools with predictable supervision had children with stronger friendship bonds and fewer incidents of minor delinquency. Schools are also used as a base for health promotion programmes.

Since the main focus of this book is on mental health amongst adults, the equally interesting literature on children in schools will be bypassed. Interested readers are referred to Fehr (1996) for a summary of children's social support processes in school. However, teachers and to a lesser extent the pupils' parents are an appropriate topic in this book.

A major social support issue is the impact of the 'disruptive behaviour disorders' of childhood and adolescence on health, social and educational services. These disorders, including oppositional, defiant and conduct behaviour problems (e.g. destroying household objects), represent over half of the referrals to mental health services, and they are increasing (Herbert, 1995). Of course, such disorders may also lead to major adult mental health problems, as well as to scholastic under-achievement, which can lead in turn to unemployment. Due to such stressors, the parents may well experience significant distress. Herbert (1995) is one of several psychologists who have attempted to resolve matters by providing consultation (training) to the parents. A major objective is to alter the reinforcement contingencies that support the antisocial behaviour of the child (e.g. stealing or bullying at school), and parents can acquire competence in the management of contingencies fairly successfully (see Milne, 1986; Sigston *et al.*, 1996 for reviews). However, Herbert (1995) stresses the value of establishing a collaborative working alliance with parents if any such training is to succeed. This includes a non-blaming, supportive, reciprocal relationship in which the parents' strengths and perspectives are an essential element in defining and implementing solutions. The collaborative process is expected to increase the parents' sense of confidence and self-sufficiency, thus helping them out in their maladaptive coping and distress, as well as ameliorating their child's conduct disorder.

Wolfendale (in Sigston *et al.*, 1996) is another who has emphasised the need to support parents so as to empower them to take control and exercise their responsibilities, but also underlined the importance of sharing expertise with parents, developing parenting skills and addressing and valuing diversity in child-rearing practices. Examples of relevant interventions include:

- *Positive parenting*: a six-module course stressing problem-solving strategies (including short-term goals);
- *Everyday problems in childhood (EPIC)*: an open learning approach based around 12 leaflets concerning everyday issues for parents (e.g. social learning theory and practice);
- *Newpin*: a voluntary organisation for parents who are depressed and isolated and which aims to break the cycle of destructive family behaviour by applying an eclectic range of psychological theories (including humanistic and psychodynamic); and
- *Parents and under-eights' programme*: an Open University distance learning course, targeting thousands of parents through a focus on child development and the parents' personal skills.

The results of these kinds of programmes tend to be positive. For instance, in a randomised controlled trial involving 97 conduct-disordered children (4–7 yrs) and 166 parents, Webster-Stratton and Hammond (1997) compared a parent-training approach against child treatment and against both interventions combined. The greatest improvements were found for the parent-training approach (92% of parents reporting desired changes in their child's behaviour), closely followed by the combined approach. The direct intervention with the children complemented the work with parents, as improvements occurred in areas not influenced by parent training (e.g. interaction with peers at school).

Some parent training has been developed through self-help groups, which provides a distinctive form of assistance. In keeping with many other findings reported in this book, the outstanding benefit is the opportunity to meet similar others to receive emotional support. This is particularly valued, as it comes from other parents with similar experiences and difficulties. However, a small local study with 43 parents indicated that the best-appreciated approach was one in which a paid worker acted as a facilitator, since this boosted the practical and informational support to parents, while keeping emotional support well above the level provided in a professional-led group (Bracken, 1997).

Mental health practitioners can contribute to the school environment in other ways, including developing home–school partnerships, fostering parental involvement, providing relevant continuing professional development to staff, and through organisational development work (e.g. enabling participative decision-making and facilitating other aspects of effective leadership) (Gersch, in Sigston et al., 1996). Gersch also argued that there was a role for action research on such topics as homework and attendance at school.

Work

The role that work sites play for adults has strong parallels with the role of schools for children, such as providing regular scheduled activity with people outside the family and providing social status. Both settings also entail grappling with stressors and a consequent role for social support. However, unlike schools, the workplace can entail unemployment, a major correlate of mental health problems, which will be discussed shortly.

There is growing evidence that employment is broadly health promoting, particularly when compared with involuntary unemployment. This is indicated by a range of outcomes, including mortality, morbidity (high levels of anxiety), superior immune functioning and even the absence of unhealthy behaviours (smoking or alcohol problems). Furthermore, contrary to popular belief, employment for women has no negative impact on their husbands' morbidity or anxiety (Carroll et al., 1993). These authors examined several possible explanations for the benefits of work, including the obvious financial gain, but noted that this is unlikely to provide a full explanation given that work fulfils complex social functions and that for some workers the social aspects may be crucial, either in offsetting inherent job stress or in compensation for impoverished social relations in other spheres of their lives. For instance, it has been found that employment was not positively associated with health amongst people who had least access to opportunities to derive support and esteem at home. This kind of interaction was studied in a fascinating analysis by Noor (1997). She considered the relationship between housework as distributed between men and employed women, hypothesising that the crucial contribution to women's wellbeing was the extent to which their husbands spent time providing support for housework. She took a sample of the 153 employed married women and correlated their perceptions of a husband's contribution to housework and the wives' wellbeing and social support. Perceived support from the husband was measured by a 12-item scale including both positive and negative items within the marital relationships (e.g. good communication, not getting enough emotional support). Noor (1997) found, as expected, that the support provided by the husband mediated the relationship between the stress of housework and wellbeing. She noted that both the message from the husband that the wife was doing the right thing and the husband's support contributed to social support.

In terms of mental health services there have been various important demonstrations of the benefits of work for people with mental health problems. In these analyses, employment is usually not regarded primarily in terms of financial income, but rather as an indicator of successful treatment outcome, and a means of enhancing the individual functioning in such areas as self-esteem and socialisation. One well-known programme, the programme of assertive community treatment (PACT: Test et al., 1985) is a comprehensive community-based programme integrating both clinical and rehabilitative services within a continuous treatment team approach. A treatment objective is improved social functioning, and a thorough back up service is provided to ensure that this objective is achieved if at all possible. PACT appears to be effective, resulting in higher than average employment levels (40–50% of PACT clients employed at any given time and 80% engaged in vocational interventions: Test et al., 1985). Within the PACT approach, the coping skills and social skills of the client are related to such factors as the stimulation and stress of the work environment, which in turn are related to such intervention strategies as analysing the quantity and type of support that clients will require over time. This includes the development of long-term supportive relationships and a weekly vocational group meeting which helps to provide support to clients within a problem-solving approach. This can include helping clients to handle criticism from co-workers, as well as skills in not discussing delusions or other problems that might interfere with the social support that may be available in work sites. A summary of the PACT model is provided by Russett and Frey (1991).

Further support for the notion that it is the availability of social support that makes an important contribution to the value of employment was reported in a study by Parry (1986). In a community survey of 193 working class mothers she found that those who had suffered a severely stressful life event in the previous year had high levels of distress. However, employment reduced this risk when social support was available, but when support was unavailable the risk of distress was even higher. Parry concluded that having paid employment outside the home does increase the threshold for tolerable stress, provided the level of social support is sufficient, particularly the availability and use of a close confiding relationship. This therefore agreed with the findings of Brown and Harris (1978).

Consistent findings have also been reported for men. Stansfield *et al.*, (1997) studied the effect of home- and work-related chronic stresses and the mediating role of social support on psychiatric sickness absence with a sample of over 10,000 London-based civil servants, 70% of whom were men. Social support at home and at work was assessed in terms of a confiding relationship and the availability of emotional, practical, and negative aspects of support. In keeping with Parry and other findings in this area, Stansfield and colleagues found that the negative aspects of social support and material problems contributed to sick leave due to mental health problems. However, when high levels of support were provided at work these served a protective function. The effect was not as clear cut for the women in the sample. A useful feature of this study was the inclusion of objective outcome measures, in the form of sicknotes from doctors.

The conclusion seems to be that social support is linked to health at work, though the effect on the sexes is different, with men being most influenced by negative support and women most affected by confiding and emotional support. Not only does this indicate that support at work can play the kind of mediating role that theory would propose, it also opens up the possibility of social support interventions at work.

Workplace interventions

There is a widespread perception that work-related stress is now of almost epidemic proportions, providing the leading cause for health problems. Surveys have suggested that 78% of respondents complained that work was the biggest source of stress, that only 35% felt that their jobs gave pleasure or satisfaction, and that more than half reported that their lives had become more stressful in the past 10 years (Rosch, 1997). A wide range of interventions have been described in relation to ameliorating the stress of working life, and these are summarised under three broad headings in Table 7.4, based on the review by Quick *et al.* (1997).

It will be seen from Table 7.4 that interventions to reduce stress at work can occur at the individual level, restructuring the workplace and the work–person fit, and through interpersonal interventions. Given that the focus of this book is on social support, it is the latter category that is of

Table 7.4 Interventions to help workers (Quick *et al.*, 1997)

Intervention category	Examples
A: *Individuals*	• Managing the work environment • Lifestyle management (e.g. fitness and diet) • Developing self-control (e.g. relaxation training) • Therapy/counselling
B: *Workplaces*	• Job and task re-design • Participative management • Flexible work schedules • Career development • Redesign of physical settings (e.g. structure; acoustics; lighting)
C: *Interpersonal*	• Role analysis (clarifying expectations) • Goal setting for performance areas • Social support • Team building (e.g. resolving interpersonal conflicts) • Diversity programmes (valuing and using varying talents and perspectives)

most interest. In terms of intervening at the social support level, Quick *et al.* (1997) identified five types of support that can occur in the workplace, as summarised below:

- *protection from stress*: direct assistance in terms of resources, time, labour or environmental modification;
- *informational*: providing information necessary for managing the job demands;
- *evaluative*: feedback on one's personal and professional role functioning;
- *modelling*: evidence of the required work performance standards from another person;
- *emotional*: displaying empathy, esteem, caring or love for another worker.

As Quick *et al.* (1997) noted, social support not only helps to protect individuals from the stress of some aspects of working life, it also can improve work effectiveness. A good example of a figure who can provide many of these support functions is the supervisor, who is noted as a powerful source of support because he or she can contribute information, support and esteem. However, support from colleagues is also important in that some may cope better with conflict or stress than the supervisor, or may afford alternative ways of managing stressors. In any case, the sense of support from one's fellow workers seems to be critical for job satisfaction and general wellbeing. In some cases support may even come from one's customers. In conclusion, Quick *et al.* (1997) noted that the positive effects of social support required that organisations take steps to implement support systems in the workplace. They can do this by modelling social support from the highest level and by designing environments in which social support of various kinds can occur. In addition, managers can provide protective support by means of capital, material or the provision of human resources on a temporary basis, to assist an individual to cope with transient adverse stress. In addition, there is a need for informal support systems to complement the formal ones, based on such models as mentoring, socialisation for new recruits (including introducing them to reliable support figures and encouraging mutually supportive relationships with other new recruits). Another avenue is that employees should be encouraged to seek support from others when this is appropriate, unlike some organisations which emphasise independence to the extent that individuals are reluctant to seek support.

An example of the elements of this model in terms of mental health have been provided by Kyronz and Humphreys (1997) who analysed questionnaire responses from 327 mental health staff working in 15 inpatient substance abuse treatment programmes. As predicted by Quick *et al.* (1997), the support provided by supervisors was an important factor in terms of the kind of treatment environment that the staff provided. In particular, low levels of supervision and supervisory support tend to be related to more symptoms of depression; while higher levels are associated with less emotional exhaustion and burn out. In addition, valuation and recognition by supervisors increase the sense of belonging to the organisation and other positive membership emotions. The study by Kyronz and Humphreys (1997) indicated that these affective and psychological consequences of the supervisory climate can spill over into the treatment environment, in the sense that staff may base their interactions with clients on the model provided by the supervisor.

Unemployment

During the 1980s, unemployment in the UK rose quite considerably, and with it came growing concern for the possible mental health consequences for individuals. In one study, based on interviews with health visitors, health education officers and social workers from around the UK, it was found that 80% of health visitors and social workers and 50% of health education officers regarded unemployment as having an impact on their day-to-day work with clients. While increased poverty was the most striking problematic feature, it was also noted that individual and family problems exacerbated the impact of unemployment. Most of these interviewees were unaware of local initiatives and indeed thought that there was little they could do. Indeed, they were apprehensive that their supervisors would not see unemployment and its effects on health as a legitimate issue for health workers to tackle (Townsend *et al.*, 1988).

The association between unemployment and mental health problems is now fairly well established, as in cross-sectional studies that show higher levels of distress amongst the unemployed and through longitudinal research showing that levels of mental health fall and rise as employment is lost and regained (Orford, 1992). As Warr (1988) stated that:

> Significant main effects of employment status have consistently been identified. Unemployed people experience higher levels of depression, anxiety and general distress, together with low self esteem and confidence. From studies examining changes in status over time, unemployment is seen to be causally implicated in the creation of these differences. (p. 64)

As ever, it should be noted that unemployment, construed as a stressor, will not impact equally on everyone since the usual moderating factors of coping and social support will have some bearing, as will the social context and meaning of unemployment for the individual. To illustrate, Heubeck *et al.* (1995) carried out a study with 94 unemployed youths in Australia, reporting significantly more depression and loss of behavioural/emotional control than their employed counterparts ($N = 87$). They found that, although there were no gender differences, attributions about responsibility for unemployment and for solving it were found to be clearly related to depression and emotional control. This supports the transactional stress model, in that it is the interpretation of the experience of unemployment itself that plays a crucial role in how people react emotionally. In keeping also with the attributional model, 'internals' (i.e. people who fundamentally thought that they were able to control a situation) reported significantly less depression and loss of emotional control than those youths with 'external' attributions (e.g. blaming the state of the economy, prejudices or lack of jobs in the area). Although these authors did not analyse the role of social support, in their discussion they did note that social support may influence the causal attributions that individuals make.

To return to the Townsend *et al.* (1988) summary of the interviews with health workers and their uncertainty about what can be done by such groups to address the problems associated with unemployment, options include the following. Health authorities can:

- monitor unemployment and its health effects;
- have a clear strategy on ameliorating it;
- relay information to staff;
- take unemployment into account, targeting resources to those in most need;

- Train staff in the benefits and facilities available to the unemployed;
- liaise with local authorities over local community initiatives; and
- create jobs and work.

In addition, Townsend *et al.* (1988) thought that all health workers should be trained in the effects of unemployment and that the NHS, as the largest employer in Europe, can create jobs and work opportunities for the unemployed.

A clear plan to address unemployment and other related challenges (especially deprivation and poor health) is the creation of 'Health Action Zones' (HAZs) in the UK, announced in the Government's White Paper *The New NHS: Modern, Dependable* (1997). HAZs are intended to bring services together in partnership, in order to find innovative ways to tackle health problems and thereby to reshape local services. The projects that the HAZs will undertake include improving job opportunities for disadvantaged young people and providing parenting skills programmes for families with vulnerable children.

SOCIAL SUPPORT IN THE HIGH STREET

In addition to the various environments covered so far in this account of the distal interventions that mental health practitioners can undertake, there is, finally, the fascinating sphere of the 'high street'. This refers to a wide range of familiar settings in which the community obtain, amongst other things, social support. This section will provide a brief outline of the opportunities and benefits of support in the high street, based on a summary of one particular town, that of Morpeth, Northumberland, where I live and work.

In Morpeth, one end of the high street has a GP surgery and the role of GPs in providing informal support has been summarised in Chapter 6. As noted there, this includes the provision of emotional support as well as other helpful transactions (e.g. the opportunity to off-load unpleasant feelings). Proceeding along the Morpeth high street one next arrives at a cafe, a place well known for its facilitation of social interaction. Although I have never studied a cafe itself as a setting for social support, nor have I encountered any other research in this setting, it bears a strong resemblance to other settings which have been analysed, such as pubs, in that both provide very well-designed opportunities for informal support within a generally up-beat environment. Another key feature of cafes and pubs is that the staff working in these settings often themselves facilitate and offer support. For example, in Cowen's (1982) seminal analysis of different groups of informal helpers, it was noted that bartenders most frequently provided social support for their clients in relation to work issues, followed by marital problems, financial worries and then emotional/psychological concerns. Their most frequent strategy in providing this support was to just listen, followed by trying to be lighthearted and then offering support and sympathy. As a result of this kind of support, three of eleven strategies reported by Cowen for bartenders, the bartenders tended to feel fairly supportive and sympathetic towards their clients.

Further up the high street are various shops. Although these appear to provide a very low frequency of social support (C. Barker *et al.*, 1990) they may nonetheless be valued by local people. A case in point is the florists, a shop which is peculiarly associated with emotion, in that a high frequency of clients will be purchasing flowers in relation to particularly happy events (e.g. anniversaries, weddings) or sad ones (e.g. funerals). As a result of this emotional colouring, florists can be expected to engage in relatively high levels of social support (e.g. showing concern and offering sympathy). For instance, in one study they were found to offer more support and sympathy than stylists or local ministers of the church. However, overall the florists provided slightly less social support than the bartenders, hairdressers and ministers in the local study (Milne, 1992b).

Further up the same Morpeth high street one comes across a building dedicated to voluntary associations such as the Northern Schizophrenia Fellowship and Age Concern. These groups make it their business to provide informational and emotional support (e.g. through group work) to the local people. The previous chapter summarised some of the evidence for this valuable effect.

Still further up Morpeth high street one will find a hair stylist, a well-established source of social support. As discussed previously in Chapter 1, hairdressers are likely to deal with some significant mental health issues in their routine work and to use important supportive strategies to try and help their clients to cope (e.g. the most commonly used strategy is offering support and sympathy). My own efforts to support and analyse what goes on in a Morpeth salon indicated that Cowen's findings from the USA are also true of the UK, in that clients do indeed make use of stylists for the purpose of obtaining social support. This does appear to alleviate some of their distress, although stylists can end up feeling burdened by the process. As regards a role for mental health practitioners in this sphere, we found that providing a workshop that helped hairdressers to give useful local information and boosted their counselling skills made them feel much better in their social support role (Milne & Mullin, 1987; Milne *et al.* 1992a).

Further along the high street in Morpeth one encounters the vets, yet another setting in which social support may occur. The case study that follows details an analysis of the vets, indicating how social support occurred.

Case study: Vets are social supporters too!*

Given the likely significance of social support in relation to older adults with pets, this small case study analysed interactions in a vet's surgery. The vet's role entails a caring and 'psychological' disposition to clients, making the vet's surgery particularly interesting (Cusack, 1988). Both objective (i.e. direct observational) and subjective data (i.e. self-report questionnaire) were used to determine whether the older adults sought or received more frequent social support from a vet, a more systematic approach than that generally pursued in evaluations of the value of companion pets.

Method

One hundred consecutive clients attending a veterinary surgery participated in the study. Fifty were 'older adults' (at least 65 years of age), and the remaining fifty were 'adults' (i.e. between 18 and 64 years of age). One (male) vet participated. These clients were observed by means of a coding system which served to classify the direction and nature of client and vet speech into five types of social support. These were 'cognitive guidance', 'social reinforcement', 'emotional support', 'tangible assistance' and 'socialising'.

The self-report questionnaire addressed the same five forms of social support. The questionnaire format was based on the Significant Others Scale (Power et al., 1988), so as to distinguish between 'perceived' and 'ideal' social support, and between different sources of support (i.e. family, vet, nurse etc). The 21 items on the questionnaire were each rated on a 1–7 frequency scale, with 1 representing 'never' and 7 'always'. For example, item 1 asked 'to what extent can you talk about a specific problem with (partner; closest parent; closest child; closest sibling; vet; vet's nurse?)'. The first such grid is completed for 'actual support'; (the support received in reality) and the second for 'ideal support' (the support that the client would like in an ideal world). This yields 'real' and 'ideal' social support profiles for each client.

Results

In order to determine the reliability of the system, 16% of observations were independently coded by a second observer. A percentage exact agreement of 87% was obtained, which is an acceptable level of reliability. The reliability of the question-

* This case study is based on the final-year dissertation of Catherine Brew, undertaken when she was a psychology undergraduate at Newcastle University. The present author supervised the project.

naire was also assessed by the split half method and yielded a significant correlation (Pearson's correlation coefficient: r = 0.91; p < 0.01).

The observational data indicated that there were no significant differences between the behaviours of older adults and the rest of the sample. However, analysis of the vet's behaviour revealed that a significantly higher frequency of 'emotional support' was provided to the older adults. This was mirrored in the questionnaire data, in that the older adults perceived themselves as receiving a significantly greater frequency of socially supportive behaviour, in this case across all five support categories. These clients also regarded 'socialising' as the main function of the support, whereas the adult sample saw 'tangible assistance' as the most important function.

Discussion

From this small study it appeared that vets may indeed play a significant role in providing social support to their clients, as indicated by prior research in the USA. More originally, the present study suggests that this is provided in a deliberate way, so as to favour the older clients. That is, older adults did not behave any differently toward the vet than their fellow adult clients. As a result of this positive bias, the older adults received more 'emotional support', as measured by a reliable and objective observation instrument; and they perceived themselves as receiving more of all five support categories, as gauged by a subjective questionnaire. This pattern of social support has been shown to raise the self-esteem of older adults (Krause & Markides, 1990) and bears out the assertion that vets fulfil a therapeutic role (Cusack, 1988).

Why should the vet be providing this kind of differential support, given that it did not appear to be a function of his clients' support-seeking behaviour? One methodological explanation is that he was indeed responding to elicitation behaviours, but these were not assessed by the present coding system (e.g. non-verbal cues). Winefield (1984) has noted that the lonely and depressed use 'restricted' non-verbal cues, such as not maintaining eye contact. The vet may have responded to such cues by providing emotional support. A second reason may be that the vet perceived the older adults as more 'needy', responding with extra sympathy and caring to what was viewed as a particularly strong bond between pet and owner. On being questioned, the vet gave some support to the later possibility, agreeing that he felt a special responsibility to provide support to the older adults amongst his clients.

These possible explanations imply the need to measure more broadly (i.e. including non-verbal behaviour and the supporters disposition towards the client) and to investigate the relationship with support elicitation and its consequences. That is, do older adults enjoy similar privileges in other community settings, or do they have to work harder to receive their support? Do pets make this work easier to accomplish? And, even if they do a better job of eliciting support with the help of a pet, is it organised in a pattern akin to that provided by the present vet? The results of such analyses would help us to better understand the role of pets and vets in relation to 'community care'.

Finally, to complete this social support tour of Morpeth, the high street ends with a river and a park in which there is encouragement to walk, and a playground including a paddling pool. This environment is another opportunity for social support, in that most noticeably the parents of young children can sit together while their children play and engage in comparisons of life as a parent. The park is also a setting in which people play together (there are tennis courts and bowling greens and the opportunity to row on the river) and I know from my own experience that the local running club who often cross the park and the high street will use the less vigorous parts of their run to talk about ongoing problems and will typically give and receive social support. Quite apart from the verbal transactions that go on in a park, one shouldn't underestimate one of the core parts of social support, which is simply the benefits of engaging in positive social interaction with similar others, leading to the vital sense of belonging to a community.

SUMMARY AND CONCLUSIONS

Although this chapter has covered such major dimensions as housing, physical environments, material resources, health education, social deprivation, the workplace and the high street, it only really provides a sketch of the relevant dimensions and findings in relation to distal interventions that might influence social support. Although wide-ranging, the occurrence of what mental health practitioners might do to facilitate social support at the distal level stop short of the widely held assumption that political action is necessary to achieve any meaningful impact. If nothing else, this chapter has hopefully raised awareness of the forces that bear down upon our clients and cause them to call upon us for assistance. Perhaps the information in this chapter will make mental health practitioners slightly more cautious in engaging solely in intrapersonally focused, one-to-one therapy.

Although there is a bewildering array of social support settings and participants, mental health practitioners may take some comfort from the existence of some recurring and core functions that are prominent. Repeatedly, the empirical literature that has analysed social support in distal environments has found that it plays an important role and that certain essential aspects of it, such as emotional support, are a powerful buffer to stress. Other variables and the associated roles that mental health practitioners can play in manipulating them are summarised in Table 7.5.

Table 7.5 A general summary of possible roles for mental health practitioners working at the distal level.

Distal environment category	Sample of possible roles
Physical (built) environment	• Encourage compatible residents to interact (the 'contact' factors that foster friendship) • Advocate, on behalf of clients, for environmental improvements (e.g. fencing; private areas: see Table 7.1)
Material and social deprivation	• Work in poorer areas • Form partnerships with residents to reform institutions • Provide acceptance and verification to individual clients • Coordinate services
Health education	• Prepare and disseminate mental health information (leaflets at exhibitions) • Develop and evaluate self-help packages • Provide a crisis help line • Contribute to the mass media (see Table 7.3)
School and work	• Form therapeutic partnerships with parents • Facilitate parents and teachers support groups • Encourage clients to engage their managers in workplace and interpersonal support (see Table 7.4) • Foster employment skills and opportunities

PART 4

Evaluating social support interventions

How might we assess the impact of social support interventions? Which instruments and criteria provide the 'best fit' with measurement standards and health service policy? What can one do to maximise the application of findings? This section tackles these and other fundamental questions in a wide-ranging account of research and evaluation, alongside the issue of how we might best develop social therapy.

Chapter 8

EVALUATION OF SOCIAL SUPPORT INTERVENTIONS

INTRODUCTION: WHAT IS 'QUALITY' IN RESEARCH AND EVALUATION?

Defining the terms 'research' and 'evaluation' is no simple matter. To begin with, they overlap with a number of closely related data collection methods designed to analyse variables of interest in mental health practice. To illustrate, Parry (1992) distinguished between service evaluation, operational research, professional audit, service audit, quality assurance and total quality management. She concluded that these methods can be creatively combined, since they all serve the principle of encouraging mental health practitioners to reflect on their practice and learn from their experience. Integral to them all is the idea that information is collected systematically and fed back in a way that encourages improvements and corrections towards some goal. This goal is normally defined following critical discussion with key participants. She concluded that there is little doubt that such methods and practices are under-used in the psychotherapy services that were the focus of her review.

A particularly timely and helpful way to think about the distinction between various forms of research is the research and development (R and D) initiative in the NHS (Peckham, 1991). This clarified the integrated roles for fundamental or discovery-orientated research, which was designed to establish the knowledge base for the NHS; pragmatic or development research, which was intended to establish whether methods such as a given therapy were effective under routine NHS conditions; and finally, implementation research, which should be conducted to determine whether those methods that have demonstrated efficacy from fundamental research and have demonstrated effectiveness from development research are actually carried out correctly under routine conditions (most clearly determined by service evaluation, action research and audit). A detailed breakdown of these approaches and their implications for mental health practitioners has been provided by Milne and Paxton (1998).

Table 8.1 summarises some of the broad characteristics of fundamental and action research.

Action research

Although it is recognised that any such characterisation is bound to be at least partly erroneous, it may, nonetheless, serve as a useful starting point in thinking about the nature of different kinds of research and the value that they may hold when applied to an issue like social support. For instance, on almost every one of the five features defined in Table 8.1, it can fairly readily be concluded that action research is a more appropriate model with which to approach the study of social support than is the academic or fundamental research alternative. To illustrate, it is an assumption in action research that data collection has to occur responsively within the context of data collection. Even the definition of a topic for research would normally arise from a careful discussion of relevant possibilities with a number of interested parties (referred to from now on as stakeholders).

Table 8.1 Some broad ways to distinguish between two general approaches to research, based on Milne (1987) and Schwandt (1990).

Features	Evaluation/action research	Fundamental/academic research
1. Research context	Highly salient: research is transactional and responds to its context	Minimised
2. Research topics	Wide range of socially important tasks (i.e. problem-solving cycle) but narrow focus on topics (i.e. evaluation)	Narrow range of tasks (see 5) but very wide range of academically respectable topics
3. Research methods	Technical quality secondary and relative to context and specific application. Methods derived heuristically (i.e. unique, problem-solving approach)	Rigour primary and relative to the standards of the 'quality' research literature (e.g. controls; instruments)
4. Research objectives	Produce useful information and procedures that are 'owned' by the stakeholders and lead to benefits for clients	Build and develop theories, by discovering new knowledge and publishing it in 'quality' (high impact) journals
5. Research relationships	Personal characteristics of the researcher as important as technical expertise	Technical expertise paramount

Another clear distinction in most cases between these two research traditions is that in action research the emphasis is on pursuing a problem-solving cycle in order to aid decision-making and improve the quality of an
intervention. Understanding the basic processes that underlie the intervention is more typically a focus of fundamental research. However, this
rather dichotomous view of research is potentially quite misleading in any
particular situation. It is more reasonable to view them as areas on a continuum, areas which may at times overlap. A case in point is the emphasis
on research methods which, as indicated in Table 8.1, stresses that rigour
and replication are a primary emphasis in fundamental research. However,
it is also the ambition of action researchers to obtain the best possible rigour
in their research (Milne, 1987). Also, to set up a distinction between an
approach that attempts to discover knowledge against a second that mere-
ly attempts to apply what is already known is fallacious. Clear examples
include the fact that action researchers do publish their work and would
regard this outcome as desirable in much the same way as would a fundamental researcher; and both styles of research require a sound grasp of
research methodology in order to cope with the demands of conducting
successful research. In this sense, action research can be regarded as a
bridge between the poles of pure research and rather crude evaluations.

As indicated by Table 8.1, action research would involve the mental
health practitioner occupying the role of consultant, collaborator, resource-
person and a problem-finder so as to facilitate the work of stakeholders in
defining objectives (Hoshmand & O'Byrne, 1996). The goals would typically be pragmatic ones that lead to decision-making, action and evaluation,
based around some kind of programme improvement or social reform.
Additionally, a less tangible objective of action research is to enhance the
problem-solving skills of those in the system, that is, to give them some of
the action research skills that will facilitate continued self-improvement
and foster a culture of inquiry. The methods that will be used are iterative,
meaning that they are based on a succession of attempts to problem-solve,
each one drawing on and building on its predecessor. The research methods used by the action researcher will be driven more by context and local
appropriateness than by the empirical literature. Referred to as 'methodological pluralism', this would involve engaging stakeholders in decisions
about the most appropriate instruments and research designs for that particular purpose. In this sense, the relevance of the information to be collected takes precedence over the rigour, as highlighted in Table 8.1 (row 3).

Philosophical frameworks

Action research, like any other research model, implicitly or explicitly
implies a certain view of knowledge or truth. The traditional view of

knowledge is the so-called 'positivist' one in which it is assumed that objective facts can be obtained and that an objective reality exists. Post-modernism has criticised this view successfully, in terms of both its logic and its context. Logically, philosophers such as Popper (1959) have shown that the idea of a rational, value-free, objective and pure knowledge of an objective reality was impossible. This was partly due to the fallacy that one could 'prove' some fact by repeatedly demonstrating a finding, through traditional research methods. As Popper pointed out, no number of confirmations of a phenomenon could ever prove it, since it would only take one disconfirmation to show that the proposed truth was unfounded. This was referred to as the principle of falsification and encouraged a line of research that took greater risks in terms of the predictions that were made and made greater efforts to find evidence for the falsification of a hypothesis.

The second major attack on positivism can be subsumed under the 'constructivist' viewpoint, which challenges the traditional separation between the notion of an objective researcher and the research focus. Rather, it is argued that the researcher constructs findings in a social, political and cultural context. On this view, researchers do not find or discover the truth, and the phenomena they purport to explain are not mechanistic or deterministic; rather the constructivist viewpoint suggests that reality and findings are perspectives that are embedded within a particular researcher's approach to a problem or question. No particular belief system (such as the positivistic method of natural science) should be given a privileged position in relation to the truth. On this view there are no objective facts or universal laws, rather a need to approach knowledge in a more tentative and contextual way, one that openly acknowledges the role of the researcher.

As a result of this post-modernist approach, differences between research in the social sciences tradition and knowledge from the humanities can become indistinguishable. For example, both may make use of 'case studies', based heavily on personal experience, introspection, life stories, first person accounts and so forth (Denzin & Lincoln, 1994). As noted by these authors, research these days is multi-paradigmatic and involves a 'dizzying pluralism'. In order to bring some sense of order to this seeming methodological chaos, they most helpfully delineated four major philosophies of science. In keeping with the action research model is the framework of post-positivism. This philosophy of knowledge assumes that it is possible to understand the nature of things and also to improve matters. However, unlike positivism, it doesn't assume that objective truth is possible, and like constructivism, acknowledges that all knowledge is ultimately personal and contextual. Its preferred methods are quantitative, including true and quasi experiments, systems analyses, cost–benefit equations, and so forth. The other major frameworks were defined as pragmatism, which emphasises utility and methods of an eclectic variety (for example survey questionnaires, interviews and observations); interpretivism, which assumes diverse understandings of reality and uses fundamentally qualitative methods (such as case studies, interviews and reviews of documents) to elucidate underlying themes and to capture the experiences of different individuals involved in a programme; and finally, Denzin and Lincoln (1994) refer to the critical or normative scientific framework. The ideological basis for this approach is one of emancipation, empowerment and social change, focusing on the beneficiaries of any programme and on empowering relatively powerless groups. It emphasises stakeholder participation and the use of unstructured quantitative and qualitative methods. To illustrate, a key objective would be to analyse ways in which the goals and activities of a service help to maintain power inequities in society. An excellent review of the Denzin and Lincoln book has been provided by Fishman (1995).

Within this frame of reference, evaluation research is regarded as standing at a crossroads between the different frameworks, sited fairly close to the centre of a post-modern, qualitative research approach. To quote Denzin and Lincoln (1994), programme evaluation is

> the critical site where theory, method ... action and policy all come together. Qualitative researchers can isolate target populations, show the immediate effects of certain programmes on such groups, and isolate the constraints that operate against policy changes in such settings. (p. 15)

Qualitative research

Qualitative research is customarily used to describe research that involves data collection and analysis, so as to contribute to the understanding of the clients' subjective experience of themselves, their relationships or their social world. A classic example in the mental health field is Goffman's (1961) book *Asylums*, which was a qualitative study of the psychiatric hospital as a total institution. Goffman's objective was to try and learn more about the social world of the hospital patient as experienced from his or her own perspective. He utilised observation to make sense of his material, but qualitative research is in essence a multi-method approach, involving :

> an interpretative, naturalistic approach to its subject matter. This means that qualitative researchers study things in their natural settings, attempting to make sense of or interpret phenomena in terms of the meanings people bring to them. (Denzin & Lincoln, 1994, p. 2)

Other characteristic features of a qualitative approach are that observations of the kind conducted by Goffman take place in the natural setting and are uncontrolled; that the observer gets close to the data and adopts an insider perspective; that the orientation is towards exploration, expansion, discovery, description and induction; and that the fundamental orientation is towards understanding process, including real, rich and deep data that cannot be generalised but which refer to a holistic vision and assume a dynamic reality (Cook & Reichardt, 1979).

The approaches used for data collection within the qualitative research tradition include the following:

- ethnography and ethnomethodology;
- grounded theory;
- protocol analysis;
- discourse analysis;
- conversational analysis;
- constructivist approaches;
- humanistic approaches;
- phenomenology and hermeneutic investigation;
- case studies;
- interview-based methodologies;
- multiple case research.

In recounting this diverse range of qualitative research activity, Stiles (1993) notes that although the qualitative study of human experience is probably as old as human experience itself, there has been a development in the last couple of decades, following the availability of the kind of high-quality audio and video recording equipment that makes the preservation of phenomena possible. In his scholarly analysis, Stiles considered that a number of key issues delineated qualitative from quantitative research. These included the use of linguistic results as opposed to quantitative data (for example, a dialogue or narrative is presented uncoded as evidence); empathy is used as an observation strategy (that is, investigators use their own feeling reactions and other inner experiences as data, and may make inferences about participants' experiences from these data); and contextual interpretation is stressed (events tend to be understood and reported in their context). Given its emphasis on the use of language, qualitative research is also polydimensional (each aspect of human experience that is analysed can be considered on a different dimension); non-linear causality is accommodated, because elements in the analysis can feed back and influence subsequent behaviour: the start point may bear little resemblance to the end point (as in a semi-structured interview that goes from a trivial question to a profound insight); empowerment is a research goal (e.g. emancipating participants is a legitimate or even central purpose of qualitative research, as in attempting to construct interpretations so as to further the participants' interests); and, finally, interpretations are treated as very tentative and probabilistic, using information to deepen and enlarge the understanding of human existence, rather than to develop prediction or control, as is characteristic of quantitative research. The results are judged by their applicability, in terms of facilitating how readers adapt ideas to their own context, rather than in terms of conclusions that have some kind of literal generalisation. Stiles (1993) concluded that these features allowed qualitative research to fill a little used epistemological space between traditional research and the methods of history and biography. The outcome is not generalised truth but rather the understanding that people who read the results of qualitative research can develop and apply to their own situation.

Quality in research

As noted by Stiles (1993) there are several continuities between traditional positivist research and the qualitative approaches, including the use of some research methods (for example, observation and interviews), and there is also a shared emphasis on such conventions as the need for reliability and validity. In both traditions, reliability refers to the trustworthiness of the observations or data that are collected; by contrast, validity refers to the trustworthiness of the interpretations or conclusions that are drawn from such data. Similarly, the underlying cannon of scepticism or objectivity is considered important in both traditions, although terms like 'permeability' may be preferred in the qualitative approach as a way of capturing the notion that any understanding is necessarily limited and should be changed in relation to observations that falsify a prior understanding. One of the features of quality research, according to Stiles (1993), is that it enhances the readers' understanding of the social and cultural context in which the research was conducted. These and other characteristics of quality in research are listed in Table 8.2. This table takes a range of characteristics found in various research traditions, and attempts to show that there does indeed appear to be considerable overlap in the criteria that such traditions would use to judge the worth of a piece of research.

An important elaboration of characteristic 1 in Table 8.2 is the way that research quality is defined within the R and D initiative (Culyer, 1994). In order for research to be funded by the NHS, there is a need for

- a design that produces new knowledge (internal validity);
- generalisable findings (external validity);
- a clear protocol;
- a peer-reviewed protocol;
- approval by the Local Research Ethical Committee;

- clear management arrangements; and
- plans for publication.

By contrast, research quality in the UK's higher education sector now revolves around publication in 'high impact' journals. Impact is determined by the frequency with which any particular journal is cited in other journals. Thus, famous journals, such as the *Archives of General Psychiatry* has an impact value of 11.2; whereas less cited journals, such as *The British Journal of Psychiatry*, score only 2.3. In these crude terms, the former journal has five times the quality of the latter.

In essence, the summary in Table 8.2 represents an integrative formulation of research, covering a wide spectrum of approaches. The differences between these approaches appear, at least to this observer, to be more semantic than real. Take the example of the first quality characteristic, sophistication. Within the tradition of discovery oriented, fundamental or academic research, there would be an emphasis on using highly reliable and valid instruments to obtain data that were collected as objectively as possible. The system for gathering the data would be set out in such a form that other people could independently obtain the same findings. Consider then the notion of triangulation from the qualitative research tradition. This also has the underlying emphasis of trying to maximise accurate or fair interpretation of information and simultaneously to minimise misinterpretation, by reliance on a limited range of sources of information. The two traditions therefore share a commitment to multiple data sources, multiple methods and an effort to assess the convergence of information across these different sources of data. Similarly, the risk of bias and distortion on the part of the researcher is just as real in qualitative as in traditional quantitative research. Selective perception reporting and self-fulfilling prophecies are risks for all research methods, as noted by Stiles (1993). As he suggests, investigators cannot eliminate their values and preconceptions, but whatever their tradition they can work to make these more permeable or falsifiable. Whether the technique that one uses as an investigator to achieve this balance is independent replication or peer debriefing is secondary to a commitment to improving our understanding of phenomena and our ability to use this understanding to improve our lot. Just as in the research process itself, researchers should engage in a dialectical process in which their observations and findings are challenged and open to refinement. This is identified in Table 8.2 under number 7, the execution process.

Summary

As noted by Schwandt (1990), the notion of quality (whether in respect of research or anything else) is capable of multiple meanings, dependent

Table 8.2   'Meta-evaluation'—some criteria by which to judge the quality of research (based on Cousins & Leithwood, 1986; Fawcett, 1991; Stiles, 1993 and Schwandt, 1990)

Quality characteristics	Definition
1. Sophistication	Rigour and elegance of the methods used (e.g. peer review and grading of an elaborate research protocol in relation to funding decisions): the 'truth value' dimension. Includes high internal validity and objectivity (e.g. independent replication)
2. Credibility	Performance of the researcher (e.g. demeanour), the characteristics of the researcher (including qualifications and affiliation); and participants involved or problems tackled (ecological validity: simulations with students versus people in natural contexts experiencing socially important problems)
3. Timeliness	Originality in the focus and methods of research; practical value of the findings in relation to a pressing practical problem (i.e. optimal timing of an intervention)
4. Utility	Practical value or relevance of research in facilitating understanding or problem-solving (e.g. data serving as informational feedback): the 'action' dimension, including being sustainable and inexpensive.
5. Conformance to product standards	Defining and meeting specifications for the technology or intervention (e.g. the 'manipulation check' on the fidelity of a therapy)
6. Customer perceptions	Vantage point of user on research findings taken into consideration skilfully and patiently. Quality is in the eyes of the user (satisfying demands or 'fitness for use')
7. Execution process	Flowchart of tasks and checkpoints detailed: checking quality while research process is unfolding. Engaging persistently and actively in seeking disconfirmation. Getting it right first time and sticking to the plan. Collaboration with stakeholders
8. Communication	Tangible (e.g. audit of a report or publication) and intangible (e.g. interpersonal skills) aspects of information transmission judged for objectivity, authenticity, completeness and influence. Investigator declares own biases and the research context

largely upon the perspective one adopts and the particular values that one endorses. No one approach is entirely acceptable to members and proponents of a second approach, although as Table 8.2 attempts to indicate, there are surprising and reassuring levels of overlap between the paradigms at a general level (e.g. the need to be as rigorous and as credible as possible). It is unproductive to debate whether one particular orientation, such as action research or qualitative research, is in some sense superior to other versions of research practice. To use Schwandt's (1990) term, it is difficult to define a list of meta-criteria that are not somehow bound in to a particular research orientation. As a result, it is difficult to provide some standard set of criteria by which to judge an evaluation, at least in a form that would be acceptable to those working in a different research paradigm.

In this respect, action research is suggested as the most appropriate orientation to research for mental health practitioners with an interest in social support, rather than in some sense being a better-quality approach. This is because it is more relevant and appropriate to research that is conducted within a service setting and is orientated to complex problems that arise in naturalistic, social contexts. But more important than this particular orientation to research is the strategic importance of adopting at least some such approach to the systematic analysis and evaluation of one's professional practice. In this sense, research quality is about specifying what one is attempting to achieve in collaboration with other stakeholders, particularly the users of one's services. It is also about subjecting these services to critical scrutiny in such a way as to provide corrective feedback, leading to improved services in the future. The research approach then allows one to demonstrate that such feedback has, in some way, informed and guided the service towards achieving better standards of execution and outcome.

On this logic, the rest of the chapter sets out to illustrate how different ways of designing a piece of research can accommodate to the action research paradigm. The emphasis is on a graded approach, beginning with very simple designs that would be a suitable starting point for mental health practitioners with little or no research experience, and proceeding through to more sophisticated designs that are still viable in an applied, service context. Within any research design there need to be appropriate instruments which measure both the intervention itself (the so-called 'manipulation check') and instruments that also measure the outcomes that these interventions are designed to produce. Finally, this chapter looks at what Table 8.2 (row 8) defined as the communication task: the need to engage energetically and skilfully in collaborating with stakeholders so that the information that is generated by research is put to best use.

RESEARCH DESIGNS: THE INEVITABLE RIGOUR VERSUS RELEVANCE TENSION

It has been suggested that there are five principal challenges facing mental health practitioners when they set out to evaluate community support programmes (Durbin *et al.*, 1995). These include selecting an appropriate research design, engaging the staff or users of a programme, obtaining an adequate study sample, involving clients and selecting measurement domains and instruments. All of these challenges will be discussed in the remainder of this chapter, starting with the question of clarifying an appropriate research design.

By definition, research design denotes when, where and on whom measurements are taken; it is the logical structure which guides the collection of data (Barker *et al.*, 1994). These authors suggest that research designs are of two fundamental types, namely the experimental and the non-experimental. Experimental designs involve some kind of intervention by the researcher, whereas non-experimental designs involve the assessment of some phenomenon without changing the situation. The most common form of non-experimental design is the correlational study, which sets out to analyse the association between two or more factors, something that has been illustrated many times in the preceding chapters. Other examples include descriptive studies, epidemiological analyses and consumer satisfaction surveys. By contrast, experimental designs entail testing out an intervention in order to discover something about a phenomenon under scrutiny. Unlike the non-experimental designs, experimental research allows one to infer whether or not a given factor (e.g. social support) has a causal influence on some other factor (e.g. depression). The factor that is varied is referred to as the independent variable or manipulation, whereas the thing that is taken as a measure of the independent variable's effect is referred to as the dependent or outcome variable.

There are many types of experimental design, and these in turn can be classified as randomised or non-randomised. The non-randomised designs are weaker, in that there is less basis for confidently inferring that an intervention has had an effect on a dependent variable. By contrast, in the randomised design the participants are allocated to groups on the basis of a random assignment process. Crucially, such randomisation rules out certain biases in how the participants are selected for respective groups. Both experimental and non-experimental research designs may use control or comparison groups: the former do not receive a crucial active ingredient, and the latter contrasts a new intervention with a viable alternative treatment. A good practical example of a control-group strategy that is available to mental health practitioners is the use of waiting-list control groups. If groups of research participants are given random assignment to either a waiting list or a treatment group, and then both groups are given some initial assessment, then this design takes care of both selection and reactivity to the process of being assessed.

In essence, such design features as control groups are attempts to minimise 'confounds' (i.e. threats to the internal validity of a study). Numerous confounds exist, including learning, maturation, underlying social trends, interfering random events and, as already illustrated, reactivity to the process of being assessed. These and other threats that will be discussed shortly were analysed exhaustively by Campbell and Stanley (1963). Before proceeding to detail some of these threats and the research designs that practitioners can use to minimise them, it is worth pausing to illustrate the nature of some of these confounding factors.

Demand characteristics

This term is used to recognise that participants are not passive responders but rather they are often motivated to identify what is expected by the researcher and either to comply or resist the influence. To illustrate, T. Anderson and Strupp (1996) examined participants' reports of the demand characteristics in a psychotherapy research study exploring the effectiveness of manualised treatment. A total of 59 of these participants were interviewed following the end of the therapy and it was found that those who were highly aware of their role as a research participant had the kind of outcomes that were consistent with the hypothesised outcomes from the study. Therefore this awareness was probably a confound, creating an alternative and plausible explanation for the obtained findings. As a result, the researcher is unable to confidently attribute results, such as an improved clinical status, to the therapy as opposed to the demand characteristic of the therapy research process. A clear example is awareness of what a specific instrument may be intended to measure (e.g. depression), which the aware participant can answer in a socially desirable direction (i.e. trying to please or thank the therapist). Equally, demand characteristics can work negatively, as in the phenomenon of the 'resentful demoralisation' of participants. Anderson and Strupp (1996) provided some transcripts from their interviews which illustrated some of the underlying feelings of participants in therapy research:

> ... it was like I was under a microscope ... I really do think you are aware that you are in a project. I want to say that it doesn't necessarily change your behaviour, but just that awareness. In the back of my mind I was wondering, you know, wanting more information, thinking there was more information about me out there than they were sharing with me. And that's frustrating. There is some more information that I could have about myself and I guess I feel resentful that that information was not available to me. (p. 780)

Credibility of interventions

Another potential confound in therapy research is that different interventions have different degrees of credibility for the recipients. In theory, careful assessment of credibility can provide an assessment of the foregoing demand characteristics and help to show that an intervention that has proved to be more effective than a control procedure has equal credibility (Shapiro, 1981). Failure to demonstrate this comparability leaves open the possibility that an apparently more effective intervention may be due to the potent arousal of the users' expectancies for improvement, rather than to any specific psychological processes that may have been triggered by the intervention.

Shapiro (1981) evaluated the expectancy-arousal hypothesis, which states that treatments differ in effectiveness only to the extent that they arouse in the users differing degrees of expectation of benefit. In one study, Shapiro asked 319 students to complete some questionnaires and then to imagine that they were suffering interpersonal anxiety and were being offered some treatment for it. The participants then read booklets describing several forms of treatment before indicating how they felt about the different treatments. This was assessed through questions such as: how logical does this treatment seem to you? how confident would you be that this treatment would be successful? and how confident would you be in recommending this treatment to a friend who was extremely prone to interpersonal anxiety? This study provided very clear-cut results favouring the expectancy-arousal hypothesis. That is, one treatment was perceived as far more credible than the others, indicating that some of the superior outcome findings obtained in prior research may, indeed, have been founded on the patients' expectancy of benefit. Based on two further studies within the same paper, Shapiro (1981) concluded that the results offered considerable evidence that differential outcomes of psychological treatments may be due to their differing levels of credibility. By implication, research designs that use simple placebo conditions cannot indemnify researchers against confounds, such as arousing positive expectancies. In addition, research should actually assess the credibility of a treatment on a routine basis so that its contribution to outcome can be taken into account.

Different research designs

There are several ways of minimising the extent of which demand characteristics and credibility, to mention but two threats to the internal validity of the study, can be limited by researchers. The essential issue is one of fitness for purpose: given a particular hypothesis or objective, which design is most appropriate, in the context of a particular study and a given set of resources? This logic is in keeping with the NHS R and D initiative, which recognises that at certain times a wide range of designs may be appropriate. However, the favoured design is the randomised controlled trial (RCT). This design analyses the comparative effectiveness of two or more interventions, based on the random allocation of participants to different treatment groups, often based on some stratification by client characteristics such as symptom severity or disability. In addition, those carrying out the assessments and receiving the intervention are blind to their membership of a particular group (the double blind procedure). A third feature of the RCT is that the interventions themselves are standardised, i.e. therapist variables and such factors as the duration of treatment are detailed in a manual and equalised across the treatment groups (Roth & Fonagy, 1996). As a result of these features, the RCT excludes many of the possible confounds, making it the 'gold standard' for research. To illustrate, Mynors-Wallis *et al.* (1995) used an RCT design to compare problem-solving treatment with Amitriptyline and with placebo for major depression presenting in primary care. Ninety-one participants with major depression were randomly allocated to one of these three treatments and the randomisation was stratified to ensure that each of the groups contained patients with depressive disorders of equivalent severity. In the drug and placebo groups, Amitriptyline and placebo were prescribed as if Amitriptyline was being given, with participants and therapists blind to the contents of capsules. The aim was to deliver the drug treatment in a way that would maximise patient compliance, in the context of a caring, therapeutic relationship. Specific psychological interventions, in particular problem-solving, were avoided, but non-specific interventions such as listening, encouraging and empathising were included. Based on this analysis, Mynors-Wallis *et al.* (1995) found that problem-solving was more effective than placebo and as effective as Amitriptyline in treating major depression in primary care. High levels of patient satisfaction with the problem-solving treatment and a low attrition rate indicated that this intervention also had credibility.

Although the RCT is an outstandingly rigorous (i.e. internally valid) research design, it is not always appropriate or feasible. Problems with the RCT include those of recruitment and randomisation. Recruitment to an RCT is only justified in situations where there is some uncertainty about the appropriate clinical interventions. Sample sizes must be large enough to establish the presence or absence of a worthwhile benefit in terms of effectiveness, cost or both. As a result, larger numbers of participants than are often available are required, leading to the involvement of several sites in order to perform the research. However, groups such as GPs have no obligation to participate in research and may, therefore, be unwilling to take part in studies that produce no immediate benefit for their patients and which may well disrupt the delivery of their health care. Because of this, those practitioners who do participate in RCTs may well be atypical, so that extrapolating findings from such an RCT may be misleading, (i.e. lack external validity).

In terms of randomisation, practitioners may also dislike giving their patients interventions that they would not normally apply. Randomisation is also likely to disrupt the customary relationship between the practitioner and the patient. A conflict of interest can arise between the role of promoting and empowering the client against the wish to recruit participants to benefit future clients, or to gain personal academic merit; and because practitioners coerce users into giving consent, long-established loyalties may be undermined or endangered. Worries about confidentiality and the risks of a new intervention are other considerations that may influence recruitment and randomisation issues.

Quasi-experimental research design

Because of these difficulties (which, it should be noted, are not unique to RCTs), other research designs may well be appropriate in a particular context. In addition to experimental designs such as the RCT, and the non-experimental designs (such as correlational analysis), there is a whole group of designs that are particularly appropriate to the mental health practitioner. These are labelled 'quasi experimental' designs. This category was introduced by Campbell and Stanley (1963) to group together those studies that have interventions and outcome measures, but which do not use random assignment. Again, various quasi-experimental designs are available and have been summarised in numerous textbooks (for example, Barker *et al.*, 1994). They include designs in which there is only one group and one assessment following intervention; assessments before and after intervention for one group; and designs in which there is more than one group or assessment. These will be discussed shortly, in terms of a graded approach to research design. In the meantime, please note that Figure 8.1 sets out some of the main types of design within a sequential model. This figure is intended to show how different designs fit different purposes. That is, in the initial exploratory phase the research involves uncontrolled evaluations such as a before and after assessments of an intervention and routine clinical projects. These have the advantages of high clinical validity (i.e. they make a lot of sense to clinicians) and they involve them usefully in the research process.

The exploratory research designs contribute to efficacy research, a phase characterised by very high internal validity, such as the RCT. In this area, tightly controlled laboratory studies are conducted to determine whether or not specific treatments and their ingredients have a clearly demonstrated causal link to certain specified outcomes. However, knowing that a treatment that is administered under laboratory conditions works is not the same as demonstrating that such a treatment is effective under service conditions, that is, it may lack external validity. For this reason it is necessary to have effectiveness studies that do such things as compare different treatments as administered under NHS conditions.

Another advantage of the sequential model that is depicted in Figure 8.1 is that practitioners should see that they can have a research role at a number of stages. The figure also helps to illustrate what might be termed the 'ecology' of clinical research, in that in reality the arrows should point round in various directions, to illustrate how problems and solutions at one stage may feed back into activities at another stage: Figure 8.1 makes the research process seem much more linear and smooth than is actually the case! While Figure 8.1 defines some research designs (for example the RCT) it leaves open the question of which designs might best fit other phases of research activity (for example evaluating the long-term outcomes of treatment). The next section suggests a viable range of designs for such studies, assuming a modest level of research sophistication and minimal resource on the part of the mental health practitioner.

Accessible designs

The decision about which research design to use to study social support (or any other manipulation) can be made using a decision-making tree. If it is possible to control all the major variables, then one would use single-subject experimental designs with systematic replication, or experimental group designs, such as the RCT. Similarly, if it is possible to randomly allocate participants to groups then large group experimental designs should be preferred. If this is not possible then the quasi-experimental designs become the best bet (Owens *et al.*, 1996). It is to these quasi-experimental designs that we now turn. There are many possible ways to determine when, where and on whom the measurements are taken within the logical structure of a research design. Table 8.3 summarises three broad classes of design, following the breakdown set out in Figure 8.1 (i.e. between exploratory, efficacy and effectiveness research approaches).

Table 8.3 summarises a few designs within each of the broad categories of research activity. The traditional case study, in which some evaluation follows an intervention with a patient, is an exploratory type of research design. Because there is no way of controlling for a large number of confounds, this design is regarded as a pre-experimental approach: it cannot be interpreted with confidence. The same applies to designs b and c. It is only when some control is introduced for some of these major threats that the designs become interpretable, as indicated by the 'interpretation threshold' in Table 8.3. Such designs would normally be used to assess the effectiveness of a treatment, but would not normally involve random allocation to groups. Finally, in the third broad row in Table 8.3 are the true experimen-

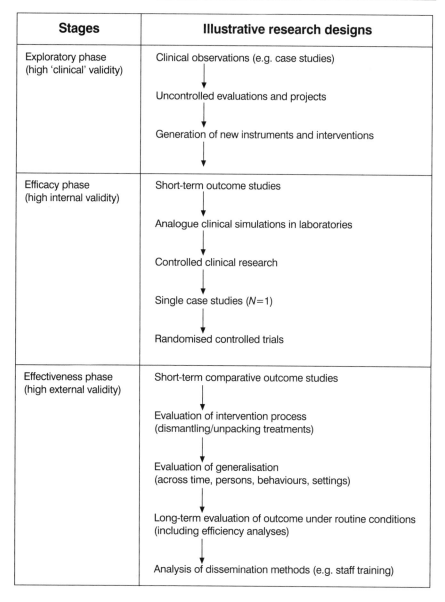

Stages	Illustrative research designs
Exploratory phase (high 'clinical' validity)	Clinical observations (e.g. case studies) ↓ Uncontrolled evaluations and projects ↓ Generation of new instruments and interventions ↓
Efficacy phase (high internal validity)	Short-term outcome studies ↓ Analogue clinical simulations in laboratories ↓ Controlled clinical research ↓ Single case studies ($N=1$) ↓ Randomised controlled trials
Effectiveness phase (high external validity)	Short-term comparative outcome studies ↓ Evaluation of intervention process (dismantling/unpacking treatments) ↓ Evaluation of generalisation (across time, persons, behaviours, settings) ↓ Long-term evaluation of outcome under routine conditions (including efficiency analyses) ↓ Analysis of dissemination methods (e.g. staff training)

Figure 8.1   A sequential model of clinical research based on Agras and Berkowitz (1980) and Salkovskis (1995), related to three broad research phases

tal designs, which would normally serve to evaluate the efficacy of a particular intervention under laboratory conditions. In these designs the crucial issue is that participants are randomly allocated to either treatment or control conditions. This randomisation is important, but the fundamental

Table 8.3　Some feasible research designs for mental health practitioners to study social support.

Exploratory research designs (implementation research)			
(a) Case study		X	O_1
(b) One group, pre-test & post-test design	O_1	X	O_2
(c) Post-test only, with non-equivalent groups		X	O_1
			O_1

Interpretation threshold: quasi-experimental designs (effectiveness research)						
(d) Time series design	OOOO	X	OOOO			
(e) Pre-test, post-test control group design	O_1 O_2	X	O_2 O_3			
(f) Repeated intervention	O_1	X_1	O_2	O_3	X_1	O_4
(g) Non-equivalent dependent variables	O_{1a} O_{1b}	X	O_{2a} O_{2b}			

True experimental designs (efficacy research)				
(h) Pre-test, post-test randomised control group design	R	O_1	X	O_2
	R	O_1		O_2
(i) Post-test only randomised control group design	R		X	O_1
	R			O_1
(j) Solomon four-group randomised control group design	R	O_1	X	O_2
	R	O_3		O_4
	R	O_1	X	O_5
	R			O_6

Key: O = assessment points (dependent variables); X = intervention (the independent variable); and R = random allocation to groups.

difference between true experiments and quasi experiments concerns their internal validity. Randomisation takes care of most of the threats to the internal validity of a study, but not all of them. By contrast, quasi experimental designs require the investigator to make threats explicit and then rule them out one by one, a laborious task (Cook and Campbell, 1976).

Threats to internal validity

As already noted, there are a number of confounds which may influence with the obtained results and mislead the investigator into believing that the improved scores following an intervention are due to the intervention. Table 8.4 indicates a number of alternative explanations for such improved scores, ones which are particularly likely to cause the results to be uninterpretable.

Table 8.4 A sample of the feasible research designs (see Table 8.3) related to the major threats to their internal and external validity. In the table, a minus indicates a definite threat (weakness in the design), a plus indicates that the threat is controlled (a strength in the design), a question mark indicates a possible source of concern and a blank indicates that the threat is not relevant (from Campbell & Stanley, 1963).

Sources of invalidity (internal)	Exploratory research designs: case study	One-group pre-test–post-test design	Quasi-experimental research designs	Time series design	Pre-test, post-test control group design	True experimental designs: pre-test–post-test control group design	Solomon four-group design
History (events between the 1st & 2nd assessment)	–	–	Interpretational threshold	–	+	+	+
Maturation (growth or change processes—e.g. becoming tired)	–	–	"	+	+	+	+
Testing (reactivity to assessment)	–	–	"	+	+	+	+
Instrumentation (changes in measurement —e.g. observer drift)	–	–	"	?	+	+	+
Regression (groups selected on basis of extreme scores regress to the mean)	–	?	"	+	?	+	+
Selection (biased/differential selection)	–	+	"	+	+	+	+
Mortality (differential loss of respondents)	–	+	"	+	+	+	+
Interaction of selection and maturation, etc. (e.g. different groups changing at different speeds)	–	–	"	+	–	+	+

Table 8.4 (*continued*)

Sources of invalidity (external)	Exploratory research designs: case study	One-group pre-test – post-test design	Quasi-experimental research designs	Time series design	Pre-test, post-test control group design	True experimental designs: pre-test–post-test control group design	Solomon four-group design
Interaction of testing and interventions (was testing situation atypical?)	?	–	"	–	–	–	+
Interaction of selection and intervention (to whom can intervention be generalised?)	–	–	"	?	?	?	?
Reactive arrangements (inc. demand characteristics)	?	?	"	?	?	?	?
Multiple intervention interference (cf. single intervention in NHS)	?	?	"	–	–	–	–

To illustrate, amongst the exploratory (or pre-experimental) research designs, such as the case study, none of the major threats to internal validity are taken into account, although with a one group pre-test post-test design the researcher can at least be confident about the absence of selection and mortality effects. The quasi-experimental designs fare better and have the basis to exclude a number of confounds. Finally, the true experimental designs have very high internal validity, although it can be noted that their external validity is questionable (Campbell & Stanley, 1963) (i.e. the extent to which findings can be generalised to other situations).

It should be noted that the kind of summary provided in Table 8.4 oversimplifies the situation. Therefore, they should be treated as a general guide to the strengths and weaknesses of the respective research designs, rather than depended upon as a reliable indicator. This is because in reality the different threats may vary significantly in terms of a particular time and context. As a consequence, it is best to think through one's design and its inevitable weaknesses carefully before commencing a study, and again when interpreting the results that one obtains: caution is the byword. As Barker *et al.* (1994) suggest, the core task is to choose a design that is appropriate to the research questions that you have in mind and to the stage of your intervention programme. In the early stages it would probably be wise to focus on exploratory (or pre-experimental), descriptive or correlational analyses which throw up promising leads. Subsequently, when a service is better defined, one can commence quasi-experimental research designs. In practice, given the way that the R and D initiative is proceeding within the NHS, it would be wise at such a stage to team up with researchers from a local university (Milne & Paxton, 1998).

Before leaving this discussion it is important to note that it has only considered in detail internal validity. As set out by Cook and Campbell (1976) there are at least four further kinds of validity, including external, temporal antecedence, statistical conclusion and construct validity. External validity is elaborated next. Most text books on research methods include an account of the threats that these different kinds of validity address, as well as some research approaches that are applicable to the work of mental health practitioners. For example, Barker *et al.* (1994) detailed a number of small sample and single case designs that are at the pre-experimental level but which provide useful information for clinicians and services. Practitioners with an interest in single subject designs would be well advised to study Hersen and Barlow (1976) or Morley (1996). Some single subject ($N=1$) designs allow the practitioner to look at very small samples (for example three clients) within a multiple baseline or multiple phase research design. This design excludes many of the threats to internal and external validity. Many researchers believe that it is these small-sample designs that are best suited to practitioners.

Discussion of the kinds of considerations that all researchers should take into account also appear in Lipsey (1990). He helpfully delineates those factors that help to increase the power of a research design, such as ensuring that the intervention is applied strongly and with high fidelity. The participants should preferably be a large sample and the dependent variables be sensitive and valid for picking up changes in those variables expected to respond to an intervention. These would be characterised by fine-grained measurement rather than coarse or categorical grouping, and be unlikely to have floor or ceiling effects. These issues of treatment fidelity and careful selection of dependent variables are discussed below. Before going on to these sections, two issues to do with research designs which have particular salience for practitioners are discussed, namely external validity and clinical significance.

External validity

External validity concerns the issue of generalisation. The central question is: to what extent can the findings from a particular study (particularly those conducted under tightly controlled conditions) be considered to apply to different samples, settings, intervention variables and measurement variables? This question is of profound importance to practitioners, who tend to have less interest in internal validity, namely the demonstration that an independent variable has unambiguously had an effect on a dependent variable. Ideally research designs are high in both internal and external validity, but in practice it is well nigh impossible to obtain this ideal. The analogy with the tax disc holder on one's car windscreen is relevant, in that one's efforts to press down on air bubbles on one part of the disc only results in the air bulges reappearing in another part. This is analogous to balancing internal and external validity; the more one emphasises rigour the less one obtains relevant results, at least as far as practitioners are concerned.

An early evaluation of the external validity of a study was conducted by Kirk (1983). She analysed the behavioural treatment of obsessive compulsive patients under routine NHS conditions, noting that in relation to efficacy research studies there were similarities between the client groups treated (for example age and problem duration) as well as some important differences (e.g. more acute NHS clients). The therapy itself also differed, in that the NHS clients were less often seen at home and were given more homework assignments and provided with a variety of ways of managing anxiety (confer the lengthy *in vivo* exposure that characterised research trials). However, comparable results were obtained and Kirk concluded that many of the aspects of rigorous research had been transferred to NHS practice with comparable results, indicating external validity. A more recent example was provided by Barkham *et al.* (1996), who extended the time-limited psychotherapy as practised in the Sheffield psychotherapy project to three NHS sites (Leicester, Huddersfield and Sheffield) for a sample of 36 clients with depression. These clients received either the 'prescriptive' or 'exploratory' treatments of the project for either 8 or 16 sessions. The initial improvements for both forms of therapy were approximately equivalent to those obtained within the Sheffield psychotherapy project proper, although poorer long-term maintenance was obtained for the NHS clients. They also concluded that this represented a generally successful external validation of the treatment.

The above two studies are rather rare, as in practice very few treatments derived from research centres have been analysed for their external validity (Shadish *et al.*, 1997). Although these authors also found from a meta-analysis of 56 outcomes studies that patients receiving therapy under routine clinical conditions do better than those who do not receive therapy, they were cautious in drawing any conclusions. One key reason for their caution was that there remains some controversy about the criteria that might best capture the notion of clinically representative conditions. They noted that the following criteria might all be applied in order to define an 'externally valid' environment;

- use of a non-university or non-research-centre setting;
- routine referral systems in operation;
- experienced professional therapists with regular case loads and without specific training for the intervention provided;
- the absence of any treatment manual;
- the absence of monitoring of the fidelity with which the intervention is implemented;
- providing interventions for demographically heterogeneous clients;
- similar services provided to clinically heterogeneous clients; and
- freedom of practitioners to use a wide variety of procedures.

This list clearly introduces another major set of potential confounds in relation to the external validity of particular research findings from laboratory settings. However, as indicated by the Barkham *et al.* study (1996), a fair degree of control can be exerted over these major threats to the external validity of the study, so that ultimately we can determine that an intervention has effectiveness as well as efficacy.

Clinical significance

Just as mental health practitioners may look with some scepticism at the results obtained with highly selected clients treated under what they may perceive to be highly favourable conditions, so they have customarily found the reliance on statistical significance that characterises fundamental research to be unconvincing. This is largely because relatively minor changes in the scores that a client obtains on one of several self-report questionnaires can prove sufficient to yield strongly significant statistical effects. Most clinicians would not be satisfied with minor numerical changes on self-report measures, looking instead for signs that somebody is in some practical sense 'improved'. Clinically significant improvement has therefore been emphasised latterly, referring to the practical importance of any changes achieved through an intervention.

Methods for judging clinical significance include evaluating changes based on social validation, and those based on the amount of change that results from an intervention, judged against some social standard. In keeping with the logic of single-subject research (which relies on visual inspection of the data to convince one of the effectiveness of a treatment), clinically important changes should be sufficiently dramatic and obvious from the data to make it unnecessary to resort to statistical tests. These include asking the recipients of an intervention to comment on whether there are socially important improvements accruing to them as a result of the intervention. Improvements include the participant's everyday functioning (e.g. resuming work, discontinuing medication) and demonstrating that the treatment itself is socially acceptable. The essential feature of social validation is to ask the participant's peer group to comment on whether or not a change has moved an individual's functioning to within some locally acceptable norm, one that no longer requires intervention (Hansen & Lambert, 1996).

A second approach to clinical significance is a statistical one in which social norms are established for functioning in both the dysfunctional and acceptable ranges, and then a client's pre- and post-intervention levels of functioning (as gauged by some relevant instrument) are compared to see whether the individual has moved from the dysfunctional to the functional range of scores. The first elaboration of how clinical significance could be determined by statistical methods of this kind was provided by Jacobson et al. (1984), whose approach resulted in an objective depiction of an individual's position in relation to a distribution of functional scores on some assessment tool, such as the Beck Depression Inventory. This approach can be used with groups or with single individuals. In both cases a cut-off score is defined as marking the difference between the dysfunctional and functional distributions, and the score of the group or individual on some psychometrically sound instrument is then plotted (see Hansen and Lambert, 1996, for further illustrations of this approach).

Fortunately for practitioners, assessments of clinical significance are now becoming more commonplace, alongside the traditional emphasis on statistical significance. To illustrate, Ogles et al. (1995) re-analysed the data from a major collaborative research programme designed to treat depression, finding that a substantial number of these clients made reliable improvements that took them to within the functional distribution of scores on the Beck Depression Inventory, the Hamilton Rating Scale for Depression and the Hopkins Symptom Checklist. However, the changes observed were not limited to the client's self-report of current symptoms of depression as measured by these instruments; they were also evident to the clinical judges and on a client self-report measure of diverse physical and psychological symptoms. The growing importance of clinical significance is reflected in a special issue of *Behavioural Assessment* devoted to the topic (1988) and to continuing refinement of the methodology (Jacobson & Truax, 1991).

A variation on the statistical method for calculating the clinical significance of an outcome is to estimate the 'number-needed-to-treat' (NNT) in order to achieve a particular clinical outcome (Gray, 1997). The NNT has become a popular measure of the effectiveness of interventions, being easier to understand than statistical calculations and providing a ready comparison of different treatments. The NNT describes the benefits of an intervention, based on the difference between specific outcome for control and experimental groups. For example, assume that 100 people were members of a carer support network, resulting in improved mood for 70 of them. A further 100 were allocated randomly to a control group, resulting in improved mood for only 20 of them. From these data, it appears that membership of the network is responsible for 50 of these 100 people obtaining relief. That is, 50% or an improvement of 50 per 100 (0.5). The NNT figure is obtained by dividing one by this value (i.e. the proportion benefiting), which gives an NNT of 2 and indicates that one of every two carers attending the support network will benefit.

MEASURING INTERVENTIONS: THE 'MANIPULATION CHECK'

As noted earlier in this chapter, an increasingly recognised part of sound evaluation is to assess whether or not a social support or other intervention was actually conducted in conformity to the specifications of that intervention. This is referred to variously as a 'manipulation check', 'treatment fidelity assessment' and the 'integrity of the independent variable assessment'. This reflects the idea that accurate and reliable description and observation of both the independent and dependent variables are necessary if one is to accurately establish a functional relationship between an intervention and an outcome (Peterson *et al.*, 1982). A number of dimensions have been suggested for the operationalisation of an intervention, including the adherence to a specific approach; the skill or proficiency with which the approach was administered; and the interpersonal effectiveness of the practitioner involved (Schaffer, 1982; Waltz *et al.*, 1993). Careful assessment of these three facets of an intervention can contribute significantly to a better understanding of whether and why our interventions work.

As noted by Waltz *et al.* (1993), assessments of the manipulation are rare. From their survey they found that only about a quarter of recently completed outcome studies used a specific treatment protocol, and of these less than half reported the amount of training or the nature of training; finally, only 13% provided documentation of the therapist's competence. Peterson *et al.* (1982) obtained similarly unsatisfactory results for a survey of several hundred articles published in the *Journal of Applied Behaviour Analysis*. The majority of these articles did not assess the implementation of the manipulation, and in a sizeable minority of cases the manipulation was not operationally defined. Even when there was a definition, no reliability checks were made to see that the manipulation occurred as defined. Examples of how manipulation checks can be conducted in a variety of settings relevant to social support are now provided.

Therapeutic interventions

A number of studies have attempted to demonstrate that the therapy provided within a research programme has fidelity. To illustrate, Startup and Shapiro (1993) assessed whether or not five therapists provided the 'prescriptive' and 'exploratory' therapies according to the respective treatment manuals. This was measured by the Sheffield Psychotherapy Rating Scale (SPRS) a system for coding the verbal utterances of therapists according to 59 items (for example 'assessing cognitive processes', 'setting homework', 'exploring feelings' and 'acknowledging affect'). The SPRS was applied to audio recordings of hour-long therapy sessions and it was found that the raters could reliably observe therapist's speech using the rating scale. More crucially, the analysis showed that the two broad forms of intervention could be differentiated almost perfectly, even though the same five therapists delivered them both. Adherence to the two approaches was also very good and did not seem to vary with the severity of the client's symptoms.

Family-based interventions

In a study by Kavanagh *et al.* (1993), therapists in standard health care settings in Australia were trained to deliver a cognitive behavioural intervention to clients and their families. Follow-up assessments taking place between 6 months and 3 years following this training were reported for a sample of 45 therapists. They reported on the number of families that they had systematically treated and the difficulties that they had encountered. According to this self-report survey, although over 80% of these therapists said they had applied elements of the intervention at least once per month, the frequencies for the cognitive and behavioural strategies fell below 40%. This indicated significant problems in disseminating the approach with fidelity to multidisciplinary settings in routine health care. The therapists indicated that amongst the difficulties in adhering to the approach was the problem of integrating family work with other responsibilities and interests, including freeing up enough time to undertake the intervention properly and the impact of staff illness or holidays on scheduling.

In a similar vein Fadden (1997) surveyed 86 therapists who had received behavioural family therapy training in the UK. Seventy percent of these respondents reported that they had used the approach in their work, but that the mean number of families seen per therapist was only 1.7. Forty percent of the families that had been seen were treated by only 8% of the trained therapists. Furthermore, a common system for maximising adherence, the use of regular supervision from a more experienced expert, was a problem for 46% of this sample. A long list of obstacles that interfered with their proper implementation of the behavioural family therapy were reported by these therapists. The most common of these was the unavailability of appropriate clients, followed by problems integrating the specialised treatment with the existing case load and other responsibilities, and by challenges in engaging clients or their families. A further 30 difficulties were recounted. This challenge of implementing treatments with fidelity will be discussed in the final chapter.

Programme integrity

Problems identified at the level of individual or family therapy also appear to arise at the level of a service system. McGrew et al. (1994), for instance, developed an index of fidelity for assessing Assertive Community Treatment programmes. They interviewed 22 experts in ACT, being individuals who had actively participated in ACT research, had held clinical and administrative positions within ACT programmes, and who were involved in implementing ACT programmes. In an initial study these experts rated the importance of 73 elements proposed as critical to ACT, also indicating ideal model specification for these elements. This led to a high level of agreement on the importance of these elements between the experts. In a second study, a 17 item summary of these critical ingredients was used to construct a fidelity index covering 3 subscales; staffing, organisation and services. Analysis of individual programmes over time indicated that there was a significant trend for the later generations of programme to drift away from the standard ACT programme.

In a similar kind of review, Dane and Schneider (1998) studied whether programme adherence was verified and promoted in evaluations of primary and early secondary prevention programmes for a series of studies conducted between 1980 and 1994. They found that only 39 of 162 such outcome studies featured specified methods for assessing adherence, and only 13 of these considered variations in adherence in drawing conclusions about the effectiveness of their programmes. Not surprisingly, it was found that lower adherence was often associated with poorer outcome. Dane and Schneider (1998) concluded that the omission of adherence data may compromise the internal validity of these outcome studies.

As these authors also noted, although there is widespread acceptance of the need to undertake manipulation checks, there is less agreement about precisely which variables should be included within such an analysis. Currently a number of dimensions have been identified, including adherence, dosage, quality of delivery, responsiveness and intervention differentiation. They advocated that researchers should ideally monitor all of these factors and conduct correlational analyses to see which of them contributes most to our understanding of the independent variable. At this stage, there is some evidence to suggest that the correlation between these various facets of a manipulation is substantial.

Dane and Schneider (1998) also drew attention to an important issue for mental health practitioners, which they refer to as the fidelity/adaptation debate. This refers to differing opinions about the feasibility and desirability of attempting to promote and verify manipulations. While researchers may wish to ensure that interventions are administered with high fidelity, the tight prescription of interventions (often developed without full knowledge of the needs and conditions under which they will be implemented) can conflict with the interests of those in a particular setting, including staff and users. For instance, rigid insistence on the strict adherence to a programme procedure may lead to animosity and ineffective implementation. The solution is a compromise labelled 'pro-adaptation' in which the local site is encouraged to make minor modifications to the intervention to accommodate local needs. The crucial issue is whether or not critical features of an intervention are retained and delivered as appropriate. By implication, intervention manuals should explicate those ingredients of the intervention that are crucial and inflexible versus those that are secondary and more flexible.

Example from social support interventions

The general principles outlined above apply equally strongly to interventions within the social support sphere. Although reviews of implementation checks have not, to the author's knowledge, been conducted in the social support field, it is likely that many of the same problems also pertain. How might a mental health practitioner conduct a manipulation check within the social support sphere? The work of Paul Toro and colleagues provides a couple of helpful examples. In one of these, Toro *et al.* (1987) analysed the social climates of mutual help and psychotherapy groups. The 22 mutual help groups in the study came from an organisation known as GROW International, which encourages the development of support networks and helps members adjust to community living. One hundred and seventy members of GROW groups completed a social climate measure, the Group Environment Scale (Moos *et al.*, 1974), as did members of 25 psychotherapy groups drawn from inpatient and outpatient settings. Comparisons between the replies of members of both groups indicated significant differences on 9 of the 10 Group Environment Scale dimensions. The mutual help members saw their groups as being higher in cohesion, leader support, independence, task orientation, order and organisation, and leader control; they were perceived as lower in expressiveness, anger and aggression, and innovation. This pattern of results is consistent in a broad way with the intentions of the two approaches, particularly since the majority of the psychotherapy groups were led by professionals adopting a psychodynamic perspective and who therefore valued the insight and the expression of negative feelings.

In a second illustration, Roberts *et al.* (1991) developed a system for observing mutual help meetings which encompassed such activities as helping behaviours, providing support, offering interpretations, suggesting ways to deal with problems, questioning, task orientation, help seeking and affective responses (agreeing or disagreeing with opinions). Roberts *et al.* (1991) found that observers could use the observation system to reliably code the 12 categories observed within the observation system. The results from administering the system indicated that the most frequent activities in the mutual help groups were information giving, impersonal questions and interpretation.

Profiles of this kind can be used to assess whether or not a social support group corresponds to its intended function, which would include relatively high levels of certain observed factors (providing support and self-disclosing) and lower frequencies of events likely to hinder the success of such a group (for example disagreeing or negative comments). Roberts *et al.* (1991) did indeed find this sort of profile, in that members tended to be supportive of one another during the meetings and that positive supportive events were seven times more frequent than their negative counterparts. This corresponds with the idea that a mutual help group creates a safe, supportive and benign environment for members.

Mental health practitioners interested in facilitating or supporting mutual help groups would therefore be able to use a system such as this to determine whether or not the group is indeed operating with fidelity, an important component of quality research.

MEASURING OUTCOMES: CHOOSING APPROPRIATE INSTRUMENTS

A second of the major challenges facing community support programmes defined by Durbin et al. (1995) is to select measurement domains and tools. The penultimate section of Chapter 4 already defines some criteria for a good instrument with which to measure social support, using the CORE instrument as a case in point. That chapter also includes numerous options for the service evaluator. The purpose of this section is to clarify a framework for selecting an instrument, including some of the key questions that one would wish to ask when determining which instrument is the most appropriate tool for the particular job in hand.

One of the problems facing the mental health practitioner is the sheer volume and diversity of measurement domains that are emphasised by different researchers. This can include physical, material and emotional well-being; quality of life; service costs; citizenship; civic involvement; personal fulfilment; hopefulness; development of loving relationships; self determination; self-esteem; daily health habits and functional effectiveness levels; psychological processes in illness; processes of natural recovery from illness; responses to controlled laboratory inductions (for example stress tests); prevention and health promotion (lifestyle process and outcome); socio-economic conditions affecting health (for example poverty and overcrowding); health care utilisation and compliance; and ecological hazards to health (for example pollutants). Within the NHS, six key areas for research and evaluation have been defined. They are a service's 'equity' (fair share of resources for all the population, based on their needs), 'appropriateness' (the service provided is what is required), 'accessibility' (needy groups are not excluded), 'effectiveness' (achieving the intended benefits), 'acceptability' (satisfying reasonable expectations) and 'efficiency' (maximum benefits from financial and other resources) (Department of Health, 1992). Each of these service objectives can then be assessed, as in applying structure, process and outcome evaluations (Parry, 1996).

Some sense can be brought to this bewildering array of potential measurement domains by adopting broad categories such as those suggested by Larson (1997), who distinguished between the categories of clinical status, functional status, humanitarian status (life satisfaction and fulfilment) and public welfare, including safety factors and prevention of harm to the community.

To make matters even more perplexing, each domain has a multiplicity of available instruments with which to measure a person's functioning. There are literally hundreds of published instruments available with which to measure common aspects of clinical status (for example assessments of anxiety and depression), and little consistency across published studies to guide one as to which instruments might best serve one's purpose (for example allowing benchmarking to take place, i.e. comparing one's own clinical outcomes with those reported by researchers in several other countries). For example, Froyd *et al.* (1996) surveyed 334 outcome studies from 21 major journals, finding that 1430 different instruments were used, of which 850 were only used once. It was for these reasons that Barkham *et al.* (1998) developed CORE, as outlined in Chapter 4.

Measurement: coping strategies for practitioners

A couple of helpful ways to cope with this diversity of options is to focus down on a limited number of considerations, and to do so in a stepwise fashion. Although there are a multiplicity of measurement domains, fortunately there does appear to be considerable consensus about those which should have pre-eminence, particularly the symptomatic status of the index patient. In this spirit, Roth and Fonagy (1996) proposed that evaluators use more than one measure to determine outcome and that this includes measuring different symptoms domains (such as affect, cognition and behaviour). They also suggest that practitioners should select instruments that take account of different perspectives on a problem (such as those of the relatives, the patient or friends) and also consider different domains of functioning (such as work and social performance). In the scientific literature this would be referred to as a 'multi-method' and 'multiple measure' approach, one that is desirable because it minimises the probability of arriving at an erroneous conclusion. To these three issues one can add several others that have gained wide acceptance in the research literature, as summarised in Table 8.5.

It can be seen that Table 8.5 incorporates the three dimensions emphasised by Roth and Fonagy (1996), while adding three additional dimensions for consideration, incorporating the multi-method approach (Clifford, 1998). Where possible, these are related to social support variables. In a further effort to facilitate the use of these instruments, the great majority of them have been drawn from two readily accessible portfolios,

Table 8.5   A summary of the outcome dimensions, with example instruments. Based on Ogles and Lunnen (1996), and Roth and Fonagy (1996).

Dimensions	Illustrative instruments related to social support
1. *Focus of assessment*	
• Thoughts	Coping Responses Inventory (Part 1: stressors: Moos, 1990)*
• Feelings	Daily hassles and uplifts (i.e. minor stressors: Kanner *et al.*, 1981)*
• Behaviours	Padua Inventory (obsessional-compulsive disorders: Sanavio, 1988)*
2. *Purpose of assessment*	
• Diagnosis (problem definition; classification; prediction)	Barthel Index (Mahoney & Barthel, 1965)[†]
• Monitoring change (intervention feedback; decision-making—e.g. assisting inter-agency communication)	Self-monitoring techniques (Johnston *et al.*, 1995)[†]
• Multi-site outcome evaluation (reviewing approach; bench-marking; cost–benefits; accountability; audit)	Interview Satisfaction Scale (Wolf *et al.*, 1978)[†]
3. *Domains of functioning*	
• Intrapersonal (clinical)	The Hospital Anxiety & Depression Scale (Zigmond & Snaith, 1983)*
• Interpersonal (proximal)	Inventory of Interpersonal Problems (Horowitz *et al.*, 1988)*
• Societal (distal)	Social Network Schedule (Becker *et al.*, 1997)
4. Perspectives	
• Client	Coping Responses Inventory (Moos, 1990)*
• Significant other	Golombok Rust Inventory of Marital State (Rust *et al.*, 1988)*
• Therapist/observer (e.g. multi-disciplinary team)	Clinical Anxiety Scale (Snaith *et al.*, 1982)*
5. *Data collection method*	
• Self-report (e.g. questionnaire; interview)	Significant Others Scale (Power *et al.*, 1988)*
• Independent observation, ratings or psychometric tests	Inventory of Depressive Symptomatology: Clinician Rated (Rush *et al.*, 1986)*
• Permanent products and archival records	*Ad hoc* tangible outcomes (e.g. work done)

Table 8.5   *(continued)*

Dimensions	Illustrative instruments related to social support
6. *Time point*	
• Past	The General Health Questionnaire (Goldberg, 1978)*
• Present	Community Oriented Programmes Environment Scale (Moos, 1987)
• Future	Goal Attainment Scale (Kiresuk & Sherman, 1968)

* denotes that this instrument is available in Milne (1992a);
† denotes this instrument is in Johnston *et al.*, 1995.

from which the defined tools can be photocopied, scored and interpreted with much greater ease than is possible through most published accounts of instruments.

Although fairly exhaustive, it should be recognised that even the dimensions listed in Table 8.5 do not cover all possible options. For example there may be occasions when physical examinations (invasive or non-invasive) and physiological analyses would be appropriate (e.g. bio feedback). However, the table does provide a very broad and adequate context for the likely range of work for a mental health practitioner interested in social support.

Step by step

Although one might surmise that most mental health practitioners will make occasional use of at least one of the kinds of instruments listed in Table 8.5, it would appear unusual for them to use instruments in a systematic way to evaluate services, whether in the social support field or under more routine conditions (Milne, 1987). A good coping strategy for progressing to a more appropriate way of measuring outcome is to develop one's approach in a gradual fashion. A good outline of such an approach has been provided by Elliott (1995) who produced a table of suggested measurement options in order of difficulty, progressing from least to most time consuming or intrusive. He suggested that three domains should be measured in relation to psychotherapy process research, namely the treatment outcomes, the therapeutic processes and the change processes. Each of these had a hierarchy of instrument options, proceeding from those that were easiest for the practitioner to introduce to those that were most demanding. To illustrate, in order to measure treatment outcomes one could start by using one widely used instrument before and after an intervention, such as the Beck Depression Inventory. On top of this, at some point one might use measures that also tap the stressors, coping and social support that contribute to a person's distress. One might then use the assessments more frequently, as in providing a diary for a client to complete on a weekly basis. To this one might then add a larger sample, and so forth. The same thing applies to measurement of therapy or change process, in that one could simply start by recording sessions on audiotape and then listening to these in a reflective way; as one becomes more systematic tapes could be coded in relation to specific instruments, such as the Sheffield Psychotherapy Project Rating Scale, as touched on earlier in this chapter.

The same developmental logic could be applied to service programmes, such as ones designed to facilitate social support in a neighbourhood. Schlenger *et al.* (1994) have described a multi-stage approach to such evaluations, and this also stresses how practitioners can gradually extend their use of dependent variables to successively develop a more comprehensive assessment of the outcomes of a programme. This builds on lessons learned over the months and years, as well as recognising the need to increase resources. In this sense, a key issue for those who wish to measure the impact of their interventions is to work collaboratively, a point to which we will return in the next section.

Which instrument?

In the spirit of working progressively towards more and more sophisticated approaches to the measurement of outcome, Table 8.6 provides a checklist of five fundamental questions to raise about instruments that a mental health practitioner may be considering applying. Although brief, this checklist does outline a healthy range of the kinds of measurement issues that have taxed researchers in mental health practice over the years.

Various authors have provided summaries of the available instruments in different fields. In terms of adult mental health, they include Groth-Marnat (1990), Hersen and Bellack (1998), Peck and Shapiro (1991), Thompson (1989) and Thornicroft and Tansella (1996). For example, the latter includes tools that can be used to assess global functioning, patient satisfaction, family and caregiver burden, quality of life, quality of care, social disability and needs assessment.

MAKING A DIFFERENCE: COLLABORATION AND FEEDBACK IN EVALUATION

Two of the additional challenges identified by Durbin *et al.* (1995) were to involve clients and to engage staff in the evaluation process. It is to these

Table 8.6   A checklist for selecting between different instruments (based on Karoly, 1985; Lipsey, 1990; Milne, 1987).

Question	Suggestions for finding an answer
1. *Does the instrument measure what I want to measure?*	Focus on variables that are defined as part of well-established conceptual models (e.g. stress, coping, social support and distress within the transactional stress model) and which are expected to change with the intervention.
2. *Is it a sound instrument?*	Select instruments with good reliability (i.e. providing a consistent assessment) and validity (i.e. measuring what the instrument is supposed to measure).
3. *Will the instrument be sensitive to improvement?*	Choose a specific instrument, with fine-grained units of assessment (e.g. five point bipolar rating scales), adapted to your sample (i.e. beware 'floor' and 'ceiling' effects) and apply it so as to assess peak response to the intervention.
4. *How can I fit it in to my assessment?*	Prioritise readily available, brief, easily scored and interpreted instruments (see Table 8.5). Start with simple measurement tasks (e.g. one self-report questionnaire before and after intervention).
5. *Why should I bother—what are the benefits?*	Good outcome data can contribute to client and professional feedback (i.e. additional knowledge of results), provide accountability data, aid decision-making, represent an intervention in its own right, and help to develop reflective and evidence-based practice.

issues that I now turn, noting that the remaining challenge that those authors identified (obtaining a suitable sample of participants) is unlikely to be an issue for mental health practitioners.

Perhaps one reason for the rather limited involvement of mental health practitioners in evaluating the outcomes of their programmes and interventions has been the under-utilisation of the results by the organisations in which they operate. It has been suggested that evaluators have not sufficiently taken into account the needs of other parties or stakeholders, for example by failing to recognise important elements in the way a programme is operated or evaluated with respect to the different kinds of organisations (Rogers & Hough, 1995). In a helpful table, these authors illustrated how four different kinds of organisational set-up may influence the kinds of answers that are deemed relevant by powerful figures within those organisations. For example, a traditional management hierarchy system (such as one would find in the NHS), would tend to regard the purpose of an evaluation as working towards achieving the objectives of a programme within the budget. By contrast, working in less well-established, community-based organisations, the objectives may be closer to those of determining how to get things done, gaining control over resources, or achieving political ends. As Ciarlo and Windle (1988) put it:

> ... frustration at seeing one's work neglected or even misused in programme administration is both expectable and understandable; what is not acceptable ... is naivety that assumes the automatic, well intentioned, and thoughtful consideration of one's evaluative efforts by those for whom the evaluation is intended. (p. 114)

In addition to naivety about one's organisation's interests in data, there has also been naivety regarding partnership and the way that information from an evaluation is disseminated. These are now discussed, in an effort to encourage a more effective way of working.

Stakeholder collaboration

As indicated by Figure 8.2, far from the traditional model whereby a researcher, based in some academic 'ivory tower', heroically conducts research against all the odds, the stakeholder collaborative process is one that is highly integrated with and dependent upon other key individuals for the success of the evaluation.

Recognising the advice of Rogers and Hough (1995), Figure 8.2 illustrates that one commences with some appropriate organisational support, leading to involvement in selecting who should carry out the evaluation and involvement in clarifying the goals or objectives of the evaluation. This in turn leads to the selection of a steering group, composed of clients, staff and others with an interest in an intervention. Together they define the problem that the evaluation is to focus on, and they then collaborate closely on the instruments to be used, the collection of information and the interpretation of the results (Ayers, 1987).

In contrast to the 'ivory tower' researcher, the role of the mental health practitioner in this stakeholder collaborative evaluation process is to:

- develop preliminary proposals for the evaluation design;
- act as a group facilitator and generator of ideas;
- re-word, clarify and specify questions generated by the steering group;
- list instruments for the steering group's consideration;
- collect, analyse and, with the group, interpret the data;
- synthesise the findings into usable conclusions for the organisation and other stakeholders;

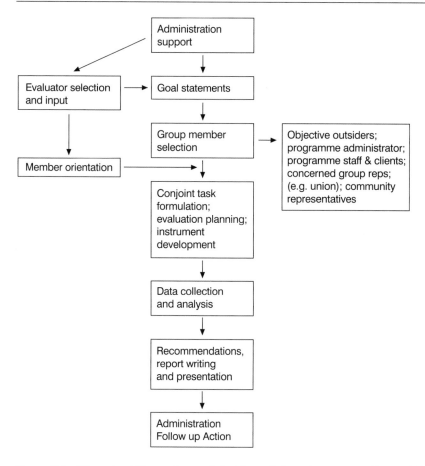

Figure 8.2   Flow chart illustrating stakeholder collaborative process (Ayers, 1987)

- draft a report and facilitate a redraft; and
- disseminate the report effectively;

This stakeholder collaborative approach has a number of costs and bene-fits. Amongst the costs are the extra time and energy required to engage with a steering group, working with unclear role boundaries and group membership, decreased evaluator autonomy, as well as the possibility of political interference and abuse. On the benefits side, however, the results of any such evaluation are likely to enjoy greater acceptance by interested parties and result in greater generalisation. Another factor relevant to the present chapter is that by engaging other people, the expertise of the eval-uator is less critical than in the traditional solo research model. Furthermore, evaluations are often 'formative' rather than one-off 'summative' analyses. That is, one evaluation should lead to another, gradually developing the technology and improving the intervention. This gives mental health practitioners the opportunity to develop competencies in evaluation, initially perhaps working alongside more experienced colleagues. Similarly, in this way more seasoned intervention evaluators amongst mental health practitioners may empower such stakeholders as clients to conduct evaluations of their own neighbourhood issues. A helpful step-by-step account of this process is provided by Papineau and Kiely (1996) who provided a detailed breakdown of a participatory evaluation process in a community organisation. Similarly, Greene (1987) has also set out the tasks and steps in a very detailed and helpful way, adding an evaluation of what stakeholders made of this process. To do this, she used a seven-item semantic differential scale with a series of bipolar terms (such as 'useful' and 'useless'; 'worthwhile' and 'worthless'; and a 'good learning experience' versus a 'waste of time'). She reported that her sample of collaborators provided a qualified confirmation of the value of participation in evaluation, noting how it helped them learn about the intervention, provided opportunities for reflecting upon it, and led to pleasurable feelings (e.g. feeling good that one's concerns were being sought out, and realising that one is not alone).

In summary, effective practice in intervention evaluation is a collaborative, developmental approach. This contrasts rather starkly with the caricature of traditional research provided by Gale (1985):

> Research ... conjures up images of beautiful scientists in white coats making brilliant discoveries. The world applauds as the King of Sweden hands over the Nobel Prize to a distinguished yet shy recipient. The prize is a large cash sum ... an appropriate reward for dedication to higher purposes ... for the scientist ... is married to truth.' (p. 187).

Providing a suitable report

Even with a successful collaborative group behind an evaluation, there remains a need to communicate the findings in a way that serves as feedback to other interested parties. Far too often, mental health practitioners have produced weighty tomes that are inaccessible to interested parties. According to Tash and Stahler (1982) one can enhance the use of one's findings by recognising the need to identify the user audience and by tailoring recommendations to such groups; by formulating any recommendations collaboratively with those audiences (e.g. by having a presentation and discussion meeting); by directing specific recommendations towards the development of specific programme changes; by assessing the impact of any recommendations over time; and by making an effort to present recommendations in an empathetic way.

An instrument has actually been developed with which one could assess some of these aspects of a written report. Russon and Koehly (1995) developed the Communication Process Scales to rate the persuasive impact of evaluation reports upon decision-makers. The scales consist of 28 Likert scale items measuring the following variables:

- attention (e.g. how wordy the report is);
- liking (e.g. how imaginative the report is);
- comprehension (e.g. containing too much information for ready understanding);
- generating related understanding (providing clear data summaries);
- learning how (e.g. ideas on ways to improve an intervention);
- attitude (e.g. how important the message is for the readership's orientation to the intervention); and
- decision-making (making acceptable recommendations).

It should be clear from these guidelines and suggestions that undertaking a successful evaluation is no simple matter. Indeed, it is a full-time profession for some specialists. However, the emphasis in this section has been upon a developmental approach, in which mental health practitioners build upon their existing skills (e.g. those derived from the assessment of the individual client) so that they can apply these self same skills at a systems level (e.g. a carers group). The principles of assessments at the individual or systems level are fundamentally identical, as illustrated by the need to select one's assessment tool with care and to use it longitudinally and formatively, both to guide oneself as an evaluator and to guide the intervention with which one is involved. In so doing, one is guided by the outcomes, such as beneficial symptomatic and other changes in the client and desirable changes in the status of a system (e.g. improved social environment in a self-help group).

Good examples of the kinds of outcomes one should look for in a service or system level intervention are that collaborators are aware of an evaluation and of its findings; that they can put this knowledge to some conceptual use (e.g. facilitating reflection on the objectives of an intervention); that it has some perceived value (e.g. the findings are instrumental in decision-making or planning); that this leads to some symbolic or practical outcomes (such as demonstrating the viability of an intervention to funding bodies or helping with implementing practical plans on site); and, finally, that the impact or consequences are desirable to staff, users and other relevant individuals in a system, such as a neighbourhood (Milne & Kennedy, 1993; Papineau & Kiely, 1996).

SUMMARY AND CONCLUSIONS

This chapter has covered a very large terrain, beginning with some philosophical issues about the nature of 'quality' in the evaluation of interventions and concluding with some very pragmatic suggestions about how to feed back the results of an evaluation. As per many other chapters within this book, I have been profoundly aware of the impossibility of doing justice to the full range of methods and possibilities, this time in the sphere of research and evaluation. However, if nothing else, this chapter should serve as a useful foundation for mental health practitioners to engage in more frequent and more systematic evaluation of their social support interventions.

The content of research

From the foregoing, two major conclusions stand out as meriting attention. The first of these concerns the fundamental structure of evaluations, and this has helpfully been summarised by Roth and Fonagy (1996). They drew the distinction between four broad content questions that are highly topical in today's mental health services. These are effectiveness questions, and assume that researchers in centres of excellence nationally are taking care of the efficacy questions.

Question 1:   *What is the right thing to do?*

This question should be answered from efficacy research and placed into clinical guidelines, protocols and intervention manuals, as in those manuals provided for 'prescriptive' and 'exploratory' therapies by the Sheffield Psychotherapy Project (Shapiro & Firth, 1987).

Question 2:   *Has the right thing been done?*

This issue can be addressed by mental health practitioners by means of clinical audit and by carrying out manipulation checks as detailed earlier in this chapter. Key questions concern whether one is adhering appropriately to a guideline or manual, as illustrated by the Cognitive Therapy Scale approach of checking adherence against a 'red line'.

Question 3:   *Has it been done right?*

Complementing the above analysis of adherence, one should also assess how competently an intervention has been implemented. This would include measuring the proficiency or skill with which one delivers a treatment, together with the interpersonal effectiveness of such an intervention. Although not discussed in this chapter, the conventional way to assess interpersonal effectiveness would be through the use of consumer satisfaction surveys (e.g. Stallard, 1994; 1996).

Question 4: *Did it result in the right outcome?*

This question takes us back to the selection and administration of appropriate dependent variables, as enumerated in Tables 8.5 and 8.6. The right outcome is what theory and prior research would predict from the competent administration of a treatment. It should also be benchmarked against those outcomes obtained by other practitioners in other parts of the country (e.g. percentage of patients with clinically significant improvements following a social therapy intervention). However, perhaps the most important benchmark is one's own prior outcomes, in the sense that effective evaluation practice is cumulative, developing both the technology of measurement and the process of evaluation over time.

The process of research

The final conclusion that appears to follow from this chapter is how the research process needs to complement its content. That is, just as social supporters are empowered within the mental health field for mutual benefit, so mental health practitioners are also empowered as researchers and evaluators, for the benefit of themselves, their services and their users. This comes close to the model of evidence-based practice, which will be discussed in the final chapter. However, as far as this chapter is concerned, the action research model summarised in the first section provides a clear statement of how we can participate collaboratively with others in a problem-solving cycle, one that uses the methods of science to guide us to better interventions over time. Such a process not only engages more of us in evidence-based practice, but also promises greater utilisation of the knowledge that comes from evaluating our interventions. Similarly, it can empower our users by providing them with rich information and even competences in conducting their own evaluations in the future. In this sense, even if one's evaluation focused on traditional mental health interventions, such as the value of drop-in mental health centres in the community, one could conceivably still be engaging in a form of social support intervention.

Chapter 9

REFLECTIONS AND IMPLICATIONS

INTRODUCTION: TIME TO GET INTO TROUBLE?

Social support is of profound importance to wellbeing and so researchers as well as professionals need to study its nature and test out ways to foster it. To illustrate, in 1992 the Health of the Nation had as one of its major mental illness objectives that services improve significantly the health and social functioning of mentally ill people. At the most fundamental personal level, social support is related to an individual's growth, in that perceiving the world as supportive makes exploration and reasonable risk taking more likely, and high levels of anxiety and self-preoccupation less likely (Sarason *et al.*, 1990). Through taking reasonable risks and succeeding people develop new competences and confidence, extend their social support encounters, and learn to thrive. In general terms, this has been described as 'the art of getting into trouble'! This seemingly paradoxical phrase is explained by Newbrough (1993, p. 166) (the sexist language is in the original).

> Life is always problematic and what you become will rest in no small measure on the kinds of problem situations that you get yourself into and have to work yourself out of ... It is deep in the nature of man to make problems for himself. Man has often been called the problem-solver, but he is even more the problem-maker. Every noble achievement ... represents a new synopsis of the human experience, deepening our understanding and enriching our spirit. But each solid noble achievement creates new problems, often of unexpected dimension and man moves eagerly on to face these new complexities and to impose his order upon them. And so it will be, world without end.

To know a person, it is useful to know what she or he has done, which is another way of defining what problems have been solved. It is even more informative, however, to know what problems people are working on now, for these will define the growing edge of their being. In practice, professionals who either provide social support to their patients or help them to be better elicitors of social support are therefore defining a 'problem'. A critical challenge for the professional is to make such problems close to their current range of competence, so that success and enhanced confidence can be achieved.

What are the situations of just manageable difficulty for mental health professionals in relation to social support? What can they do to increase the likelihood that they will solve problems in relation to social support? It has been suggested that, since it is impossible to separate our work from the social order within which it takes place (Sarason, 1981), an appropriate problem for professionals concerns the nature and consequences of the social order for their own practice. Such a vision construes mental health professionals as moving into a field of public health, as opposed to a focus on the intrapersonal determinants of mental health (Kelly, 1990). On this reasoning, just as professionals within the physical health field have demonstrated how 'at risk' patients can be identified and assisted in relation to such problems as coronary heart disease (i.e. identifying those who exercise infrequently, smoke and eat a high-fat cholesterol diet), so mental health professionals are encouraged by Kelly (1990) to identify and attend to the precursors of mental health difficulties. As he noted, a prime candidate for such a public health strategy is social support. From such an analogy, inspiring visions of our future practice can be delineated. Kelly (1990) sees practitioners as public-health-orientated professionals who are recognised as a community resource, participate in preventive interventions, develop and undertake research designed to enhance policy and practice, and engage in generally more accessible, proactive, and local community-focused approach. In this way, the long-standing ambition to 'give psychology away' (Miller, 1969) could be realised.

Plausible and even inspiring as such visions are, they do not obviously represent the next achievable problem for mental health professionals. Nor do 'prescriptions' of this kind make much difference to the behaviour of mental health professionals, any more than they are likely to modify the behaviour of their patients. For these reasons, the next two sections of this chapter provide a more psychologically informed approach to developing our practice. Only by a more thoughtful approach are professionals likely to engage more frequently and effectively in social therapy. In essence, if we are to get deeper into the kind of trouble that grappling with social support problems entails, we need to be unusually reflexive in our approach. Reflexivity refers to the application of the kinds of principles and methods that mental health professionals would use with their patients to themselves (e.g. a gradual approach to problem resolution).

COPING STRATEGIES FOR PROFESSIONALS

Many articles and texts have encouraged professionals to play a more active role in promoting social support. For instance, the main text that relates to the present one (Gottlieb, 1983) concluded by noting that professionals need to recognise that their work represents only a fraction of the pool of resources available to citizens and to recognise their role in supplementing such resources. However, this otherwise marvellous introduction to the kind of work we might do in the social support field did not detail how we might ensure that we actually conduct this important work. While providing fairly inspirational and practical information to professionals may result in a small proportion of them toying with a new approach, it is unlikely to prove successful. Since the earliest analyses of innovation, it has been recognised that:

> There is nothing more difficult to carry out, nor more doubtful of success, nor more dangerous to handle than to initiate a new order of things. (Machiavelli, *circa* 1513)

A popular and more recent attempt to tackle the innovation challenge is referred to as the 'myth of the hero innovator' (Georgiades & Phillimore, 1975). The myth is that through training or other means we can create veritable knights in shining armour who will bring about changes in organisations at a stroke. As these authors noted, such a view is over-simplistic; the fact of the matter is that large organisations, such as hospitals, will, like dragons, eat hero innovators for breakfast. To counteract this unpleasant consequence, Georgiades and Phillimore (1975) propose six guidelines for a more successful approach to innovation. Some of these guidelines are most relevant at the individual level, while others are more to do with service systems and larger organisational units. For convenience, these two levels will be tackled separately, starting in this section with strategies for coping with change at the level of the individual professional and his or her immediate colleagues.

A broad coping strategy: be reflexive

Reflexivity in professional practice is surprisingly uncommon. It has been suggested that the scarcity of reflexive accounts of professional practice reflects a somewhat elitist stance. But if we have a theory of human behaviour, then surely it should be applied to professionals as well as to the rest of the world, and to behave as if this were not true can make us look ridiculous (Bernstein, 1995). It can also make us appear clumsy, in the sense that we have ignored approaches which have both empirical support and with which we have considerable fluency and competence. To illustrate reflexivity, Gale (1990) applied psychology to the psychology degree, concluding that it deserved not so much first class honours as a miserable failure. To obtain a better class of degree, Gale asked what aspects of psychological know-how could be applied to the way that we teach students on psychology degree programmes. Amongst the numerous answers that he was able to generate to this profound question from psychology itself were such things as developing selection assessments that had predictive validity, applying methods of learning that fostered intellectual enjoyment and reinforcement from a system, not to mention developing better systems for continuous assessment and feedback.

Based on such reflexivity, the wise professional would undertake an assessment and formulation of his or her own behaviour in order to better understand the variables that contribute to both the status quo and to incremental developments in his or her practice (see for an example Milne & Paxton, 1998). In contrast to sweeping visions and naive prescriptions, this strategy would include a clear recognition of those factors that represent barriers and disincentives to change in professional practice. Consider, by contrast, the advice of the Working Party of the College of General Practitioners (see Goldberg & Huxley, 1980) whose advice to GPs was that they should engage more in what was termed 'simple psychotherapy' based on a tolerant attitude and a general counselling approach to patients. The report of the working party admitted that this advice may be hard to implement in large urban practices, but nevertheless insisted that the better the doctors the nearer they approached it.

A helpful step beyond such exhortation and prescription has been indicated in the study by Fadden (1997) which analysed some of the barriers to a professional's engagement in behavioural family therapy. In trying to make sense of the low level of implementation of this therapy following careful training, she summarised the results of a survey of 86 trained therapists. This indicated that their greatest obstacles included

- unavailability of appropriate clients;
- difficulty integrating family work with caseload and other responsibilities;
- engaging clients or families;
- insufficient time allowed from the service to do the therapy;
- non-applicability of the therapy to the needs of specific families; and
- limited knowledge and skills in family intervention.

As per other similar surveys, Fadden (1997) did however note that a number of opportunities and reinforcers also existed for engaging in family therapy, such as collaboration with a co-therapist and a clear intervention manual. This reflects another of the guidelines promulgated by Georgiades and Phillimore (1975), who noted that some factors and individuals are actually supportive of professional change. These might be referred to as 'the natural ecology' of any large system, since it is improbable that all such factors will represent barriers. Beyond a reliance on the natural ecology of a service system to provide reinforcement for professional change, it is important that individual professionals also exert some self-regulation over their own behaviour (Milne & Paxton, 1998). Table 9.1 summarises a number of ways in which professions can exert control over the development of their own practice. This is based on identifying four main avenues to change, derived from Kolb's (1984) marvellous summary of experiential learning. This identifies four main variables, namely: reflection, conceptualisation, planning and experiencing. As listed and defined in Table 9.1, these four variables can be related to a number of ways that professionals can develop their practice. Not apparent from this table is the very important fact that professionals would need to engage in the full experiential learning cycle in order to expect any real change to take place. That is, they would have to engage repeatedly in a cycle involving all four avenues to change, and in addition they would probably require a package of the change methods listed under the examples in order to make important changes.

Table 9.1 draws on a number of helpful accounts of changing professional behaviour, which are broadly part of the current emphasis on 'evidence-based practice' (Roth & Fonagy, 1996). Evidence-based practice (EBP) is the process of systematically reviewing, appraising and using clinical research findings to aid the delivery of optimum clinical care to patients (Rosenburg & Donald, 1995). As set out by Roth and Fonagy (1996), EBP is to be supported by a range of methods, including relevant research, clinical guidelines, consensus amongst clinicians as to best practice and continuing professional development. EBP should be followed by audits, designed to ensure that the practice corresponds to some predetermined standards; and to clinical benchmarking studies, which establish the relative effectiveness of local practice. Ultimately, EBP and its supports are intended to improve the quality of care to our patients. In addition to the EBP logic, Table 9.1 also draws on ideas for disseminating good practice from the Department of Health (1995) and from the service innovation literature (Porras & Hoffer, 1986).

Where is the evidence?

Although the approach encapsulated in Table 9.1 is much more reflexive than simply prescribing or advocating new ways of working, there is not

Table 9.1   Ways that professionals can change their own professional activities (based on Department of Health, 1995; Kolb, 1984; Porras & Hoffer, 1986; Roth & Fonagy, 1996)

Avenues to change	Examples
1. *Reflection* (Constructive re-interpretation of one's experience of professional practice from one's own perspective)	• Using supervision (the non-directive, 'counselling' phase). • Developing a vision of new approaches (e.g. using a reflective diary). • Collaborating with similarly minded colleagues (i.e. inquiring and reflective).
2. *Conceptualisation* (Reformulating one's experience in the light of theory, research findings, and the explanations of colleagues)	• Inquiring into alternatives (e.g. studying or discussing conflicting approaches). • Participating in continuing professional development (including various educational methods, such as workshops and reading/writing literature reviews). • Reviewing research and development activity collaboratively (e.g. clinical guidelines; clinical consensus statements).
3. *Planning* (Applying the ideas from reflection and conceptualisation so as to make choices, decisions and plan new ways of working and testing out ideas)	• Setting up clinical audit and linked feedback systems. • Devising a service evaluation. • Designing a new service (e.g. intended to reach the materially disadvantaged with new approaches).
4. *Experiencing* (Heightened awareness and acceptance of affect, related to key elements of professional practice; derived from action)	• Engaging in local consensus processes (collaborating with others to solve problems; taking lead responsibility; communicating discomfort openly—e.g. anxiety). • Experimenting with new approaches in a tentative way. • Acting as an opinion-leader or 'champion' of a new approach

a lot of convincing evidence that they would be successful. While early reviews of continuing professional development, for example, indicated that various methods such as workshops and conferences could improve the professional's competence, later and more rigorous evaluations suggested that little benefit accrued to the patient. For example, Haynes *et al.* (1984) reported that only 13% of continuing professional development analyses were based on randomised trials, and only 20% of these trials had bothered to assess the impact of continuing professional development on client outcome. Of these, only one actually demonstrated any improvement in the patient's condition as a result of continuing professional development. Subsequent reviews have been similarly cautious, tending to conclude that continuing professional development on its own may have some small benefits for the professional, but has to be combined with other interventions if it is to prove advantageous for the patient.

The evidence for a second approach to developing professional practice, the use of clinical guidelines, is also unfortunately not yet well supported by research. To illustrate, Grimshaw and Russell (1993) conducted a systematic review of 59 careful evaluations of clinical guidelines of which 55 reported improvements in the professional's clinical practice. Of these, 11 had measured the benefits for the patients, and only 9 reported statistically significant improvements. Grimshaw and Russell (1994) concluded that guidelines can improve practice and lead to health gains for patients. However, the authors noted that there was considerable variability in the performance of professionals who were following these clinical guidelines. This led them to suggest ways to improve guidelines in the future, including consensus meetings between professionals. This illustrates how different methods of promoting change amongst professionals can be integrated, as per Table 9.1.

In terms of the value of audit, the story is somewhat similar in that the initial and less systematic reviews indicated that audit and associated feedback of results could have an influence on professionals (Walshe and Buttery, 1995). However, surveys suggest that only about 20% of professionals attribute any change in their practice to audit (Robinson, 1996) and a systematic review of the 13 randomised studies located by 1988 (Lomas & Haynes, 1988) suggested that professionals' perceptions of change in their practice exaggerated actual change, and that benefits for patients had been demonstrated in only three studies.

INNOVATION IN PROFESSIONAL SERVICES

One plausible reason for the relative lack of success for the kinds of methods outlined in Table 9.1 is that they have been used in isolation, rather than as part of a systematic programme. To be reflexive once more, professionals would rarely utilise only one discrete intervention method in their work with patients, tending to prefer packages such as exemplified by anxiety management. In the same way, a reflexive approach to the development of the work done by professionals in relation to social therapy requires a more programmed approach. This brings us on to a recognition of a second related factor, namely that we must take account of the system in which the behaviour change is to take place.

Reference was made earlier in this chapter to the 'myth of the hero innovator'. What do the guidelines provided by Georgiades and Phillimore (1975) and others who have studied the process of change in organisational and professional systems indicate would be relevant in the present context? Again, a table has been used to summarise the main ideas that appear to be relevant, set out once more with what are hopefully clear examples of action that can be taken to develop the kind of system that would support change at the personal level.

Table 9.2   Important factors in the work systems of professionals, together with suggestions for creating a supportive system (based on Porras & Hoffer, 1996)

Innovation variable	Suggested actions
1. *Organisational structure* (Coordination and control elements in a system; resources; policies and procedures; information and reward systems)	• Collaboration with service partners (including policy makers). • Developing and maintaining a shared vision. • Setting up informational feedback systems (e.g. regular service satisfaction surveys).
2. *Social factors* (Norms and values; informal communication; individual factors)	• Respecting and supporting colleagues. • Shaping perceptions of 'problems' and 'solutions'. • Fostering 'evidence-based practice' and an experimental, action research approach.
3. *Technological factors* (Tools, equipment, job design, compatibility and control variables)	• Pooling, designing and devolving instruments to audit and evaluate new work practices. • Supporting social supporters. • Working in small, effective groups.
4. *Physical setting factors* (Configuration of work space; work ambience or 'atmosphere')	• Creating neighbourhood teams, based in pivotal places (e.g. high rise flats). • Developing environments that foster creativity and involvement (e.g. open-plan offices; coffee periods, for chatting)

The list of innovation variables identified in Table 9.2 are obviously only one possible way of defining important factors in a work system. Similarly, the suggested actions in the right-hand column of Table 9.2 imply consistently that mental health professionals should exercise a significant degree of self-regulation. In reality, it is reasonable to assume that others, such as service managers and purchasing health authorities, will also play a significant role in creating an environment that is conducive to change. Of course, since the actions of professionals cannot occur in some kind of vacuum, it is highly probable that even were other groups disinterested in fostering change, then the activity of professionals (along the lines suggested by Table 9.2) would result in an interaction effect, resulting in greater participation and involvement from other groups. This is indicated in a study by West (1989), which analysed innovation amongst 92 health visitors. The results indicated that they had engaged in a significant level of innovation over the past year: 38% had changed their work objectives, 31% had changed their work methods, and a further 17% had changed their working relationships. Amongst the barriers to their innovation were over-work and time pressures, lack of resources and management policies and styles. Counterbalancing these barriers were some powerful reinforcers for innovation, including how senior nurses listened to and supported the health visitors, particularly at a time of crisis. Even more pronounced was the effect of support from colleagues, including feedback about good practice. Somewhat paradoxically, West (1989) concluded that innovation was widespread and seemed to occur most when workload was high. The explanation for this seeming paradox is that innovation can be seen as a coping strategy with which to deal with exceptional work stress. The second major factor was that the health visitors themselves received good social support. Similar findings have been reported for other professional groups.

What are the implications of all this for the ways in which innovation at work can be fostered? Three major options are now considered, namely the roles of training, re-organising and forming partnerships.

Training

A further example of the interaction between personal and system level changes was provided by McDonald (1991), in relation to an organisational analysis of in-service staff training. Twenty conditions necessary for the generalisation of this training were identified from the literature and built into a questionnaire that was administered to almost 300 staff. Analysis of their replies indicated that five factors were important to the success of the training. The most powerful of these was the amount of commitment that was made by the administration, including the need for supervision and communicating to staff their support for the training endeavour. The second most important factor was how other agencies viewed the training, for example how credible or acceptable it was perceived to be. The three remaining factors were work incentives, the personal attribute of the individual professional and the competence that individuals regarded themselves as possessing.

It seems self-evident that if organisations (such as Higher Education or the NHS) are to encourage the kind of developments in services that would lead to social therapy on a larger scale, then both initial professional training and continuing professional development need to be given an appropriate shift of emphasis. In an early consideration of what this might entail, Moffic *et al.* (1979) suggested that initial training should concentrate on developing generalists who draw on core principles and competences; refer to a theory base drawn from more than one social science (i.e. sociology, anthropology and political science); develop specialist skills relevant to community work; and undertake mini-clinical placements that are in a relevant training site. Table 9.1 lists some ways in which continuing professional development could then build on this initial foundation.

Two further aspects of training are worth mentioning: the developments of shared learning and the incorporation of evidence-based practice in training. Professional training for mental health staff is carried out overwhelmingly on a single-discipline basis in the UK, despite strong evidence that there are significant elements of similarity between the various programmes (Sainsbury Centre, 1997). The Centre's analysis of future roles and training for mental health staff suggested defining a common training agenda based on the needs of service users, carers and the general public. The traditional emphasis on 'cure' should be succeeded by a focus on community level work, collaborative working, life-long learning and a shared interprofessional programme of both initial and continuing professional development. The Centre recognised that identification of core competences across and within the different professional groups would greatly facilitate a programme of shared learning, and Table 9.3 records some of those core skills that are most relevant to social therapy. The Centre's review also suggested that the specific training of all mental health professionals be attended to in specific ways. For instance, it was recommended that in the case of clinical psychologists greater attention be given to community-based services, multidisciplinary working and training in management, consultancy, staff facilitation and communication skills. Similar recommendations were made for social work, mental health nursing, occupational therapy and psychiatry.

Turning to the question of evidence-based practice (EBP), surveys in America suggest that training programmes under-emphasise the procedures for which there is strong evidence (Crits-Christoph *et al.*, 1995). As outlined earlier in this chapter, the advent of an EBP emphasis within the new NHS provides a great opportunity for facilitating the integration of research knowledge with practice. Furthermore, EBP has the advantage that it should facilitate the initial acquisition of skills, due to the increasingly widely available training guidelines and protocols, as well as enhancing the reliability with which these procedures are applied (for example through audit and feedback). In addition to manuals describing in detail the EBP methods, supporting material such as video tapes are

Table 9.3　Core skills that could form the basis of shared learning about social therapy (based on the Sainsbury Centre, 1997)

1. Management	• Knowledge of current systems of care and the policy background (for example care management procedures) • Understanding of the roles of the various disciplines and agencies involved in the provision of community mental health care
2. Assessment	• Skill in conducting a collaborative, needs-based assessment • Ability to develop a treatment or care plan, based on a thorough and comprehensive assessment of the client, family and social system
3. Treatment and care management	• Knowledge of crisis intervention, theory and practice • Knowledge of basic current cognitive behavioural strategies to assist users, carers and family networks to contain and manage a severe and enduring mental illness
4. Collaborative working	• Awareness of the need to work in partnership with carers and social networks • Ability to work effectively as a member of a multidisciplinary mental health team.

also becoming increasingly available (Calhoun *et al.*, 1998). An emphasis on EBP carries other advantages, including a clearer theoretical conceptualisation for interventions; greater appreciation of the relationship between the rigour with which research is conducted and the confidence one can have in the findings; streamlining curricula by de-emphasising less essential and outdated elements; the careful design of EBP procedures facilitates the use of 'vertical supervision' in which more senior trainees act as supervisors for their more junior colleagues; and finally, evidence on effective training methods can be used to design the training programmes (Calhoun *et al.*, 1998). These authors concluded their article on EBP (referred to in America as 'empirically supported treatments') by listing seven guidelines that emerge from the literature on how to conduct successful training. These are summarised in Table 9.4.

As Calhoun *et al.* (1988) noted, the design, implementation and dissemination of evidence-based training programmes in EBP is new territory and should be developed in keeping with a scientific approach.

Reorganising

Unlike the preceding sections, for the sake of variety this one draws on newspaper reports appearing at the time of writing. For example, in one

Table 9.4 Some guidelines for developing evidence-based practice amongst professionals

Guidelines for training	Justification
1. Include video material	• Tapes provide rich detail on how best to conduct EBP, answering many questions that learners may have to a level of detail that even the most conscientious of trainers cannot anticipate.
2. Base supervision on tape recordings	• Just as videos provide learners with rich information so they also provide supervisors with the most accurate information possible on the correctness and completeness of a learner's implementation of EBP. Tapes also allow for responsive and contextual learning, and can allow the learner to convey to the supervisor their style and status during the taped session.
3. Evaluate progress systematically and frequently	• Strengthening the above point on the use of tapes, the use of published systems for judging whether or not a learner has adhered to EBP can facilitate mutual learning. For example, such ratings can clearly identify aspects of an intervention that a learner is omitting or failing to implement fully or correctly. This provides the basis for individualised supervision, as well as for an ongoing index of learning.
4. Provide training material illustrating common errors	• In order to help learners appreciate some of the pitfalls and coping strategies, helpful materials also illustrate a range of competence levels.
5. Use group supervision and learning methods	• There appear to be several advantages to using group approaches on at least an occasional basis, including efficient use of the trainer's time and learning from peers.
6. Provide training in a sufficient number of cases	• It is suggested that in order to develop adequately learners develop skills in relation to at least four fairly typical cases and a similar number of atypical cases.
7. Include instruction in evaluating outcomes	• Because EBP is typically associated with published evaluations, measures are usually available with which to also assess the effectiveness of the learner's work.

of these the *Observer* (5 April, 1998) provides a report on how powerlessness is a public health issue. Specifically, the report details how the residents of tower blocks in Birmingham were joined by mental health professionals, in order to turn a flat into the estate's mental health lifeline. The flat became the base for a range of activities, such as a mother and toddler group, bingo, and drop-in support from two workers. It was reported that the flat had become a powerful symbol of the growing power that people on the estate can exert over mental health resources. Through their involvement with the new centre local people have been empowered to develop their own social support role and with it their self-esteem (for example mothers are encouraged to form their own support groups). A health visitor and two support workers, funded by the local NHS, staff the flat, encouraging teenagers to go for training and serving as a network for self-improvement and mutual help. In addition, Birmingham Council provides the flat rent free. The scheme has worked well, and there are now plans to have community psychiatric nurses and a range of other professionals operating from the flat. The Health Authority chairman, interviewed by the author (Melanie Phillips) for the article, concluded that this fresh organisational arrangement symbolised an end to the residents' fatalism and a route to better health provision.

A second item in another paper provided a photograph from a hairdressing salon. The accompanying note stated that hairdressers had been recruited for a health project in Kirkby, Merseyside. The project involved 31 hairdressers in five salons, each of whom had been trained to advise customers on screening programmes and the importance of health checks. The initiative was established by the Regional Health Promotion Unit, to encourage more women to accept invitations for breast screening in an area where uptake rates were very low.

A third and final topical example is a £2 million initiative launched to improve mental health services in areas with some of the highest social deprivation in London. The project, financed and supported by the Sainsbury Centre for Mental Health, the Kinds Fund and the Department of Health, will link organisations across health, local government and the voluntary sector. The aim is to break down traditional boundaries and to develop an integrated service for those suffering from severe mental illness in the community. The initiative will provide special assertive outreach teams of social workers, psychiatrists, nurses and outreach workers, to help people in need of 24-hour support in the community, using social inclusion principles and concentrating on practical ways of fostering their coping.

Forming partnerships

As already emphasised, the innovation guidelines suggest how crucial it is to form working alliances with key colleagues within ones organisational system and with key individuals in the neighbourhood social support systems. In addition, particularly in an era of evidence-based practice and R and D initiatives, some mental health professionals may find it advantageous to form links with centres for applied psychology and other higher education groupings. Such centres can bring together a community of like-minded professionals; promote the knowledge base needed to guide research and apply interventions; provide a focal point for professionals to access academic expertise; remove barriers between academics and the potential users of that knowledge (for example by providing public demonstrations and lectures that are free); and, more proactively, by infusing collaborating sectors with students and researchers and by providing a full range of services (including continuing professional development, research and consultancy) (Gale, 1997).

Such centres and affiliations can provide the basis for action research in local neighbourhoods. A case in point was described by Riley (1997) who developed a system for promoting child care for school-aged children in local American communities. Based on a model of close collaboration with key members of the local community, this academic not only helped many hundreds of parents to feel more confident about their parenting skills, but also motivated local citizens to act on the knowledge from these local projects. As a result, they developed a stronger psychological 'sense of community' or 'cohesion'. For example, existing community groups that were floundering were given much needed structure, focus and motivation by participating in a joint project. Riley (1997) drew out guidelines for successful innovation by comparing his initial failures with later successes (for example learning to act as a facilitator, rather than as an outside expert).

CONCLUDING COMMENTS

Inspired by the imaginative work of Emery Cowen (1982) on the nature of informal help, guided by the scholarly accounts of the possibilities by Jim Orford (1992) and pricked into action by the rhetoric of David Smail (1991), this book represents my attempt to put forward a viable way to deal with what Smail has referred to as the fundamental dilemma for mental health professionals. On the one hand this dilemma is between our explanations of why people suffer, which tend to refer to the material world; and on the other hand our emphasis on the creative powers of intrapersonal therapy, far removed from the material world. The 'third way' of addressing this dilemma has hopefully become clear from this text, which is to show how a relatively minor shift of emphasis would result in significantly greater recognition of the role of the material and social world, particularly in the realm of social support that impinges so powerfully on our patient's lives. Chapters 5–7 attempted to detail increasingly systemic interventions that mental health professionals could undertake to foster what I have termed social therapy. It has been recognised that, in their functioning as therapists, professionals were never oblivious to the significance of the material world, with its poverty and hardship, inequality and oppression, ideology and cultural differences (Salmon, 1991). Rather, as suggested by Salmon, the problem for therapists has been the lack of a language with which to formulate the meaning of these socio-cultural realities in relation to their work. Building on this understanding, the present book has recognised too that not only did they require a clearer grasp of these interrelationships, but they also required an adequate formulation of how they could intervene effectively into this matrix. It is hoped that this book has provided some of the formulation and guidance that Salmon invited.

However, I am under no illusion about the scale of the change that would be required in professional practice in order to produce a significant change in the way that we provide social therapy. Two examples should serve. One of these concerns the almost unbounded range of influences on social support, an unlimited range that makes the mind of the service developer boggle. To illustrate, Masterton and Mander (1990) studied psychiatric emergencies presenting at the Royal Edinburgh Hospital during the time that Scotland were playing in the World Cup Finals. From analysing the number of psychiatric emergencies over the period before, during and after the World Cup, they found that reductions in emergency psychiatric presentations to hospital occurred during and after the finals of the World Cup, an effect evident in women as well as men, and more marked among the mentally ill than those who were not. They believed that increases in the numbers of schizophrenic and neurotic men presenting before the competition could be due to the football, which they attributed to a period of increased stress in the form of anticipation and excitement before the World Cup, allied to the outlet that this competition provides for an acceptable expression of collective nationhood during and after the event. They speculated that such a common focus of interest and endeavour, fused with a surge of nationalism, might enhance social cohesion in the same way that one might explain the decreased suicide rates during times of war.

A second sobering antidote to one's enthusiasm for social support comes from the negative aspects of social relationships. This has been noted in some detail elsewhere in the book, in relation to such issues as expressed emotion (EE) amongst carers. The powerful examples of the negative potential of human relationships include bullying, harassment, conflict and violence (see special issue of the *Journal of Community and Applied Social Psychology*, **7**(3), 1997. This negative aspect is nicely summarised in the titles of two new books. One is entitled *The Dark Side of Close Relationships* (Spitzberg & Cupach, 1998) and includes sections on fatal attractions, jealousy, envy, misunderstanding, gossip, co-dependence, sexual coercion, stalking, relationship termination and unrequited love. The second, called *Dangerous Relationships* (Russell, 1998) examines the association between pornography, misogyny and rape, and contends that these relationships are indeed dangerous to women. It is clear from these that interpersonal relationships are at least a two-sided coin, which is one of the reasons for preferring the term social therapy to the term social support; i.e. one is more accustomed to associating negative possibilities with therapy than with the term social support.

Forward to the past

In one of the seminal texts addressing the issues of social therapy, Rappaport (1977) noted how the experience of writing his book transformed his understanding of the field and resulted in a book that ended where community psychology should begin. Specifically, he urged professionals to study, experience and understand what was missing from the text regarding communities and the naturally occurring helping systems in families, neighbourhoods and social networks. Only by understanding these systems, he suggested, could we do more to provide help to those who do not fit into our existing and rather limited set of options.

The present text revisits many of the issues outlined by Rappaport over two decades ago. Hopefully, however, in keeping with the kind of experiential learning cycle outlined in Table 9.1, the present text deepens and extends in a pragmatic way how professionals can actually offer a greater range of helping options to their work neighbourhoods.

Although one might feel paralysed by the great range of social support phenomena or by the potential of social interactions to be negative, in keeping with Rappaport (1977) the present text also recognises certain core processes on which social therapy can be founded. Fundamentally, these include a shift away from the traditional exercise of power within a therapeutic relationship that has a largely intrapersonal focus, and a move towards collaboration with local neighbourhoods. This carries an implicit emphasis on empowerment and innovation processes, and it de-emphasises professionalism, while remaining true to such important sources of professional knowledge as the methods of action research. It is only by emphasising such core processes that one can hope to justify the inevitably limited coverage of the literature that a book such as this will contain. Given this context, it is perhaps best to end with a piece of folk wisdom:

Go to the people
Live among them
Love them
Start with what they know
Build on what they have

But of the best leaders
When their task is accomplished
Their work is done
The people all remark: 'we have done it ourselves'.

(Rogers, 1986)

REFERENCES

Agras, W.S. & Berkowitz, R. (1980). Clinical research in behaviour therapy: halfway there? *Behaviour Therapy*, **11**, 472–487.

Albee, G.W. (1986). Toward a just society: lessons from observations on the primary prevention of psychopathology. *American Psychologist*, **41**, 891–898.

Alloway, R. & Bebbington, P. (1987). The buffer theory of social support—a review of the literature. *Psychological Medicine*, **17**, 91–108.

American Psychiatric Association (1994). *Diagnostic and Statistical Manual of Mental Disorders (4th edn)*. Washington, DC: APA.

Anderson, J., Dayson, D., Willis, W., Gooch, C., Margoulis, O., O'Driscoll, G. & Leff, J. (1993). The TAPS project 13: Clinical and social outcomes of long-stay psychiatric patients after one year in the community. *British Journal of Psychiatry*, **162** (suppl. 19), 45–56.

Anderson, R.K., Hart, B.L. & Hart, L.A. (1984). *The Pet Connection*. Minneapolis: University Press.

Anderson, T. & Strupp, H.H. (1996). The ecology of psychotherapy research. *Journal of Consulting & Clinical Psychology*, **64**, 776–782.

Antonucci, T.C. & Akiyama, H. (1987). An examination of sex differences in social support among older men and women. *Sex Roles*, **17**, 737–749.

Archer, J. & Winchester, G. (1994). Bereavement following death of a pet. *British Journal of Psychology*, **85**, 259–271.

Atkinson, J.M. & Coia, D.A. (1995). *Families Coping with Schizophrenia*. Chichester: Wiley.

Audit Commission. (1986). *Making a Reality of Community Care*. London: HMSO.

Ayers, T.D. (1987). Stakeholders as partners in evaluation: a stakeholder-collaborative approach. *Evaluation and Programme Planning*, **10**, 263–271.

Balestrieri, M., Williams, P. & Wilkinson, G. (1988). Specialist mental health treatment in general practice: a meta-analysis. *Psychological Medicine*, **18**, 711–717

Balint, M. (1964). *The Doctor, his Patient and the Illness*. London: Pitman.

Barker, C., Pistrang, N., Shapiro, D.A., & Shaw, I. (1990). Coping and help seeking in the UK adult population. *British Journal of Clinical Psychology*, **29**, 271–285.

Barker, R.G. (1968). *Ecological Psychology: Concepts and Methods for Studying the Environment of Human Behaviour*. Stanford: University Press.

Barker, R.G. & Wright, H.F. (1955). *Midwest and its Children: The Psychological Ecology of an American Town*. New York: Harperdraw.

Barker, C., Pistrang, N. and Elliott, R. (1994). *Research Methods in Clinical and Counselling Psychology*. Chichester: Wiley.

Barkham, M., Rees, A., Shapiro, D.A., Stiles, W.B., Agnew, R.M., Halstead, J., Culverwell, A. and Harrington, V.M.G. (1996). Outcomes of time limited psychotherapy in applied settings: replicating the second Sheffield Psychotherapy Project. *Journal of Consulting & Clinical Psychology*, **64**, 1079–1085.

Barkham, M., Evans, C., Margison, F., McGrath, G., Mellor-Clark, J., Milne, D. & Connell, J. (1998). The rationale for developing and implementing core batteries for routine use in service settings and psychotherapy outcome research. *Journal of Mental Health*, **7**, 35–47.

Barnes, M.K. & Duck, S. (1994). Everyday communicative contexts for social support. In: B.R. Burleson, T.L. Albrecht, & I.G. Sarason (eds). *Communication of Social Support*. London: Sage.

Barrerra, M. and Ainley, S.L. (1983). The structure of social support: A conceptual and empirical analysis. *Journal of Community Psychology*, **11**,133–143.

Barrera, M., Sandler, I.N. & Ramsay, T.B. (1981). Preliminary development of a scale of social support: studies on college students. *American Journal of Community Psychology*, **9**, 435–447.

Barrowclough, C. & Parle, M. (1997). Appraisal, psychological adjustment and expressed emotion in relation of patients suffering from schizophrenia. *British Journal of Psychiatry*, **171**, 26–30.

Barrowclough, C. & Tarrier, N. (1992). *Families of Schizophrenic Patients: Cognitive–Behavioural Intervention*. London: Chapman & Hall.

Baxter, L.A. (1986). Gender differences in the heterosexual relationship rules embedded in break-up accounts. *Journal of Social and Personal Relationships*, **3**, 289–306.

Beck, A.T. (1991). Cognitive therapy: a 30 year perspective. *American Psychologist*, **46**, 368–375.

Becker, T., Thornicroft, G., Leese, M., McCrane, P., Johnson, S., Albert, M. & Turner, D. (1997). Social networks and service use among representative cases of psychosis in South London. *British Journal of Psychiatry*, **171**, 15–19.

Bender, M.P. (1976). *Community psychology*. Methuen: London.

Bernstein, G.S. (1995). Toward a functional analysis of the behaviour of behaviour therapists. *The Behaviour Therapist*, **February**, 35–36.

Beutler, L.E. & Kendall, P.C. (1995). Introduction to the special section: the case for training in the provision of psychological theory. *Journal of Consulting & Clinical Psychology*, **63**, 179–181.

Billings, A.G., Cronkite, R.C. & Moos, R.H. (1983). Social-environmental factors in unipolar depression: comparisons of depressed patients and non-depressed controls. *Journal of Abnormal Psychology*, **92**, 119–133.

Birchwood, M. & Tarrier, N. (1994). *Psychological Management of Schizophrenia*. New York: Wiley.

Birchwood, M., Smith, J., Cochrane, R., Wetton, S. & Copestake, S. (1990). The Social Functioning Scale. The development and validation of a new scale of social adjustment for use in family intervention programmes with schizophrenia patients. *British Journal of Psychiatry*, **157**, 853–859.

Bledin, K.D., MacCarthy, B., Kuipers, L. & Woods, R.T. (1990). Daughters of people with dementia: expressed emotion, strain and coping. *British Journal of Psychiatry*, **157**, 221–227.

Bowling, A. (1991). *Measuring Health: A review of quality of life measurement scales*. Milton Keynes: Open University Press.

Bracken, A. (1997). Parental support groups and the role of professionals. Unpublished Educational Psychology MSc Dissertation, University of Newcastle upon Tyne.

Brewin, C.R. In: T.S. Brugha (ed.) (1995). *Social Support & Psychiatric Disorder: Research Findings & Guidelines for Clinical Practice*. Cambridge: Cambridge University Press.

Brodaty, H. & Gresham, M. (1989). Effect of a training programme to reduce stress in carers of patients with dementia. *British Medical Journal*, **299**, 1375–1379.

Brodaty, H., Gresham, M. & Luscombe, G. (1997). The Prince Henry Hospital dementia caregiver's training programme. *International Journal of Geriatric Psychiatry*, **12**, 183–192.

Brody, E.M. & Farber, B.A. (1989). Effects of psychotherapy on significant others. *Professional Psychology: Research & Practice*, **20**, 116–122

Brown, G. & Harris, T. (1978). *Social Origins of Depression: a Study of Psychiatric Disorder in Women*. London: Tavistock.

Brown, G.W., Andrews, B., Harris, T., Adler, Z. & Bridge, L. (1986). Social support, self-esteem & depression. *Psychological medicine*, **16**, 813–831.

Brugha, T.S. (1988). Social support. *Current Opinion in Psychiatry*, **1**, 206–211.

Burgoyne, R.W., Staples, F.R., Yamamoto, J., Wolkon, G.H. & Kline, F. (1979). Patients' requests of an outpatient clinic. *Archives of General Psychiatry*, **36**, 400–403.

Burns, T. (1997a). TV Counselling. *Journal of Mental Health*, **6**, 381–387.

Burns, T. (1997b). Case management, care management and care programming. *British Journal of Psychiatry*, **170**, 393–395.

Buunk, B.P. & Hoorens, V. (1992). Social support & stress: the role of social comparison & social exchange processes. *British Journal of Clinical Psychology*, **31**, 445–447.

Calhoun, K.S., Moras, K., Pilkonis, P.A. & Rehm, L.P. (1998). Empirically supported treatments: implications for training. *Journal of Consulting & Clinical Psychology*, **66**, 151–162.

Campbell, D.T. & Stanley, J.C. (1963). *Experimental & Quasi-experimental Designs for Research*. Chicago: Rand McNally.

Cape, J.D. (1996). Psychological treatment of emotional problems by general practitioners. *British Journal of Medical Psychology*, **69**, 85–99

Caplan, G. (1964). Principles of Preventive Psychiatry. New York: Basic Books.

Caplan, G. (1974). *Support Systems & Community Mental Health*. New York: Behavioural Publications.

Carroll, D., Niven, C.A. & Sheffield, D. (1993). Gender, social circumstances and health. In: C.A. Niven & D. Carroll (eds) *The Health Psychology of Women*. Reading: Harwood Academic Publishers.

Carver, C.S., Scheier, M.F., & Weintraub, J.K. (1989). Assessing coping strategies: a theoretical-based approach. *Journal of Personality & Social Psychology*, **56**, 267–283.

Cassel, J. (1974). Psychosocial processes and stress: theoretical formulations. *International Journal of Health Services*, **4**, 471–482.

Cassel, J. (1994). Psychosocial processes & stress: theoretical formulations. *International Journal of Health Services*, **4**, 471–482.

Cauce, A.M., & Srebnik, D.S. (1990). Returning to social support systems: a morphological analysis of social networks. *American Journal of Community Psychology*, **18**, 609–618.

Champion, L.A. & Power, M.J. (1995). Social and cognitive approaches to depression: towards a new synthesis. *British Journal of Clinical Psychology*, **34**, 485–504.

Cherulnik, P.D. (1993). *Applications of Environment–Behaviour Research*. Cambridge: University Press.

Christensen, A. & Jacobson, N. S. (1994). Who (or what) can do psychotherapy: the status and challenge of non professional therapies. *Psychological Science*, **5**, 8–14.

Ciarlo, J.A. & Windle, C. (1988). Mental health programme evaluation and needs assessment. In: H.S. Bloom, D.S. Cardray and R.J. Light (eds) *New Directions in Programme Evaluation*. San Francisco: Jossey-Bass.

Clifford, P. (1998). M is for outcome: the CORE outcomes initiative. *Journal of Mental Health*, **7**, 19–24.

Cobb, J.P., Mathews, A.M., Childs-Clarke, A. & Blowers, C.M. (1984). The spouse as co-therapist in the treatment of agoraphobia. *British Journal of Psychiatry*, **144**, 282–287.

Cobb, S. (1976). Social support as a moderator of life stress. *Psychosomatic Medicine*, **38**, 300–314.

Cohen, S. & Wills, T.A. (1985). Stress, social support and the buffering hypothesis. *Psychological Bulletin*, **98**, 310–357.

Collerton, D., Cooper, T., Milne, D. & Rowley, D. (1991). Psychologists at an exhibition. *Clinical Psychology Forum*, **34**, 5–6.

Connell, J., Barkham, M., Evans, C., Margison, F., McGrath, G. & Milne, D. (1997). *Clinical Outcomes in Routine Evaluation Outcome Measure: Guidelines for Use*. Leeds: Psychological Therapies Research Centre.

Cook, T.B. & Reichardt, C.S. (1979). *Qualitative and Quantitative Methods in Evaluation Research*. Beverly Hills, CA: Sage.

Cook, T.D. & Campbell, D.T. (1976). The design and conduct of quasi-experiments and true experiments in field settings. In: M.D. Dunnett (ed.): *Handbook of Industrial and Organisational Psychology*. New York: Wiley.

Cousins, J.B. & Leithwood, K.A. (1986). Empirical research on evaluation utilisation. *Review of Educational Research*, **56**, 331–364.

Cowen, E.L. (1982). Help is where you find it. *American Psychologist*, **37**, 385–395.

Cowen, E.L., Gesten, E.L., Boike, M., Norton, P., Wilson, A.B. & DeStefano, M.A. (1979). Hairdressers as caregivers: 1. A descriptive profile of interpersonal help-giving involvements. *American Journal of Community Psychology*, **7**, 633–648.

Coyne, J. (1976). Toward an interactional description of depression. *Psychiatry*, **39**, 28–39.

Coyne, J. C. and DeLongis, A. (1986). Going beyond social support: the role of social relationships in adaptation. *Journal of Consulting and Clinical Psychology*, **54**, 454–460.

Crits-Christoph, R., Frank, E., Chambless, D.L., Brody, C. & Karp, J.F. (1995). Training in empirically validated treatments: what are clinical psychology students learning? *Professional Psychology: Research & Practice*, **26**, 514–522.

Crowe, M., Ridley, J. & Skynner, R. (1990). *Therapy with couples: A behavioural Systems Approach to Marital and Sexual Problems*. Oxford: Blackwell.

Culyer, A. (1994). *Supporting R & D in the NHS: Implementation Plan*. London: Department of Health.

Cusack, O. (1988). *Pets and Mental Health*. London: Haworth Press.

Cutrona, E.E. (1996). *Social Support in Couples*. London: Sage.

Dalgard, O.S. & Tambs, K. (1997). Urban environment and mental health. *British Journal of Psychiatry*, **171**, 530–536.

Dalgard, O.S., Bjørk, S. & Tambs, K. (1995). Social support, negative life events and mental health. *British Journal of Psychiatry*, **166**, 29–34.

Dane, A.V. & Schneider, B.H. (1998). Programme integrity in primary and early secondary prevention: are implementation effects out of control? *Clinical Psychology Review*, **18**, 23–45.

Deasy, L.C. & Quinn, O.W. (1955). The wife of the mental patient and the hospital psychiatrist. *Journal of Social Issues*, **11**, 49–60.

Denzin, N.K. & Lincoln, Y.S. (eds) (1994). *Handbook of Qualitative Research.* Thousand Oaks, CA: Sage.

Department of Health (1990). *National Health Service & Community Care Act.* London: HMSO.

Department of Health (1992). *The Health of the Nation: A Strategy for Health in England.* London: HMSO.

Department of Health (1995). *Methods to Promote the Implementation of Research Findings in the NHS.* Leeds: Department of Health

Department of Health (1996). *NHS Psychotherapy Services in England: Review of Strategic Policy* Wetherby: NHSE.

Donnan, P., Hutchinson, A., Paxton, R., Grant, B. & Firth, M. (1990). Self-help materials for anxiety: a randomised controlled trial in general practice. *British Journal of General Practice*, **40**, 498–501.

Dunn, M., O'Driscoll, C., Dayson, D., Willis, W. & Leff, J. (1990). The TAPS Project 4: An observational study of the social life of long stay patients. *British Journal of Psychiatry*, **157**, 842–848.

Durbin, J., Goering, P., Wasylenki, D. & Roth, J. (1995). Meeting the challenge: field evaluations of community support programmes. *Psychiatric Rehabilitation Journal*, **19**, 19–25.

Durlak, J.A. (1979). Comparative effectiveness of paraprofessional and professional helpers. *Psychological Bulletin*, **86**, 80–92.

Egan, G. (1990). *The Skilled Helper*, Pacific Grove, California: Brooks/Cole.

Elliott, R. (1995). Therapy process research and clinical practice: practical strategies. In: M. Aveline & D.A. Shapiro (eds). *Research Foundations for Psychotherapy Practice.* Chichester: Wiley.

Elliott, V. & Milne, D. (1991). Patients best friend? *Nursing Times*, **87**, 34–35.

Ewles, L. & Simnett, I. (1987). *Promoting Health: A Practical Guide to Health Education.* Chichester: Wiley

Fadden, G. (1997). Implementation of family interventions in routine clinical practice following staff training programmes: a major cause for concern. *Journal of Mental Health*, **6**, 599–612.

Fairbanks, L.A., McGuire, M.T., Cole, S.R., Sbordone, R., Silvers, F.M. & Richards, M. (1977). The ethological study of four psychiatric wards: patient, staff and system behaviours. *Journal of Psychiatric Research*, **13**, 193–209.

Falloon, I.R.H., Kydd, R.R., Coverdale, J.H. & Laidlaw, T.M. (1996). Early detection and intervention for initial episodes of schizophrenia. *Schizophrenia Bulletin*, **22**, 271–281.

Faust, D. & Zlotnik, C. (1995). Another dodo bird verdict? Revisiting the comparative effectiveness of professional and paraprofessional therapist. *Clinical Psychology & Psychotherapy*, **2**, 157–167.

Fawcett, S.B. (1991). Some values guiding community research and action. *Journal of Applied Behaviour Analysis*, **24**, 621–636.

Fehr, B. (1996). *Friendship Processes*. London: Sage.

Fishman, D.B. (1995). Postmodernism comes to programme evaluation II: a review of Denzin & Lincoln's Handbook of Qualitative Research. *Evaluation and Programme Planning*, **18**, 301–310.

Fox, R.E., (1994). Training professional psychologists in the 21st century. *American Psychologist*, **49**, 1042–1050.

Fox, R.E., Kovacs, A.L. & Graham, S.R. (1985). Proposals for a revolution in the preparation and regulation of professional psychologists. *American Psychologist*, **40**, 1042–1050.

Frank, J.D. & Frank, J.B. (1991). *Persuasion & Healing: a Comparative Study of Psychotherapy (3rd edn)*. Baltimore: Johns Hopkins University Press.

Froland, C., Pancoast, D.L., Chapman, N.J., & Kimboko, P.J. (1981). *Helping Networks & Human Services*. Sage: Beverly Hills.

Froyd, J.E., Lambert, M.J. & Froyd, J.D. (1996). A review of practices of psychotherapy outcome measurement. *Journal of Mental Health*, **5**, 11–15.

Fryer, D. (1998). Editor's Preface (to a Special Issue: Mental health consequences of economic insecurity, relative poverty and social exclusion). *Journal of Community and Applied Social Psychology*, **8**, 75–180.

Galanter, M. (1988). Zealous self-help groups as adjuncts to psychiatric treatment: a study of recovery, Inc. *American Journal of Psychiatry*, **145**, 1248–1253.

Galanter, M. (1990). Cults and zealous self-help movements: a psychiatric perspective. *American Journal of Psychiatry*, **147**, 543–551.

Gale, A. (1985). On doing research: the dream and the reality. *Journal of Family Therapy*, **7**, 187–211.

Gale, A. (1990). Applying psychology to the psychology degree: pass with first class honours or miserable failure? *The Psychologist*, **11**, 483–488.

Gale, T. (1997). The reconstruction of British psychology. *The Psychologist*, **January**, 11–15.

Garbarino, J. (1983). Social support network: Rx for the helping professions. In: J.K. Whittaker & J. Garbarino: *Social Support Network*, New York: Aldine.

Gelsthorpe, S. (1997). Conflict, collusion, co-operation and trying to be constructive. *Clinical Psychology Forum*, **103**, 34–38.

Georgiades, N.J. & Phillimore, L. (1975). The myth of the hero-innovator and alternative strategies for organisational change. In: C.C. Kierman & F. P Woodford (eds). *Behaviour Modification with the Severely Retarded*. London: Associated Scientific Publishers.

Gilgen, A.R. (1982). *American Psychology Since World War II: A Profile of the Discipline*. Westport, C.T: Greenwood Press.

Goffmann, E. (1961). *Asylums*. Harmondsworth: Pelican.

Goldberg, D. (1978). *Manual of the General Health Questionnaire*. NFER, Slough.

Goldberg, D. & Huxley, P. (1980). *Mental Illness in the Community: The Pathway to Psychiatric Care*. Tavistock: London.

Goldberg, D., & Williams, P. (1988). *A User's Guide to the General Health Questionnaire*. Windsor: NFER-Nelson.

Goldiamond, I. (1978). The professional as a double agent. *Journal of Applied Behavioural Analysis*, **11** 178–184.

Goss, S. (1996). Bringing housing into community care. *Journal of Inter Professional Care*, **10**, 231–239.

Gottlieb, B.H. (1983). *Social Support Strategies: Guidelines for Mental Health Practice*. London: Sage Publications.

Grant, G. & Nolan, M. (1993). Informal carers: sources & concomitants of satisfaction. *Health & Social Care in the Community*, **1**, 147–159.

Gray, J.A.M. (1997). *Evidence Based Healthcare: How to make policy and management decisions*. London: Churchill-Livingstone.

Greene, J. (1987). Stakeholder participation in evaluation design : is it worth the effort? *Evaluation and Programme Planning*, **10**, 379–394.

Grencavage, L.M. & Norcross, J.C. (1990). Where are the commonalities among the common factors? *Professional Psychology*, **21**, 372–378.

Grimshaw, J.M. & Russell, I.T. (1993). Effective clinical guidelines in medical practice: a systematic review of rigorous evaluations. *The Lancet*, **342**, 1317–1322.

Grimshaw, J.M. & Russell, I.T. (1994). Achieving health gain through guidelines II: Ensuring guidelines change medical practice. *Quality in Health Care*, **3**, 45–52.

Groth-Marnat, G. (1990). *Handbook of Psychological Assessment*. Chichester: Wiley.

Guay, J. (1994). Bridging the gap between professionals and the community in mental health services: findings and policy implications of two demonstration projects. *Health & Social Care in the Community*, **2**, 95–103.

Haan, N. (1977). *Coping & Defending: Processes of Self-Environment Organisation*. New York: Academic Press.

Hagan, T. & Smail, D. (1997). Power-mapping—1. Background and basic methodology. *Journal of Community and Applied Social Psychology*, **7**, 257–267.

Haley, W.E., Levine, E.G., Brown, S., Berry, J.W. & Hughes, G.H. (1987). Psychological, social and health consequences of caring for a relative with senile dementia. *Journal of the American Geriatrics Society*, **35**, 405–411.

Halpern, D. (1995). *Mental Health and the Built Environment*. London: Taylor & Francis.

Hansen, N.B. & Lambert, M.J. (1996). Clinical significance: an overview of models. *Journal of Mental Health*, 5, 17–24.

Harchik, A.E., Sherman, J.A., Hopkins, B.L., Strouse, M.C., & Sheldon, J.B. (1989). Use of behavioural techniques by paraprofessional staff: a review and proposal. *Behavioural Residential Treatment*, 4, 331–357.

Hardy, G.E. & Shapiro, D.A. (1985). Therapist response modes in prescriptive and exploratory psychotherapy. *British Journal of Clinical Psychology*, 24, 235–245.

Harries, C., Frois, M. & Healey, J. (1984). The 'hidden society': the practical use of multi-dimensional scaling to illuminate the pattern of relationships between long-stay psychiatric residents. *Journal of Advanced Nursing*, 9, 619–625.

Hattie, J.A., Sharpley, C.F., & Rogers, H.J. (1984). Comparative effectiveness of professional and paraprofessional helpers. *Psychological Bulletin*, 95, 534–541.

Haughie, E., Milne, D., & Elliott, V. (1992). An evaluation of companion pets with elderly psychiatric patients. *Behavioural Psychotherapy*, 20, 367–372.

Hayes, S.C., Nelson, R.O. & Jarrett, R.B. (1987). The treatment utility of assessment. *American Psychologist*, 42, 963–974.

Hayes, S.C., Follette, W.C., Dawes, R.D. & Grady, K. (1995). *Scientific Standards of Psychological Practice*. Reno, NV: Context Press.

Haynes, R.B., Davis, D.A., McKibbon, A. & Tugwell, P. (1984). A critical appraisal of the efficacy of continuing medical education. *Journal of American Medical Association*, 251, 61–64.

Heitzmann, C.A. & Kaplan, R.M. (1988). Assessment of methods for measuring social support. *Health Psychology*, 7, 75–109.

Heller, K. (1979). The effects of social support: prevention and treatment implications. In A.P. Goldstein & F.H. Kanfer (eds). *Maximising Treatment Gains: Transfer Enhancement in Psychotherapy*. New York: Academic Press (pp. 353–382).

Heller, K. (1990). Social and community interventions. *Annual Review of Psychology*, 41, 141–168

Heller, K., Swindle, R.W. & Dusenbury, L. (1986). Component social support processes: comments & integration. *Journal of Consulting & Clinical Psychology*, 54, 466–470.

Henderson, P. & Thomas, D.N. (1987). *Skills in Neighbourhood Work*, London: Allen & Unwin.

Henderson, S., Duncan-Jones, P., Bryne, D.G. & Scott, R. (1980). Measuring social relationships: the Interview Schedule for Social Intervention. *Psychological Medicine*, 10, 723–734.

Herbert, M. (1995). A collaborative model of training for parents of children with disruptive behaviour disorders. *British Journal of Clinical Psychology*, **34**, 325–342.

Herink, R. (ed.) (1980). *The Psychotherapy Handbook*. New York: Meridian.

Hersen, M. & Barlow, D.H. (1976). *Single Case Experimental Designs: Strategies for Studying Behaviour Change*. New York: Pergamon.

Hersen, M. & Bellack, A.S. (1988). *Dictionary of Behavioural Assessment Techniques*. Oxford: Pergamon.

Heubeck, B.G., Tausch, B. & Mayor, B. (1995). Models of responsibility and depression in unemployed young males and females. *Journal of Community and Applied Social Psychology*, **5**, 291–309.

Hewstone, M., Carpenter, J. Franklyn-Stokes, & Routh, D. (1994). Intergroup contact between professional groups: two evaluation studies. *Journal of Community & Applied Social Psychology*, **4**, 347–363.

Hobbs, N. (1968). The art of getting into trouble. Commencement address, Peabody Demonstration School, Nashville, TN (cited in Newborough, 1993).

Hogarty, G.E., Anderson, C.M., Resh, D.J., *et al.* (1991). Family psychoeducation, social skills training, and maintenance chemotherapy in the aftercare treatment of schizophrenia. *Archives of General Psychiatry*, **48**, 340–347.

Holahan, C.J., Moos, R.H. and Schaeffer, J.A. (1996). Coping, stress resistance and growth: conceptualizing adaptive functioning. In M. Zeidner and N.S. Endler (eds). *Handbook of Coping*. New York: Wiley.

Holdsworth, N., Paxton, R., Seidel, S., Thomson, D. & Shrubb, S. (1994). Improving the effectiveness of self-help materials for mental health problems common in primary care. *Journal of Mental Health*, **3**, 413–422.

Holloway, F. (1991). Case management for the mentally ill: Looking at the evidence. *International Journal of Social Psychiatry*, **37**, 2–13.

Holmes, T.T & Rahe, R.H. (1967). The social readjustment rating scale. *Journal of Psychosomatic Research*, **11**, 213–218.

Holmes-Eber, P. & Riger, S. (1990). Hospitalization and the composition of mental patients' social networks. *Schizophrenia Bulletin*, **16**, 157–164.

Horowitz, L.M., Rosenberg, S.E., Baer, B.A., Ureno, G. & Vellasnor, V.S. (1988). Inventory of interpersonal problems: psychometric properties and clinical applications. *Journal of Consulting & Clinical Psychology*, **56**, 885–892.

Hoshmand, L.T. and O'Byrne, K. (1996). Reconsidering action research as a guiding metaphor for professional psychology. *Journal of Community Psychology*, **24**, 185–200.

Howells, E. (1993). Unconditional positive regard. *Clinical Psychology Forum*, **62**, 10.

Humphreys K. (1996). Clinical Psychologists as psychotherapists; history, future and alternatives. *American Psychologist*, **51**, 190–197.

Huxley, P. (1990). *Effective Community Mental Health Services*. Aldershot: Avebury.

Jacquet, C.H. (ed.). (1984). *Year book of American and Canadian Churches*. Nashville: Abingdon.

Jacobson, N.S. & Truax, P. (1991). Clinical significance: a statistical approach to defining meaningful change in psychotherapy research. *Journal of Consulting & Clinical Psychology*, **59**, 12–19.

Jacobson, N.S., Follette, W.C. & Revenstorf, D. (1984). Psychotherapy outcome research: methods for reporting variability and evaluating clinical significance. *Behaviour Therapy*, **15**, 336–352.

Jahoda, M. (1988). Economic recession and mental health: some conceptual issues. *Journal of Social Issues*, **44**, 13–24.

Johnston, M., Wright, S. & Weinman, J. (1995). *Measures in Health Psychology: a User's Portfolio*. Windsor: NFER-Nelson.

Kahaha, E., Kahana, B., Hard, Z. & Rosner, T. (1988). Coping with extreme trauma. In: J.P. Wilson, Z. Hazel & B. Kahana (eds). *Human Adaptation to Extreme Stress*. New York: Plenum Press.

Kalsy, S. & McDonnell, J. (1997). Four month evaluation of the Crossroads – Tynedale pilot befriending scheme for older people suffering from dementia. Unpublished document, available from the first author, c/o Clinical Psychology, Ridley Building, Newcastle University, Queen Victoria Road, Newcastle NE1 7RU.

Kane, J.M. & McGlashan, T.H. (1995). Treatment of Schizophrenia. *The Lancet*, **346**, 820–825.

Kanner, A.D., Coyne, J.C., Schaeffer, C. & Lazarus, R.S. (1981). Comparison of two models of stress management: daily hassles and uplifts versus major life events. *Journal of Behavioural Medicine*, **4**, 1–39.

Karoly, P. (1985). The logic and character of assessment in health psychology: perspectives and possibilities. In: P. Karoly (ed.) *Measurement Strategies in Health Psychology*, New York: Wiley.

Katz, J., Beach, S.R.H. and Anderson, P. (1996). Self-enhancement versus self-verification: does spousal support always help? *Cognitive Therapy and Research*, **20**, 345–360.

Kavanagh, D.J., Piatkowska, O., Clark, D. *et al.* (1993). Application of cognitive behavioural intervention for schizophrenia in multidisciplinary teams: what can the matter be? *Australian Psychologist*, **28**, 181–188.

Kazdin, A.E. (1986). Comparative outcome studies of psychotherapy: methodological issues and strategies. *Journal of Consulting & Clinical Psychology*, **54**, 95–105.

Kelly, J.G. (1990). Changing contexts and the field of community psychology. *American Journal of Community Psychology*, **18**, 769–792.

Kiresuk, T. & Sherman, R. (1968). Goal Attainment Scaling: a general method of evaluating comprehensive mental health programmes. *Community Mental Health Journal*, **4**, 443–453.

Kirk, J.W. (1983). Behavioural treatment of obsessional-compulsive patients in routine clinical practice. *Behaviour Research & Therapy*, **21**, 57–62.

Kitson, A.L. (1987). A comparative analysis of lay-caring and professional (nursing) caring relationships. *International Journal of Nursing Studies*, **24**, 155–165.

Kitwood, T. (1996). A dialectical framework of dementia. In R.T. Woods (ed.) *Handbook of the Clinical Psychology of Ageing*. Chichester: Wiley.

Kolb, D.A. (1984). *Experiential Learning: Experience as the Source of Learning and Development*. Englewood Cliffs, NJ: Prentice-Hall.

Krause, N. & Markides, K. (1990). Measuring social support among older adults. *International Journal of Ageing and Human Development*, **30**, 37–53.

Kuipers, E. (1998). Working with carers: interventions for relative and staff carers of those who have a psychosis. In: T. Wykes, N. Tarrier & S. Lewis (eds) *Outcome and Innovation in Psychological Treatment of Schizophrenia*. Chichester: Wiley.

Kyronz, E.M. & Humphreys, K. (1997). Do health care work places affect treatment environments? *Journal of Community and Applied Social Psychology*, **7**, 105–108.

Lago, D., Connell, C.M. & Knight, B. (1983). A companion animal programme. In M.A. Smyer & M. Gatz (eds). *Mental Health and Ageing*. London: Sage.

Lago, D., Kaper, R., Delaney, M. & Connell, C. (1988). Assessment of favourable attitudes toward pets. *Anthrozoos*, **1**, 240–254.

Lane, C. & Hobfoll, S.E. (1992). How loss affects anger and alienates potential supporters. *Journal of Consulting & Clinical Psychology*, **60**, 935–942.

Larson, J.S. (1997). Medical outcomes research: improving measurement in mental health. *Evaluation and The Health Professions*, **20**, 109–112.

Lazarus, R. & Folkman, S. (1984). *Stress, Appraisal & Coping*. New York: Springer.

Leadbetter, C. (1998). I think I've found it (Labour's 'third way'). *The Observer*, **10.5.98**, p. 23.

Leff, J. (1997). The future of community care. In J. Leff (ed): *Care in the Community: Illusion or Reality?* Chichester: Wiley.

Leff, J., Berkowitz, R., Sharit, N., Strachan, A., Glass, I. & Vaughan, C. (1990). A trial of family therapy versus a relatives group for schizophrenia. *British Journal of Psychiatry*, **157**, 571–577.

Lester, N., Smart, L. & Baum, A. (1994). Measuring coping flexibility. *Psychology & Health*, **9**, 409–424.

Levy, L.H. (1984). The metamorphosis of clinical psychology: towards a new chapter as human service psychology. *American Psychologist*, **39**, 486–494.

Lewin, K. (1951). *Field Theory in Social Science*. New York: Harper.

Liang, B. & Bogat, G.A. (1994). Culture, central & coping: new perspectives on social support. *American Journal of Community Psychology*, **22**, 123–147.

Liem, J.H. & Liem, G.R. (1977). Life events, social support & physical and psychological wellbeing. Paper presented to the annual meeting of the American Psychological Association, Montreal, Canada.

Lipsey, M.W. (1990). *Design Sensitivity*. London: Sage.

Lomas, J. & Haynes, R.B. (1988). A taxonomy and critical review of tested strategies for the application of clinical practice recommendations from 'official' to 'individual clinical policy'. *American Journal of Preventive Medicine*, **4**, 77–94.

Longabaugh, R., Wirtz, P.W., Beattie, M.C., Noel, N. & Stout, R. (1995). Matching treatment focus to patient social investment and support: 18 month follow-up results. *Journal of Consulting & Clinical Psychology*, **63**, 296–307.

Lovett, S. & Gallagher, D. (1988). Psychoeducational interventions for family caregivers: preliminary efficacy data. *Behaviour Therapy*, **19**, 321–330.

Lundberg, A. (1998). *The Environment and Mental Health*. London: Lawrence Erlbaum.

McCullagh, A. & Rich, C. (1996). Local heroes. *Health Service Journal*, **14th March**, 37.

McDonald, R.M. (1991). Assessment of organisational context: a missing component in evaluations of training programmes. *Evaluation and Programme Planning*, **14**, 273–279.

McGrew, J.H., Bond, G.R., Dietzen, L. & Salyers, M. (1994). Measuring the fidelity of implementation of a mental health programme model. *Journal of Consulting & Clinical Psychology*, **62**, 670–678.

McKee, K.J., Whittick, J.E., Bollinger, B.B., Gilhooly, M.M.L., Gordon, D.S., Mutch, W.J. and Philp, I. (1997). Coping in family supporters of elderly people with dementia. *British Journal of Clinical Psychology*, **36**, 323–340.

McPherson, F.M. & Murphy, S. (1997). Deprivation & health: an audit of equity of access to a clinical psychology service. *Clinical Psychology Forum*, **104**, 16–18

Mahoney, F.I., Barthel, D.W. (1965). Functional evaluation: the Barthel Index. (In: Johnston *et al.*, 1995) *Maryland State Medical Journal*, **41**, 61–65.

Marshall, M., Gray, A., Lockwood, A. & Green, R. (1996). Case management for people with severe mental disorders. In: C. Adams, J. De Jesus Maris & P. White (eds). *Schizophrenia Module of the Cochrane Database of Systematic Reviews*. Oxford: Cochrane Library.

Maslow, A.H. (1970). *Motivation and Personality*. New York: Harper & Row.

Masson, J. (1989). *Against Therapy*. London: Fontana.

Masterton, G. & Mander, A.J. (1990). Psychiatric emergencies, Scotland and the World Cup Finals. *British Journal of Psychiatry*, **156**, 475–478.

Maton, K.I. (1989). Community settings as buffers of life stress? Highly supportive churches, mutual help groups and senior centres. *American Journal of Community Psychology*, **17**, 203–232.

Meissen, G.J., Gleason, D.F. & Embree, M.G. (1991). An assessment of the needs of mutual help groups. *American Journal of Community Psychology*, **19**, 427–442.

Merton, R. (1968). *Social Theory & Structure*. New York: Free Press

Metzer, E., Kemp, P. & Smith, B. (1994). Social networks in a cluster of three group homes for the mentally ill. *Journal of Mental Health*, **3**, 263–270.

Miller, G.A. (1969). Psychology as a means of promoting human welfare. *American Psychologist*, **24**, 1063–1075.

Milne, D. L. (1986). Planning and evaluating innovations in nursing practice by measuring the ward atmosphere. *Journal of Advanced Nursing*, **11**, 203–210.

Milne, D.L. (ed.) (1987). *Evaluating Mental Health Practice: Methods and Applications*. London: Croom-Helm.

Milne, D. (ed.) (1992a). *Assessment: A Mental Health Portfolio*. Reading: NFER-Nelson.

Milne D.L. (1992b). Promoting mental health through social support. In D. Trent (ed.) *Promotion of Mental Health*. Aldershot: Avebury.

Milne, D.L. (1993). *Psychology & Mental Health Nursing*. London: Macmillan.

Milne, D. (1994). Behavioural psychotherapists in practice: a survey of UK practitioners. *Behavioural and Cognitive Psychotherapy*, **22**, 247–257.

Milne, D. & Kennedy, S.J. (1993). The utility of consumer satisfaction data: a case study in organisational behaviour management. *Behavioural & Cognitive Psychotherapy*, **21**, 281–291.

Milne D. & Mullin, M. (1987). Is a problem shared a problem shaved? An evaluation of hairdressers and social support. *British Journal of Clinical Psychology*, **26**, 69–70.

Milne, D.L. & Netherwood, P. (1997). Seeking social support: an observational instrument and illustration. *Behavioural and Cognitive Psychotherapy*, **25**, 173–185.

Milne, D.L. & Paxton, R. (1998). A psychological re-analysis of the scientist–practitioner model. *Clinical Psychology & Psychotherapy* (in press).

Milne, D & Ridley, N. (1994). A review of behavioural psychotherapy in the 1980s: On course? *Behavioural and Cognitive Psychotherapy*, **22**, 75–85.

Milne, D., Jones, R. & Walters, P. (1989a). Anxiety management in the community: a social support model and preliminary evaluation. *Behavioural psychotherapy*, **17**, 221–236.

Milne, D.L., Pitt, I. & Sabin, N. (1989b). Evaluation of a Carer Support Scheme for elderly people: the importance of coping. *British Journal of Social Work*, **23**, 157–168.

Milne, D.L., Cowie, I., Gormly, A., White, C. & Hartley, C. (1992a). Social supporters and behaviour therapists: three studies of the form and functions of their help. *Behavioural & Cognitive Psychotherapy*, **20**, 343–354.

Milne, D.L., Fife, J. & Elliott, V. (1992b). A process of evaluation. *Journal of District Nursing*, **10**, 16–20.

Mitchell, R.E. & Trickett, E.J. (1980). Task force report: social networks as mediators of social support. *Community Mental Health Journal*, **16**, 27–44.

Moffic, H. S., Barrios, F. X., Cheney, C.C. & Adams, G.L. (1979). Training in community mental health. *Community Mental Health Review*, **4**, 1–11.

Moos, R.H. (1976). Evaluating and changing community settings. *American Journal of Community Psychology*, **4**, 313–326.

Moos, R.H. (1987). *Community Oriented Programmes Environment Scale Manual* (2nd edn). Palo Alto, CA: Consulting Psychologist Press.

Moos, R.H. (1990). *Coping Responses Inventory*. In: Milne (1992a).

Moos, R.H. (1991). Life stressors, social resources and the treatment of depression. In: J. Becker & A. Kleinman (eds). *Psychosocial Aspects of Depression*. Hillsdale, NJ: Lawrence Erlbaum

Moos, R.H. (1997). Coping Responses Inventory. In: C.P. Zalaquett & R. J. Woods (eds). *Evaluating Stress: A Book of Resources*. Lanham, Md: Scarecrow.

Moos, R.H. & Lemke, S. (1980). Assessing the physical and architectural features of sheltered care settings. *Journal of Gerontology*, **35**, 571–583.

Moos, R.H & Schaefer, J.A. (1993). Coping resources & processes: current concepts & measures. In L. Goldberger & S. Brezniz (eds). *Handbook of Stress: Theoretical & Clinical Aspects*. New York: Free Press.

Moos, R.H., Insel, P.M. & Humphrey, B. (1974). *Family, Work, and Group Environment Scales: Combined Preliminary Manual*. Palo Alto, California: Consulting Psychologists Press.

Morley, S. (1996). Single case research. In: G. Parry & F.N. Watts (eds). *Behavioural and Mental Health Research: A Handbook of Skills and Methods* (2nd edn). Hove: Erlbaum, Taylor & Francis.

Morris, R. & Carstairs, V. (1991). Which deprivation? A comparison of selected deprivation indexes. *Journal of Public Health Medicine*, **13**, 318–326.

Morris, L.W., Morris, R.G. & Britton, P.G. (1988). Factors affecting the emotional wellbeing of the caregivers of dementia sufferers: a review. *British Journal of Psychiatry*, **153**, 147–156.

Mosher, L. & Burti, L. (1994). *Community Mental Health: A Practical Guide.* New York: Norton.

Mowbray, C.T. (1990). Community treatment for the seriously mentally ill: is this community psychology? *American Journal of Community Psychology*, **18**, 893–902.

Mueser, K.T. (1996). Helping families manage severe mental illness. *Psychiatric Rehabilitation Skills*, **1**, 21–42.

Murray, A., Shepherd, G., Onyett, S. & Muijen, M. (1997). *More than a friend: The role of support workers in community mental health services.* London: Sainsbury Centre.

Murray, V., Walker, H.W., Mitchell, C. & Pelosi, A.J. (1996). Needs for care from a demand-led community psychiatric service: a study of patients with major mental illness. *British Medical Journal*, **312**, 1582–1586.

Mynors-Wallis, L.M., Gath, D.H., Lloyd-Thomas, A.R. & Tomlinson, D. (1995). Randomised controlled trial comparing problem-solving treatment with amitriptyline and Placebo for major depression in primary care. *British Medical Journal*, **310**, 441–445.

Nagar, D. & Paulus, P.B. (1997). Residential crowding experience scale: assessment and validation. *Journal of Community & Applied Social Psychology*, **7**, 303–319.

Neuchterlain, K.H. (1987). Vulnerability models for schizophrenia: state of the art. In: H. Hafner, W.F. Gattaz and W. Janzarik (eds). *In Search of the Causes of Schizophrenia*. Berlin: Springer.

Newbrough, J.R. (1993). David Charis—community action psychologist: the troublesome artist. *American Journal of Community Psychology*, **21**, 165–170.

Newcomb, M.D. & Chou, C.P. (1989). Social support among young adults: latent-variable models of quantity and satisfaction within six life areas. *Multivariate Behavioural Research*, **24**, 233–256.

Nolan, M.R. & Grant, G. (1989). Addressing the needs of informal carers: a neglected area of nursing practice. *Journal of Advanced Nursing*, **14**, 950–961.

Noor, N.M. (1997). The relationship between wives' estimates of time spent doing housework, support and wives' wellbeing. *Journal of Community & Applied Social Psychology*, **7**, 413–423.

O'Connor, D.W., Pollitt, P.A., Roth, M., Brook, C.P.B. & Reiss, B.B. (1990). Problems reported by relatives in a community study of dementia. *British Journal of Psychiatry*, **156**, 835–841.

O'Donnell, J.M. & George, K. (1977). The use of volunteers in a community mental health centre emergency and reception service: a comparative study of professional and lay telephone counselling. *Community Mental Health Journal*, **13**, 3–12.

O'Driscoll, C., Wills, W., Leff, J. & Marogolis, O. (1993). The TAPS Project 10: The long stay population of Friern & Claybury Hospitals. The baseline survey. *British Journal of Psychiatry*, **162** (supp. 19), 30–35.

Oei, T.P.S. & Shuttlewood, G.J. (1996). Specific and non-specific factors in psychotherapy: a case of cognitive therapy for depression. *Clinical Psychology Review*, **16**, 83–103.

Ogles, B.M., & Lunnen, K.M. (1996). Assessing outcomes in practice. *Journal of Mental Health*, **5**, 35–46.

Ogles, B.M., Lambert, M.J. & Sawyer, J.D. (1995). Clinical significance of the National Institute of Mental Health Treatment of Depression Collaborative Research Programme Data. *Journal of Consulting and Clinical Psychology*, **63**, 321–326.

Orford, J. (1992). *Community Psychology: Theory and Practice*. Chichester: Wiley.

Owens, R.G., Slade, P.D. & Fielding, D.M. (1996). Patient series and quasi-experimental designs. In: G. Parry & F.N. Watts (eds). *Behavioural and Mental Health Research*. Hove: Erlbaum.

Papineau, D. & Kiely, M.C. (1996). Participatory evaluation in a community organization: fostering stakeholder empowerment & utilization. *Evaluation and Programme Planning*, **19**, 79–93.

Pargament, K.I., Ensing, D.S., Falgout, K. & Warren, R.K. (1988). Consultation with churches and synagogues. In: P.A. Keller & S.R. Heyman (eds). *Innovations in Clinical Practice*. Sorasota, FL: Professional Resource Exchange.

Parry, G. (1986). Paid employment, life events, social support, and mental health in working class mothers. *Journal of Health & Social Behaviour*, **27**, 193–208.

Parry, G. (1992). Improving psychotherapy services: applications of research, audit and evaluation. *British Journal of Clinical Psychology*, **31**, 3–19.

Parry, G. (1996). Service evaluation and audit methods. In: G. Parry & F.N. Watts (eds). *Behavioural and Mental Health Research*. Hove: Erlbaum Taylor & Francis.

Parry, G. & Watts, F.N. (1996). *Behaviour and Mental Health Research: A Handbook of Skills and Methods* (2nd edn). Hove: Erlbaum.

Peck, D. & Shapiro, C. (1991). *Measuring Human Problems: A Practical Guide*. Chichester: Wiley.

Peckham, M. (1991). Research and development for the National Health Service. *The Lancet*, **338**, 367–371.

Perry, J. & Felce, D. (1995). Objective assessments of quality of life: how much do they agree with each other? *Journal of Community & Applied Social Psychology*, **5**, 1–19.

Peterson, D.R. (1995). The reflective educator. *American Psychologist*, **50**, 975–983.

Peterson, L., Homer, A.L. & Wonderlich, S.A. (1982). The integrity of independent variables in behaviour analysis. *Journal of Applied Behaviour Analysis*, **15**, 477–492.

Phillimore, P., Barker, C. & Rutter, C. (1994). Widening inequality of health in Northern England, 1981–91. *British Medical Journal*, **308**, 1125–1128.

Pierce, G.R. (1994). The quality of relationships inventory: assessing the interperson context of social support. In: B.R. Burleson, T.L. Abbrecht & I.G. Sarason (eds). *Communication of Social Support: Messages, Interactions, Relationship & Community*. London: Sage.

Pierce, G.R., Sarason, I.G. & Sarason, B.R. (1996). Coping & social support. In: M. Zeidner & N.S. Endler (eds). *Handbooks of Coping: Theory, Research, Applications*. New York: Wiley.

Pistrang, N. & Barker, C. (1995). The partner relationship in psychological response to breast cancer. *Social Science and Medicine*, **40**, 789–797.

Pistrang, N., Barker, C. & Rutter, C. (1997). Social Support as conversation: analysing breast cancer patients' interactions with their partners. *Social Science & Medicine*, **5**, 773–781.

Popper, K.R. (1959). *The Logic of Scientific Discovery*. London: Hutchinson.

Porras, J.I. & Hoffer, S.J. (1986). Common behaviour changes in successful organisation development efforts. *Journal of Applied Behavioural Science*, **22**, 477–494.

Power, M.J., Champion, L.A., & Aris, S.J. (1988). The development of a measure of social support: the Significant Others (SOS) Scale. *British Journal of Clinical Psychology*, **27**, 349–358.

Procidano, M.E. (1992). The nature of perceived social support: findings meta-analytic studies. In: C.D. Spielberger & J.N. Butcher (eds). *Advances in Personality Assessment* (Vol. 4). Hove: Lawrence Erlbaum.

Procidano, M.E. & Heller, K. (1983). Measures of perceived social support from friends and from family: three validation studies. *American Journal of Community Psychology*, **11**, 1–24.

Quick, J.C., Quick, J.D., Nelson, D.L. & Hurrell, J.J. (1997). *Preventive Stress Management in Organisations*. Washington DC: American Psychological Association.

Quine, L. & Pahl, J. (1991). Stress and coping in mother's caring for a child with severe learning difficulties: a test of Lazarus' transactional model of coping. *Journal of Community & Applied Social Psychology*, **1**, 57–70.

Rachman, R. (1995). Community care; changing the role of the hospital social worker. *Health & Social Care in the Community*, **3**, 163–172.

Rappaport, J. (1977). *Community Psychology: Values, Research & Action*. New York: Holt, Rinehart & Winston.

Rappaport, J. (1994). Commentary on 'Community Psychology & Politics', by David Smail. *Journal of Community and Applied Social Psychology*, **4**, 15–20.

Reissman, F. (1990). Restructuring help: a human services paradigm for the 1990s. *American Journal of Community Psychology*, **18**, 221–230.

Revicki, D.A. & Mitchell, J. (1986). Social support factor structure in the elderly. *Research on Ageing*, **8**, 232–248.

Reynolds, A., Pilts-Brown, S., Thornicroft, G. (1976). Everybody needs good neighbours. *Health Service* Journal, **14 March**, 32–33.

Riley, D.A. (1997). Using local research to change 100 communities for children and families. *American Psychologist*, **52**, 424–443.

Roberts, L.J., Luke, D.A., Rappaport, J., Seidman, E., Toro, P.A. & Reisch, T.M. (1991). Charting uncharted terrain: a behavioural observation system for mutual help groups. *American Journal of Community Psychology*, **19**, 715–737.

Robinson, S. (1996). Audit in the therapy professions: some constraints on progress. *Quality in Health Care*, **5**, 206–214.

Rogers, A. (1986). *Teaching Adults*. Milton Keynes: Open University Press.

Rogers, C.R. (1957). The necessary and sufficient conditions of personality change. *Journal of Consulting Psychology*, **21**, 95–103.

Rogers, C.R. (1975). Empathic: an unappreciated way of being. *Counselling Psychology*, **5**, 2–10.

Rogers, P.J. & Hough, G. (1995). Improving the effectiveness of evaluations: making the link to organisational theory. *Evaluation and Programme Planning*, **18**, 321–332.

Rosch, P.J. (1997). Foreword. In: J.C. Quick, J.D. Quick, D.L. Nelson & J.J. Hurrell (eds) *Preventive Stress Management in Organisations*. Washington DC: American Psychological Association.

Rosenberg, W. & Donald, A. (1995). Evidence-based medicine: an approach to clinical problem-solving. *British Medical Journal*, **310**, 1122–1126.

Roth, A. & Fonagy, P. (1996). *What Works for Whom?* London: Guilford.

Rotter, J. (1966). Generalized expectancies for internal versus external control of reinforcement. *Psychological Monographs*, 609, **80**, 1–28.

Rush, A.J., Giles, D.E., Schlesser, M.A., Fulton, C.L., Weissenburger, J. & Burns, C. (1986). The Inventory of Depressive Symptomatology (IDS): Preliminary findings. *Psychiatry Research*, **18**, 65–87.

Russell, D.E. (1998). *Dangerous Relationships*. London: Sage.

Russett, M.G. & Frey, J.L. (1991). The PACT vocational model: a step into the future. *Psychosocial Rehabilitation Journal*, **14**, 7–18.

Russon, C. & Koehly, L.M. (1995). Communication process scales. *Evaluation & Programme Planning*, **18**, 165–177.

Rust, J., Bennum, I., Crowe, M. & Golombok, S. (1988). *The Golombok Rust Inventory of Marital State*. Windsor: NFER-Nelson.

Sainsbury Centre for Mental Health (1997). *Pulling Together: The Future Roles and Training of Mental Health Staff*. London: Sainsbury Centre (134–138 Borough High Street, London SE1 1LB).

Salkovskis, P.M. (1995). Demonstrating specific effects in CBT. In: M. Aveline & D.A. Shapiro (eds). *Research Foundations for Psychotherapy Practice*. New York: Wiley.

Salmon, P. (1991). Psychotherapy and the wider world. *The Psychologist*, **2**, 50–51.

Sanavio, E. (1988). Obsessions and compulsions: The Padua Inventory. *Behaviour Research & Therapy*, **26**, 169–177.

Sarason, B.R., Sarason, I.G. & Pierce, G.R. (1990). *Social Support: An Interactional View*. New York: Wiley.

Sarason, B.R., Pierce, G.R. & Sarason, I.G. (1992). Personality, relationship and task-related factors in parent-child interactions. Unpublished manuscript, cited in Pierce (1994).

Sarason, I.G., Levine, H.M., Basham, R.B. & Sarason, B.R. (1983). Assessing Social Support: The Social Support Questionnaire. *Journal of Personality and Social Psychological*, **44**, 127–139.

Sarason, I.G., Sarason, B.R., Shearin, E.N., & Pierce, G.R. (1987). A brief measure of social support: practical and theoretical implications. *Journal of Social and Personal Relationships*, **4**, 497–510.

Sarason, S.B. (1981). An asocial psychology and a misdirected clinical psychology. *American Psychologist*, **36**, 827–836.

Savage, S.A., Hollin, C.R. & Hayward, A.J. (1990). Self-help manuals for problem drinking: the relative effects of their educational and therapeutic components. *British Journal of Clinical Psychology*, **29**, 373–382.

Schaffer, N.D. (1982). Multidimensional measures of therapist behaviour as predictors of outcome. *Psychological Bulletin*, **92**, 670–681.

Schlenger, W.E., Roland, E.J., Kroutil, L.A., Dennis, M.L., Magruder, K.M. & Ray, B.A. (1994). Evaluating services demonstration programmes: a multi-stage approach. *Evaluation & Programme Planning*, **17**, 381–390.

Schmaling, K.B., Fuzzetti, A.E. & Jacobson, N.S. (1989). Marital Problems. In: K. Hawton, P.M. Salkovskis, J. Kirk & D.M. Clark (eds): *Cognitive Behaviour Therapy for Psychiatric Problems*. Oxford: University Press.

Schreurs, K.M.G. & de Ridder, D.T.D. (1997). Integration of coping and social support perspectives: implications for the study of adaptation to chronic diseases. *Clinical Psychology Review*, **17**, 89–112.

Schwandt, T.A. (1990). Defining 'quality' in evaluation. *Evaluation & Programme Planning*, **13**, 177–188.

Scogin, F., Bynum, J., Stephens, G. & Calhoon, S. (1990). Efficacy of self-administered treatment programmes: meta-analytic review. *Professional Psychology: Research & Practice*, **21**, 42–47.

Scott, J. & Leff, J. (1994). Social factors, social interventions and prevention. In: E.S. Paykel, & R. Jenkins (eds). *Preventions in Psychiatry*. London: Gaskell.

Shadish, W.R., Matt, G.E., Navarro, A.M., *et al.* (1997). Evidence that therapy works in clinically representative conditions. *Journal of Consulting & Clinical Psychology*, **65**, 355–365.

Shapiro, D.A. (1981). Comparative credibility of treatment rationales: three tests of expectancy theory. *British Journal of Clinical Psychology*, **20**, 111–122.

Shapiro, D.A. & Firth, J. (1987). Prescriptive v exploratory psychotherapy: outcomes of the Sheffield psychotherapy project. *British Journal of Psychiatry*, **151**, 790–799.

Shinn, M. (1987). Expanding Community Psychology's domain. *American Journal of Community Psychology*, **15**, 555–573.

Shinn, M. (1992). Homelessness: what is a psychologist to do? *American Journal of Community Psychology*, **20**, 1–24.

Shure, M. & Spivack, G. (1982). Interpersonal problem-solving in young children: a cognitive approach to prevention. *American Journal of Community Psychology*, **10**, 341–356.

Sigston, A., Curran, P., Labram, A. & Wolfendale, S. (eds) (1996). *Psychology in practice: with young people, families and schools*. London: David Fulton.

Silver, E.J., Ireys, H.T., Bowman, L.J. & Stein, R.E.K. (1997). Psychological outcomes of a support intervention in mothers of children with ongoing health conditions: the parent-to-parent network. *Journal of Community Psychology*, **25**, 249–264.

Sloggett, A. & Joshi, H. (1994). Higher mortality in deprived areas: community or personal disadvantage? *British Medical Journal*, **309**, 1470–1474.

Smail, D. (1991). Towards a radical environmentalist psychology of help. *The Psychologist*, **2**, 61–65.

Smail, D. (1993). *The Origins of Unhappiness*. London: Harper-Collins.

Smail, D. (1995). Power and the origins of unhappiness: working with individuals. *Journal of Community & Applied Social Psychology* **5**, 347–356

Smith, C.A., Smith, C.J., Kearns, R.A. & Abbott, M.W. (1993). Housing stressors, social support and psychological distress. *Social Science and Medicine*, **37**, 603–612.

Smith, G.D. & Egger, M. (1993). Socioeconomic differentials in wealth and health: widening inequalities in health—the legacy of the Thatcher years. *British Medical Journal*, **307**, 1085–1086.

Smith, G. D. & Morris, J. (1994). Increasing inequalities in the health of the nation. *British Medical Journal*, **309**, 1453–1454.

Smith, J., Standinger, U.M. & Baltes, P.B. (1994). Occupational settings facilitating wisdom-related knowledge: the sample case of clinical psychologists. *Journal of Consulting & Clinical Psychology*, **62**, 989–999.

Smith, J.B. (1989). Companion animals in society. *Journal of Advanced Nursing*, **14**, 257–258.

Smith, T.E., Bellack, A.S. & Liberman, R.P. (1996). Social skills training for schizophrenia: review and future directions. *Clinical Psychology Review*, **16**, 599–617.

Snaith, R.P., Baugh, S.J., Claydon, A.D., Husain, A. & Sipple, M.A. (1982). The Clinical Anxiety Scale: an instrument derived from the Hamilton Anxiety Scale. *British Journal of Psychiatry*, **141**, 518–523.

Sobell, L.C. (1996). Bridging the gap between scientists and practitioners: the challenge before us. *Behaviour Therapy*, **27**, 297–320.

Solomon, P., Draine, J., Mannion, E., & Meisel, M. (1996). Impact of brief family psycho-education on self efficacy. *Schizophrenia Bulletin*, **22**, 41–45.

Spielberger, C., Jacobs, G., Russell, S. & Crane, R. (1983). Assessment of anger: the State-Trait Anger Scale. In: J.N. Butcher & C.D. Spielberger (eds), *Advances in Personality Assessment* (Vol. 2). Hillsdale, N.J: Erlbaum.

Spitzberg, B.H. & Cupach, W.R. (1998). *The Dark Side of Close Relationships*. London: Lawrence Erlbaum.

Stallard, P. (1994). Monitoring and assuring quality: the role of consumer satisfaction. *Clinical Psychology & Psychotherapy*, **4**, 233–239.

Stallard, P. (1996). The role and use of consumer satisfaction surveys in mental health services. *Journal of Mental Health*, **5**, 333–348.

Stansfeld, S.A., Rael, E.G.S., Head, J. (1997). Social support and psychiatric sickness absence: a prospective study of British civil servants. *Psychological Medicine*, **27**, 35–48.

Startup, M. and Shapiro, D.A. (1993). Therapist treatment fidelity in prescriptive versus exploratory psychotherapy. *British Journal of Clinical Psychology*, **32**, 443–456.

Stein, L.I., & Test, M.A. (1980). Alternative to mental hospital treatment. *Archives of General Psychiatry*, **37**, 392–397.

Stiles, W.B. (1993). Quality control in qualitative research. *Clinical Psychology Review*, **13**, 593–618.

Stiles, W.B., & Shapiro, D.A. (1989). Abuse of the drug metaphor in psychotherapy process—outcome research. *Clinical Psychology Review*, **9**, 521–543.

Stiles, W.B., Shapiro, D.A. & Elliott, R.K. (1986). Are all psychotherapies equivalent? *American Psychologist*, **41**, 165–180.

Stokes, G. & Goudie, G. (1990). *Working with Dementia*. Bicester: Winslow Press.

Strupp, H.H. (1978). Psychotherapy research and practice: an overview. In: A.E. Bergin & S.L. Garfield (eds): *Handbook of Psychotherapy & Behaviour Change* (2nd edn). New York: Wiley.

Sturmey, P. (1986). *Functional Analysis in Clinical Psychology*, Chichester: Wiley.

Susser, E., Valencia, E., Conover, S. (1997). Preventing recurrent homeless-ness among mentally ill men: A 'critical time' intervention after dis-charge from a shelter. *American Journal of Public Health*, **87**, 256–262.

Sussman, S. (1997). The community's response to mentally ill people: can be improved. *British Medical Journal*, **314**, 458.

Swindle, R., Cronkite, R., & Moos, R. (1989). Life stressors, social resources, coping and the four year course of unipolar depression. *Journal of Abnormal Psychology*, **48**, 468–477.

Tardy, C.H. (1985). Social support measurement. *American Journal of Community Psychology*, **13**, 187–202.

Tarrier, N., Sharpe, L., Beckett, R., Harwood, S., Baker, A. & Yusopoff, L. (1993). A trial of two cognitive behavioural methods of treating drug-resistant residual psychotic symptoms in schizophrenic patients. *Social Psychiatry and Psychiatric Epidemiology*, **28**, 5–10.

Tash, W.R. & Stahler, G.J. (1982). Enhancing the utilisation of evaluation findings. *Community Mental Health Journal*, **18**, 180–189.

Test, M.A., Knoedler, W., Allness, D. & Senn-Burke, S. (1985). Characteristics of young adults with schizophrenic disorders treated in the community. *Hospital and Community Psychiatry*, **36**, 853–858.

Thoits, P.A. (1982). Conceptual, methodological & theoretical problems in studying social support as a buffer against life stress. *Journal of Health and Social Behaviour*, **23**, 145–159.

Thoits, P.A. (1983). Dimensions of life events, that influence psychological distress: an evaluation and synthesis of the literature. In H.B. Kaplan (ed.). *Psychosocial Stress Trends in Theory and Practice*. New York: Academic Press.

Thoits, P.A. (1986). Social support as coping assistance. *Journal of Consulting & Clinical Psychology*, **54**, 416–423.

Thompson, C. (1989). *The Instruments of Psychiatric Research*. Chichester: Wiley.

Thornicroft, G. & Tansella, M. (eds) (1996). *Mental Health Outcome Measures*. New York: Springer.

Toro, P.A. (1986). A comparison of natural and professional help. *American Journal of Community Psychology*, **14**, 147–159.

Toro, P.A., Rappaport, J. & Seidman, E. (1987). Social climate comparison of mutual help and psychotherapy groups. *Journal of Consulting and Clinical Psychology*, **55**, 430–431.

Townsend, P., Davidson, N. & Whitehead, M. (eds) (1988). *Inequalities in Health: 'The Black Report' & 'Inequalities in Health'*. London: Penguin.

Townsend, P., Whitehead, M. & Davidson, N. (eds) (1992). *Inequalities in Health: the Black Report & the Health Divide*. London: Penguin.

Tracy, T.J. & Toro, P.A. (1989). Natural & professional help: a process analy-sis. *American Journal of Community Psychology*, **17**, 443–458

Veiel, H.O.F. (1993). Detrimental effects of kin support networks on the course of depression. *Journal of Abnormal Psychology*, 102, 419–429.

Wahler, R.G. (1980). The insular mother: her problems in parent–child treatment. *Journal of Applied Behaviour Analysis*, 13:207–219.

Walker, A. (1996). Environment: a new key area for the Health of the Nation? *British Medical Journal*, 313, 1197–1199.

Walker, R.G. (1980). The insular mother: her problems in parent–child treatment. *Journal of Applied Behaviour Analysis*, 13, 207–219.

Walkey, F.H., Seigert, R.J., McCormick, I.A. and Taylor, A.J.W. (1987). Multiple replication of the factor structure of the Inventory of Socially Supportive Behaviours. *Journal of Community Psychology*, 15:513–519.

Walshe, K. & Buttery, Y. (1995). Measuring the impact of audit and quality improvement programmes. *Journal of the Association for Quality and Health Care*, 2, 138–147.

Waltz, J., Addis, M.E., Koerner, K., & Jacobson, N.S. (1993). Testing the integrity of a psychotherapy protocol: assessment of adherence and competence. *Journal of Consulting & Clinical Psychology*, 61, 620–630.

Warr, P.B. (1980). An introduction to models in psychological research. In: A.J. Chapman & D.M. Jones (eds) *Model of Man*. Leicester: British Psychological Society.

Warr, P. (1987). *Work, Unemployment and Mental Health*. Oxford: Clarendon Press.

Webster-Stratton, C. & Hammond, M. (1997). Child and parent training sessions led to improved child behaviour in child conduct disorder. *Journal of Consulting & Clinical Psychology*, 65, 93–109.

Weinman, J., Wright, S. & Johnston, M. (1995). *Measures in Health Psychology: A users' portfolio*. Windsor: NFER-Nelson.

Weiss, R.S. (1972). Helping relationships: relationships of clients with physicians, social workers, priests and others. *Social Problems*, 20, 319–328.

Weissman, M.M. (1987). Advances in psychiatric epidemiology: rates and risks for major depression. *American Journal of Public Health*, 77, 445–451.

West, M.A. (1989). Innovation amongst health care professionals. *Social Behaviour*, 4, 173–184.

Whalan, G.S. & Mushet, G.L. (1990). Service requests of acute in-patients and perceived pattern of provision at discharge. *British Journal of Medical Psychology*, 63, 311–318.

White, J. (1995). 'Stresspac': a controlled trial of a self help package for the anxiety disorders. *Behavioural & Cognitive Psychotherapy*, 23, 89–108.

White, J. & Ross, M.K. (1997). Stress control large group didactic therapy for anxiety: an approach for managed care systems? *The Behaviour Therapist*, 20, 192–196.

Whitehead, A. (1991). Twenty years a-growing: some current issues in behavioural psychotherapy with elderly people. *Behavioural Psychotherapy*, **19**, 92–99.

Wilkinson, R.G. (1996). *Unhealthy Societies: the Affliction of Inequality.* London: Routledge.

Williams, J. (1996). Social inequalities and mental health: developing services and developing knowledge. *Journal of Community & Applied Social Psychology*, **6**, 311–316.

Wilson, J. (1994). Vital yet problematic. Self help and professionals—a review of the literature in the last decade. *Health and Social Care in the Community*, **1**, 211–218.

Winefield, H.R. (1984). The nature and elicitation of social support: some implications for the helping professions. *Behavioural Psychotherapy*, **12**, 318–330.

Winefield, H.R. (1987). Psychotherapy and social support: parallels and differences in the helping process. *Clinical Psychology Review*, **7**, 631–644.

Winefield, H.R. & Burnett, P.L. (1996). Barriers to an alliance between family and professional caregivers in chronic schizophrenia. *Journal of Mental Health*, **5**, 223–232.

Winefield, H.R. & Harvey, E.J. (1993). Determinants of psychological distress in relatives of people with chronic schizophrenia. *Schizophrenia Bulletin*, **19**, 619–625.

Wolf, M.H., Putnam, S.M., James, S.A. & Stiles, W.B. (1978). The medical interview satisfaction scale: development of a scale to measure patient perceptions of physician behaviour. *Journal of Behavioural Medicine*, **1**, 391.

Zarit, S.H., Anthony, C.R. & Boutselis, M. (1987). Interventions with care givers of dementia patients: comparison of two approaches. *Psychology and Aging*, **2**, 225–232.

Zarit, S.H. & Edwards, A.B. (1996). Family care giving: research and clinical intervention. In: R.T. Woods (ed.), *Handbook of the Clinical Psychology of Ageing*. Chichester: Wiley.

Zigmond, A.S. & Snaith, R.P. (1983). The Hospital Anxiety and Depression Scale. *Acta Psychiatrica Scandinavica*, **67**, 361–370.

INDEX